STRIFE ON THE WATERFRONT
The Port of New York since 1945
VERNON H. JENSEN

"A measured, thorough approach to one of the most complicated and sensitive problems of the industrial relations sphere. . . . All the drama of the waterfront is here: the factional fights within the union, crime and corruption in union halls and shippers' offices, and the looming specter of technological change. . . . However, the study's goal is not to dramatize, but rather to trace in all its complexity how the International Longshoremen's Association and the New York Shipping Association have largely failed in the industrial relations process."

— *Library Journal*

FEDERAL SERVICE AND THE CONSTITUTION
The Development of the Public Employment Relationship
DAVID H. ROSENBLOOM

"Rosenbloom . . . explores the constitutional relationship between the state and the civilian employee in the executive branch of the federal government. . . . The work is well documented, particularly with Supreme Court case material, and the author makes use of appropriate analogies to foreign countries to help the reader to judge what is the best political role for the bureaucrat in modern democracy."

— *Library Journal*

CORNELL UNIVERSITY PRESS
ITHACA AND LONDON

D1480851

RACE RELATIONS AND THE NEW YORK CITY COMMISSION ON HUMAN RIGHTS

RACE RELATIONS AND THE NEW YORK CITY COMMISSION ON HUMAN RIGHTS

GERALD BENJAMIN

CORNELL UNIVERSITY PRESS

ITHACA AND LONDON

First published 1974 by Cornell University Press.
Published in the United Kingdom by Cornell University Press Ltd., 2-4 Brook Street, London W1Y 1AA.

International Standard Book Number 0-8014-0826-1
Library of Congress Catalog Card Number 73-20790

Printed in the United States of America by Vail-Ballou Press, Inc.

For Helise and Elizabeth

Foreword

Few domestic subjects have received as much attention from scholars in all of the social sciences and from the press during the last decade as race relations. Sociologists and psychologists have defined the nature of the problem and the need to act in solving it. Historians have traced its roots in the past. Lawyers have written volumes about the legislation needed. Political scientists have set forth the political impact of racial discontent. There have been suggestions for changes in public policy resulting from this research. Rarely, however, has any scholar considered the administrative problems involved, particularly those which must be faced at the local level.

Gerald Benjamin has made a major contribution to this neglected area by examining the circumstances that led to the establishment of the Commission on Human Rights in New York City and by analyzing its operations over the first three decades of its existence. Not only was this Human Rights Commission one of the first such municipal agencies, but also it has had the largest budget of any similar municipal organization and wide formal powers.

New York City has had experience with several different kinds of agencies concerned with minority problems. Some, having neither formal powers nor public funds, attempted to achieve their goals through good will and voluntary compliance. Later agencies were given wider powers and substantial budgets. A study of the varied New York experience may help us anticipate the problems that various types of human rights commissions in other cities may face.

Given the political realities of the environment in which human rights agencies must operate, one may ask if any commission of this character can be as successful as its sponsors hope. Here, too, the New York experience may shed light, for Professor Benjamin examines the function of the New York commission in the context of the politics of the city as a whole. The political posture of the mayor and the needs of minority groups that the commission sought to serve were not necessarily compatible. Also, conflicts among the minorities who made up the agency's constituency brought on additional problems, as did the very size and representative nature of the commission itself.

Students of urban politics and administration will find this study useful because it deals with one of the most challenging aspects of modern city government. It questions the approaches to race relations which officials frequently adopted without fully understanding the administrative difficulties of implementing progressive, well-intended legislation.

As the late Lindsay Rogers once said, "Democracies are slow in learning that public popular control rests on two pillars: terms of reference precisely defined—in other words, the clear formulation of policy—and vigilant and tireless scrutiny of implementation—in other words, judgment of results." The New York City Commission on Human Rights originally was established to discover instances where human rights were denied, but it had no legal power to redress discriminatory actions. Later, it was given administrative functions without precise definitions. And the results of its operation were not subject to vigorous and tireless scrutiny.

There are other questions about administration and bureaucracy that one may properly ask. Can a particular administrative organization succeed in dealing with the human rights problem at one stage of the city's development only to be ineffective at a later stage? Does the problem take on different dimensions of importance and thus outgrow the early organization's structure? Agencies once established are difficult to abolish or modify; they tend to continue to operate in the way in which they were originally headed. To what extent has this tendency inhibited innovative change in the goals and methods of municipal human rights agencies? This study, which covers almost three decades of the history of the New York commission, provides insights into these aspects of bureaucracies.

ROBERT H. CONNERY

New York, New York

Acknowledgments

During the three years I spent in preparing this book I incurred many debts, both intellectual and personal. Because of the intangible nature of the aid I received—time expended, energy spent, ideas exchanged and sharpened, good advice given—I can never hope to repay it. I can only acknowledge receipt of these kindnesses and give them freely in my own relationships with students, colleagues, and friends.

My greatest debt is to Professor Robert Connery, who guided this work from inception to completion, always insisting upon clarity and rigor in the analysis, from the framing of the questions to the conclusions. The late Professor Wallace Sayre was the first to suggest to me that the City Commission on Human Rights might be a fruitful area for analysis, and his work provided me with a conceptual framework within which to proceed. I benefited too from the critical readings of Professors Demetrios Caraley, Charles V. Hamilton, and Stuart Bruchey, and from the comments of two anonymous readers for Cornell University Press. My friends and colleagues, both at Columbia and the State University College at New Paltz, served as constant sources of encouragement and valuable testing grounds for ideas. The comments of Professor Donald Roper on an earlier draft of this work were especially helpful.

In gathering the data for this study, I was aided by the staffs of many libraries throughout the city, both public and private, and especially by the librarians at the Municipal Archives and the Municipal Reference Library. I am grateful to Fioravante Perrotta, then an assistant to the mayor and now in private law practice, for permission to look at documents pertinent to the Human Rights Commission from the Wagner administration. In addition, this

11

study could not have been completed without the cooperation of the fifty-seven interviewees. Some of these have expressed the wish to remain anonymous. The names of others appear in footnotes. Four who were especially helpful were Stanley Lowell, William Booth, Morris Sass, and Will Maslow.

I am appreciative, too, of the financial aid for the early work on this study extended by the Columbia University Urban Center under its small-grants program. Before the University supported my efforts, my parents gave me considerable assistance, and I am grateful for their indispensable support of my career.

In preparing this manuscript for publication, I had great help from the editorial staff of Cornell University Press. I also appreciate the editorial assistance of Ernest Elliott and the aid of Susan Taber in typing several drafts of this work.

Finally, I thank my wife, Helise, without whose infinite understanding and encouragement this project would not have been successfully completed. She has adjusted, persevered, and proofread, and she has even, I think, taught me to spell "recommend."

GERALD BENJAMIN

New Paltz, New York

Contents

Tables and Charts

TABLES

CHARTS

RACE RELATIONS AND THE NEW YORK CITY COMMISSION ON HUMAN RIGHTS

1

Metropolitan Human Rights Commissions: The New York City Case

Problems of race relations have become matters of central concern in most American cities for almost two decades. Despite the manifest growth in the intensity of black-white differences, however, the role of human rights agencies, the organizations that have traditionally been used by municipalities to deal with minority problems, has not been reassessed.

Even though there has been little evaluation of the successes and failures of these agencies, they have been proliferating throughout the smaller cities of the United States in recent years. Between 1960 and 1973 over three hundred such agencies were established; this represented a fourfold increase in those operating in the country in the late 1950's.[1] In New York State alone, sixty-two human rights agencies had been established by January 1973, most of them in the state's smaller urban centers.[2]

New York City's experience with the human rights commission structure provides an invaluable point of reference for the cities that are just now establishing such agencies in response to pervasive racial problems. New York established its first commission in 1943, in response to the Harlem riots. Since that time, its agency has gone through many permutations, paralleling and reflecting the changing

[1] U.S. Conference of Mayors, *Official Local Community Relations Commissions*, National Survey and Supplement (Washington: Community Relations Service, 1965), p. 2; communication by the author with the Office of the Director of State and Local Relations, U.S. Equal Employment Opportunities Commission, Sept. 21, 1973.

[2] New York State Division of Human Rights, "Active County and Municipal Agencies in New York State," Jan. 1973.

nature of the national civil rights movement. Consequently, over the past thirty years, New York has had considerable experience with different types of human rights agencies, with varying formal powers, kinds of organizations, and roles in the city's social and political system.

One early agency functioned without any staff, budget, or formal powers. Another was strictly a creature of the mayor's office with a limited staff, no public funds, and no power to enforce its decisions. Later, after the agency became a commission, it acquired a statutory base and became the largest and most powerful city human rights agency in the country. Although the agencies recently established in other cities vary in their structure, their formal powers, and the degree of budgetary and staff support they have received from their respective administrations, almost all of them could learn from New York's experience.

Why, then, has this experience been largely ignored? The reasons appear to be twofold. First, in the larger cities such as New York, where most human rights commissions have operated, one of the results of the riots of the mid-1960's was a general disenchantment with all pre-riot administrative devices in the area of race relations. Critics, such as former commission chairman Stanley Lowell and Eugene Callender of the Urban Coalition, argued that these agencies were the products of the civil rights movement of the 1950's and that they were inadequate to meet the problems of the 1960's and 1970's. These problems, it was said, were qualitatively different, and if human rights commissions had worked the riots would not have occurred.[3]

Disenchantment with local human rights commissions is only part of the reason for ignoring their experience. Even the most severe critics of these agencies are ambivalent about their value. The National Advisory Commission on Civil Disorders, for example, while harshly critical of the "ineffective" and "ignored" grievance mechanisms in several riot-torn cities, nevertheless called for the "strengthening of those agencies, such as the Equal Employ-

---

[3] Interview with Stanley Lowell. During the course of this study many interviewees expressed this opinion.

ment Opportunities Commission, charged with eliminating discriminatory practices." [4] The implication is, of course, that given the proper powers, the existing institutions can do the job.

This ambivalence may be due, in part, to the unfortunate fact that specialists in government organization have paid little systematic attention to the operation of municipal human rights agencies.[5] Until recently, the administration of race relations has been a peripheral concern for most city governments. Even the New York City commission, the largest in the nation, with a budget of over a million dollars and a staff of more than ninety people, tends to be swallowed up in a city government that spends more than ten billion dollars annually and has more than 300,000 employees.

What little writing there has been concerning official human rights agencies has been focused on the state level and has appeared primarily in law reviews.[6] Little is known, even among serious students and practitioners of local government, about what city civil rights agencies are supposed to do, and what their actual political, social, and administrative roles have been. This shortcoming in the literature has long been noted by social scientists. In reviewing the literature of the 1950's, sociologist Herbert Blumer wrote: "In my judgement, race relations research in the decade has not contributed a great deal to policy knowledge. . . . Such policy knowledge usually arises in the wake of action taken to change race relations rather than arising from research undertaken prior to such action efforts." It is still true, as it was when Blumer wrote, that "research in race relations is rarely devoted explicitly to providing policy knowledge." [7]

To be sure, some political scientists have noted in passing the

[4] Tom Wicker, ed., *Report of the National Advisory Commission on Civil Disorders* (New York: Bantam, 1968), pp. 7, 24.

[5] Lewis Killian and Charles Grigg have examined one such agency in a small town in *Racial Crisis in America* (Englewood Cliffs: Prentice-Hall, 1964).

[6] This literature is discussed in Chapter 7.

[7] Herbert Blumer, "Research in Race Relations in the United States of America," in UNESCO, *Research on Race Relations* (New York, 1966), pp. 117–118.

multiple and conflicting roles of the public human rights agency in city government. Banfield and Wilson, for example, say:

A public human relations commission occupies a crucial but ambiguous role in the politics of race relations. On the one hand, it is a staff agency created to advise the mayor; on the other hand, it is looked to for "action" by various individuals and groups who have grievances in this field. Furthermore, it has its own conception—ingrained in the staff—of its mission to remedy certain conditions even if no one organizes a formal complaint and the mayor does not ask for advice; in such cases the human relations agency does not act as the trans-mission belt which carries reports of outrages suffered . . . nor does it provide the mayor with advice . . . and then sit back and wait. . . . On the contrary, the commission is usually engaged simulta-neously in stimulating protest and then proposing solutions to the mayor to eliminate the protest thus stimulated. This, of course, entails an elaborate pattern of negotiation and organizational ability to face in several directions at once.[8]

Such comments provide useful insights, but they almost exhaust the political science literature in the field, and they are based more upon impressionistic evidence than upon detailed analysis of the agencies themselves.

It is the premise of this analysis that by examining the conditions of the emergence and perpetuation of the New York City agency, one can begin to understand the role this organization has played in the social and political systems of the city. To maintain the continuity and comparability of the analysis, it is important to examine the city commission, and its antecedent organizations, in its total milieu for four basic time periods, 1943–55, 1955–60, 1961–65, and 1966–69. An examination of one agency over time allows a rich data base, and chronological division of the study presents the opportunity for comparative analysis. Comparing the organization to itself minimizes the effect of many extraneous vari-ables that normally have to be taken into account in such a study. This approach has been recommended by William H. Starbuck, a

---

[8] Edward Banfield and James Q. Wilson, *City Politics* (New York: Vin-tage, 1963), pp. 310–311.

leading student of organizational growth and change. He writes: "The best approach is to work with multiple observations of each organization, taking maximum advantage of opportunities to compare each organization with itself." [9]

The first period under examination here begins with the establishment of New York's semiofficial human rights agency and closes with the creation of the statutory agency in this field. The remaining chronological breaking points were chosen because they mark changes in the leadership of the commission and because analysis by administration provides the clearest organizing principle for an understanding of the agency.

For each of these periods, four sets of questions are raised. The first set, designed to establish a common frame of reference throughout the study, is concerned with the agency's structure, leadership, constituency groups, and role in the political process in the city. Why was the commission structure chosen for the city human rights agency, and why was it retained? How did the characteristics of the agency leadership change over time? What was the agency's original approach to minority problems, and how and why was this approach altered? During each period, what were the agency's constituency groups and how was it tied to them? What kind of relationship did the commission have with its sister agencies and with similar agencies functioning at other levels of government? What were its relations with the major political actors of the city?

A second set of questions is concerned with the internal political process of the commission as a bureaucratic unit, and with the agency as an actor in the civil rights policy-making arena in the city. Did the commission serve as a vehicle for minority-group access into city government, and, if so, how? Did the agency help legitimize minority affairs as a proper concern for local government in the city? In what manner was the vague mandate originally given the commission translated into specific substantive policies? Through what process was the agency able to augment its formal powers? Through what processes were the functions that the com-

---

[9] "Organizational Growth and Development," in James G. March, ed., *Handbook of Organizations* (Chicago: Rand-McNally, 1965), p. 520.

mission was expected to perform diminished during the late 1960's? How was the locus of power within the agency altered over time?

Sayre and Kaufman, in their book *Governing New York City,* provide the impetus for the consideration of the City Commission on Human Rights as part of a self-contained political arena:

Governmental decisions affecting the people of the city of New York emerge from many decision centers, each center a cluster of officials and employees and associated nongovernmental group leaders. . . .

Many small islands of decision-making may develop, and they are self-reinforcing because nongovernmental groups then discover that partial monopolies are advantageous tactical arrangements for them. The pattern, having evolved, persists.[10]

The City Commission on Human Rights may be viewed as the center of one such "small island," and the relationships between it and its constituency groups may be examined in this context. Who are the contestants who perceive the commission as an important decision-making arena? What are the stakes and prizes that these contestants seek? What happens when, in seeking these stakes and prizes, the different contestants come into conflict?

The final set of questions is evaluative. What were the objectives of the commission and how successful has it been in meeting these objectives? The effectiveness of the commission will be measured both by examining the answers to the questions posed above and by looking closely at how the commission has acted in four substantive areas during each of the periods under study. These areas are employment discrimination, housing discrimination, educational integration, and "tension control."

Ultimately, one has to consider whether there is still a need for a commission on human rights in New York City. Critics of present agencies of this type say that they do not work properly because they need strengthening. Professor Kent Lloyd, writing in the British journal *Public Administration,* bases his prescription for local commissions on an examination of several state agencies:

---

[10] Wallace Sayre and Herbert Kaufman, *Governing New York City* (New York: Russell Sage Foundation, 1960), pp. 512–513.

"Two decades' experience with state intergroup relations legislation indicates that success is possible only with the proper tools that include: a) enforceable laws and ordinances; b) independent public administrative organizations supplemented by private intergroup agency efforts; c) qualified policy-making commissioners and professionally trained administrative and intergroup relations agency personnel; d) carefully defined policy-making and administrative roles; e) adequate finance and planning for major programme activities of research, enforcement, and community organization and education." [11] On the basis of the experience of New York City, Lloyd's prescription may well be naïve.

Experts acknowledge that governmental reorganization is often necessary.[12] Carrying this further, there may well be times when a governmental agency has failed and mere reorganization is not sufficient. There may be many reasons for agency failure. The original structure and philosophy of an agency, adequate for the time in which it was established, may become obsolete. There may have been a misconception of the scope and nature of the job to be done. These problems are fundamental, and a mere increase in budget or staff will not solve them. It is possible that the New York City Commission on Human Rights has become nonfunctional for all the major actors in the civil rights arena of city politics and ought to be abolished and have its responsibilities reallocated to other city agencies.

The terms "functional," "dysfunctional," and "nonfunctional," now familiar to most social scientists, are borrowed from Robert Merton and used to describe the relationship between the commission and other major actors in the civil rights policy arena in New York.[13] In addition to Merton's categories, throughout this discussion the commission is portrayed as taking the role of either "advocate" or "apologist" in this arena. It is seen as acting in its

[11] "Urban Race Riots vs. Effective Anti-Discrimination Agencies: An End or a Beginning," *Public Administration,* 45 (Spring 1967), 52–53.

[12] Frederick C. Mosher, *Governmental Reorganizations* (Indianapolis: Bobbs-Merrill, 1967), pp. 493–512.

[13] See his *Social Theory and Social Structure,* rev. and enl. ed. (New York: The Free Press, 1957), pp. 51ff.

advocate role when it publicly or within the city government presses for policy decisions or other action favorable to a particular minority group. In fact, most commission advocacy was for the cause of the black minority. The commission is seen as acting in its apologist role when its seeks to minimize conflict and protect the interests of the mayor or other major political actors in the city. Although the advocate and apologist roles of the commission sometimes converge and it is conceivable that the agency could do both at once, they are most often viewed as being in basic conflict with each other.

One uncommon term, "tension control," is borrowed from the jargon of the commission and is treated as one of the agency's basic substantive policy areas. All commission activity may be viewed as including some degree of tension control—that is, the avoidance of interracial conflict that results in violence.

2

The Establishment of the Unity Committee

The movement for the institutionalization of city involvement in minority affairs in New York began as a result of an outburst of midsummer racial violence, violence that flared up in Harlem on the first day of August 1943.[1] It began during the early evening hours at the Braddock Hotel in the heart of the city's largest black district. A policeman from the West 135th Street Precinct had been assigned to the lobby of the Braddock for several days before the evening of the incident, though the reason for the stakeout is unclear. That night, the patrolman on duty, James Collins, attempted to arrest Miss Marjorie Polite, a thirty-five-year-old black woman who lived in the neighborhood, for disorderly conduct in the hotel lobby. Her boyfriend, Robert Bandy, a private in a black military police battalion on leave from his outfit in Jersey City, grabbed the policeman's nightstick and wrestled him to the ground in an attempt to prevent the arrest. He was joined in this attempt by his mother, Mrs. Florence Roberts, who was visiting from her home in Connecticut.

Collins, to fend off Bandy, drew his postol and fired one shot. The black soldier fell, a bullet lodged in his left shoulder. The scuffle had drawn a crowd, and soon rumors began to spread. A white cop, it was believed, had shot a black soldier in the back and had killed him.

Groups of young men gathered in the streets of Harlem, threat-

[1] *New York Times,* Aug. 2 and 3, 1943, p. 1; New York City Police Department, "Report to the Mayor on the Disturbances in Harlem" (New York: the Department, 1943). La Guardia Papers, Municipal Archives, box 714. All documents cited in this chapter are from the Municipal Archives.

ening to rush the Bellevue Hospital prison ward where the wounded soldier had been taken. They began throwing bottles and stones at police and passing vehicles, and soon gangs of forty or fifty youths, often including women and children, roamed the streets, smashing store windows, looting, and setting fires.

Mayor La Guardia ordered all traffic diverted from West Harlem and appealed on the radio for calm, cooperation, and a clearing of the streets by the citizenry. Five thousand police were rushed to the scene, firemen were held on duty, and six truckloads of army M.P.'s entered the area to remove military personnel. Subway police rode the famous "A train" below Harlem's streets, one to a car, to prevent the violence from spreading.

Soon La Guardia was in the riot-torn community, surveying the scene with black leaders and appealing for order. Ferdinand Smith of the National Maritime Union, Murray Yeargan of the National Negro Congress, and Walter White of the NAACP accompanied the mayor and asked the people again and again to return to their homes, but garbage was thrown at them and the shouts of the crowds drowned out their pleas. Similar appeals were made by these leaders and the mayor on WABC radio the next morning. La Guardia promised a thorough investigation of grievances, but, he said, first there would have to be order.

By noon on August 2, a tense calm prevailed; 554 blacks had been arrested, hundreds injured, and five killed. Four hundred policemen had required hospital treatment, but no whites had been taken into custody.[2]

Measures to meet the crisis continued the next morning. Governor Thomas E. Dewey, standing by at the Roosevelt Hotel, ordered the commander of the State Guard to have his 8,000 men report for drill and stand in readiness. A 1,500-person civilian volunteer corps was organized in Harlem and equipped with armbands and nightsticks; three hundred women were included in this group. The mayor announced a 10:30 P.M. curfew, the suspension of liquor sales, and the lifting of the wartime dim-out in West Harlem.

[2] *New York Times,* Aug. 2, 1943, p. 2.

La Guardia continued to seek the advice of black leaders during the afternoon of the second day, but he also consulted with military authorities and with the police and fire commissioners. By 9:45 in the evening, he felt confident enough to assure the worried city, in his fourth broadcast within twenty-four hours, that "at this moment the situation is under control." [3] Black merchants were not that certain; "Colored store—peace" signs began to appear in their shop windows.

Perhaps these appeals and preventatives had worked, or perhaps the violence had run its course. In any event, the large-scale rioting was over. The post mortems now began.

Background

The entry of the United States into World War II triggered a series of events that brought the racial inequalities within the nation more clearly into focus.[4] In the context of a war in support of the European democracies and against a nation with an overt racist ideology, discriminatory practices within the American armed forces tended to weaken the moral position of the United States. Furthermore, these practices served as the catalyst for a debate within the American black community over whether this was indeed "a black man's war." Incidents near southern military bases between whites who resented "uppity niggers" in uniform, and black soldiers, especially officers, who resisted discrimination in public places, added fuel to this fire.

Inequalities in the armed forces were not the only problems that exacerbated racial tensions in the nation during the war. The military draft, combined with the vast increase in demand for goods to support the war effort, created a labor shortage in the North and Northeast. Opportunities for well-paying employment intensified the migration of blacks from the rural South, who, when they arrived in northern urban centers, found that they were not in the "promised land." Employment discrimination continued, and as

---

[3] *Ibid.*
[4] For this summary I rely upon John Hope Franklin, *From Slavery to Freedom* (New York: Knopf, 1947), pp. 557–580.

blacks and whites competed for living space, racial tensions flared. Government officials were concerned both about the possible effect of these tensions upon the war effort and about the implications of possible racial clashes at home for the image of the United States abroad.[5] Occasionally, civil rights leaders were able to capitalize on these concerns. By threatening a march on Washington, for example, they were able to convince President Franklin D. Roosevelt that he should speak out against discrimination in war industries and should establish a Fair Employment Practices Committee.

The committee was a beginning, but it could hardly be expected to deal with the general problems of tension and prejudice on the local level. Concern continued, and its presence is indicated by the volume of literature published during the war years on such subjects as "Negro life," "what the Negro really wants," and "black war aims." [6] It is perhaps not accidental that Gunnar Myrdal and his team of researchers were working on their monumental study, *An American Dilemma,* during the early years of World War II. This intellectual activity reflects a growing concern with the American racial problem during this period and an emerging awareness of its implications.

In short, the racial unrest of 1943 in New York occurred during a time of war and national crisis, and this set of circumstances gives the governmental attempts to deal with this unrest an uncommon relevance for the 1970's. This relevance increases when the 1943 violence is examined closely.

Two Models

Even at the height of the disorders in Harlem on the first and second days of August, Mayor La Guardia denied that they were

[5] For an example of this concern see a letter of Attorney General Francis Biddle to President Roosevelt quoted in A. M. Lee and Norman D. Humphrey, *Race Riots* (New York: Octagon, 1968), pp. 60–61.

[6] Many books can be cited to illustrate this point. Two are: Roi Ottley, *New World A'Coming* (Boston: Houghton-Mifflin, 1943) and Rayford W. Logan, ed., *What the Negro Wants* (Chapel Hill: University of North Carolina Press, 1944).

"race riots." [7] They did not, he said, fit into the familiar pattern of black and white gangs fighting on the streets. No white vigilante groups were formed to take retribution in Harlem. Property damage was great, especially on the main avenues and cross streets of West Harlem (estimated at five million dollars by the Uptown Chamber of Commerce), but relatively few lives were lost.

La Guardia was right. The Harlem violence was qualitatively different from the clashes between the races to which America had become accustomed in the early twentieth century, and reason for believing this can be found in the fact that this event did not easily fit into the typology developed to explain these earlier manifestations of prejudice by psychologist Gordon Allport. [8] Some factors in the development of the Harlem riots, like the importance of rumor and the key role of the trivial igniting incident, correspond to the Allport model, but basically this was a different kind of phenomenon from those for which he accounted. Allport describes a growing crescendo of prejudice culminating in a physical attack by the "in-group" upon the "out-group." In Harlem, the mass violence was engaged in by the "out-group" and directed more at property than at persons.

A more adequate model for the racial disorders in Harlem in 1943 is one developed at the Lemberg Center for the Study of Violence from data based upon episodes of urban violence in the 1960's. [9] Four stages are posited. The "precipitating event" was trivial and involved an encounter with the police. Rumors caused "confrontation," and although local leaders and city officials attempted to calm the situation, it escalated. The third, "Roman Holiday," stage, with bottle and rock throwing, looting, and high tension, was reached by the early-morning hours of the next day. At this point, the city's "firm but restrained response" (no undue violence, saturating the area with reserves, holding the state troops

---

[7] *New York Times,* Aug. 2, 1943.

[8] Gordon Allport, *The Nature of Prejudice* (Garden City: Doubleday, 1958), pp. 56–57.

[9] U.S. Senate, Committee on the Judiciary, *Hearings on H.R. 421 (Anti-Riot Bill),* 90th Cong., 1st Sess., pp. 784–785.

in readiness, imposing a curfew) averted the fourth, or "war," stage.

As in the disorders of the 1960's, grievances in 1943 ran deep. Among the conditions most complained about were these: police brutality, the high price of food in Harlem, the indignities that black draftees were made to experience in the army, and the failure of the city to implement the recommendations of a group that had investigated an earlier outbreak in 1935. Even the by-products of the 1943 violence seem familiar, from the store window signs, to the newspaper speculations about "insidious propaganda" at work,[10] to the police commissioner's concern over "outside agitators." [11]

The Committee Takes Form

Both within the black community and in the city at large, the level of tension and concern pointed to the need for some action by the mayor in the wake of the violence. La Guardia, always a champion of minorities, was receptive. In fact, he had been concerned with problems of race before the riots and was greatly respected by black leaders. In 1941, he had served on the Federal Fair Employment Practices Committee (FEPC) and had advised the national government's Committee on Discrimination in Employment. Both A. Philip Randolph and Walter White had endorsed La Guardia for chairman of the FEPC. A letter from White to the mayor clearly expressed his feelings: "The people, and especially Negroes, have faith in you not only so far as your integrity and your sincere interest in this issue is concerned, but because labor unions, employers, and government officials in Washington and elsewhere would not dare try to pull anything on a board of which you are chairman." [12]

The idea of government action in the area of race relations had long been in the air in New York City. In 1941, an interracial citywide Citizens' Committee on Harlem was organized under the cochairmanship of Algernon Black of the Ethical Culture Society

---

[10] *New York World Telegram,* Aug. 2, 1943, p. 1.
[11] *New York Times,* Aug. 3, 1943, p. 1, col. 1.
[12] Walter White to La Guardia, July 14, 1941, box 808.

and Adam Clayton Powell, Sr., of the Abyssinian Baptist Church in Harlem. This nongovernmental organization worked through many subcommittees to study problems and recommend solutions to the government. Between 1941 and 1943, the liberal press and minority-group leaders repeatedly urged upon La Guardia the creation of a race relations agency, and minor legislation in this area was considered by the city council.

The disastrous Detroit riots of the early summer of 1943 added to the climate of concern about racial matters in the city. In a radio speech delivered about a month before the Harlem outbreak, La Guardia urged calm and asked that the city's ministers preach racial good will and understanding to their congregations.[13] The mayor sought to tap all possible sources of aid to avoid violence in the streets. He dispatched two police officers to Detroit to study the situation there, met with black leaders to explore the possibility of establishing a committee on race relations, and prevailed upon Langston Hughes to participate in a radio show promoting "peace and neighborliness." [14]

After the violence, demands for governmental action in the field of race relations increased dramatically in number and visibility. The *New York Times,* though it did not call for the establishment of a commission, urged an inquiry into the police system for dealing with Negro problems.[15] The NAACP urged the establishment of a permanent interracial committee, a position in which it was joined by several liberal union leaders.

A. Philip Randolph, head of the Brotherhood of Sleeping Car Porters, advised La Guardia to meet with the Citizens' Committee on Better Race Relations to consider the plan of a group constituted as a result of the riots.[16] In a manifesto to the mayor, this committee urged, as one of its points, a commission on race relations. This group was to represent all creeds, colors, and nationalities, and would be made up of representatives of labor and tenant groups

[13] La Guardia, radio address of June 22, 1943, box 808.
[14] La Guardia to Hughes, June 28, 1943, box 808.
[15] *New York Times,* Aug. 3, 1943, p. 20 (editorial).
[16] A. P. Randolph to La Guardia, Aug. 3 and Aug. 9, 1943, box 714.

and social agencies. It was to have a full-time staff and an adequate budget and was to coordinate, promote, and recommend for action the program that was produced by the investigation of the 1935 Harlem riots. The proposed agency could, in addition, "accept recommendations from other agencies and groups in the city for better race relations." A similar proposal was presented to the mayor in an editorial by the liberal daily, *PM*.

Despite these available models, La Guardia's concept of the commission was different from that of black leaders and liberal newspaper men. Whereas they desired a governmental structure oriented toward easing racial tensions, working for racial justice within the city, and perhaps providing a point of entry for minority-group spokesmen into the governmental process, he envisioned an organization almost totally apart from the city government that would study the basic causes of racial prejudice, publish its findings, and advise the city of possible ameliorative long-range actions. The mayor's view was succinctly expressed in his invitation to John D. Rockefeller, Jr., in December 1943, to chair the proposed committee: "I want to appoint a Committee on Inter-racial relations composed of men and women who are able to contribute some thought to this perplexing problem. It is to be something more than a committee, rather an institution. What I have in mind is a thorough study to be made and complete information obtained on the cause of discrimination, prejudice, and exploitation, that the study be so thorough and the information so accurate that the Committee's work or data be considered authoritative by all. I contemplate a staff of experts to do the necessary research and make studies and surveys, thus providing the material for the board." [17] In order to assure the neutral reputation of his committee, the mayor proposed to fund it from diverse nongovernmental sources. The use of public funds, he thought, would be "dangerous" because it would make the proposed committee "political." [18]

La Guardia's initial plans for membership were ambitious. He

[17] La Guardia to Rockefeller, Dec. 27, 1943, *ibid.*
[18] La Guardia to several individuals, March 6, 1944, *ibid.* The financial aim was $50,000 per year for two years.

envisioned a central committee of fifteen very prominent New York ers, bolstered in their efforts by voluntary advisory committees and a paid staff. But snags appeared almost immediately. First Beardsley Ruml and then John D. Rockefeller, Jr., turned down the chairmanship because, they said, of the press of other business.[19] Finally, La Guardia settled upon Charles Evans Hughes, Jr., son of the Supreme Court justice and former solicitor general. Others, like Anne O'Hare McCormick of the *New York Times,* refused service on the committee, and it was not until February 28, 1944, seven months after the riots, that the membership, expanded to nineteen, was revealed to the press.[20]

In his appointments to the committee, La Guardia upheld his reputation as a master of New York's ethnic politics.[21] All races and creeds were represented, and balance was provided with a liberal sprinkling of "ethnic neutrals." Overlapping group membership often makes categorization of the committee appointees difficult, but people appointed primarily for their affiliation with Jewish groups included two judges, Edward Lazansky and Nathan Perlman, and noted author Fannie Hurst, who was also active in the Urban League. Black appointees included Channing Tobias of the YMCA; Dr. William Granger, a Brooklyn physician; and the Reverend John Johnson, an Episcopal clergyman. To represent the Roman Catholic interest, La Guardia selected Father Raymond Campion; Edmund Borgia Butler, former president of the St. Vincent de Paul Society; Alfred McCosker, president of the Mutual Broadcasting System (and the only businessman on the committee); and Dorothy Hendrickson, a grade-school assistant principal. The labor interest was not forgotten; the final two appointees were Dorothy Bellanca of the CIO and Thomas Murtha, president of the Central Trades Council of the AFL.

White Protestants seem to have been selected by the mayor because of their religious stature, their humanitarian interests, or their

---

[19] Ruml to La Guardia, Dec. 8, 1943; Rockefeller to La Guardia, Dec. 30, 1943, *ibid.*

[20] McCormick to La Guardia, n.d., *ibid.*

[21] Press release, mayor's office, Feb. 27, 1944, *ibid.*

community work during his administration. They included, besides the chairman, Dr. Henry Sloane Coffin, President of the Union Theological Seminary; Morris Hadley, prominent lawyer and president of the New York Public Library; Judge Charles Colden of the New York State Supreme Court; George Z. Medalie, former U.S. attorney; Colonel Allan Pope of the Protestant Welfare Council; and Henry C. Turner, former head of the Board of Education.

It is evident from this group of original appointees that the mayor failed in his effort to attract people to his committee from the very top levels of New York business and humanitarian life. The appointees were, for the most part, "local notables" rather than "national notables." The Jewish and black leaders were prominent in New York City minority affairs, but, except for Channing Tobias, they were not the executive officers of New York–based national organizations. Catholic lay and ecclesiastical leaders were prominent men in New York circles, but they were not the most prominent such men. The same can be said for the Protestant ministers (with the exception of Henry Sloane Coffin), laymen, and businessmen, both black and white.[22] Many of the appointees were long-time La Guardia associates. In fact, some were so responsive to his wishes that the mayor informed the newspapers of their selection before even consulting with them. He took it for granted that they would accept and appear at the ceremony for the committee's initiation.[23]

Implicit Contradictions

The August 1943 outbreak in Harlem was one of the first racial disturbances that fits into the pattern of the ghetto violence of the 1960's.[24] The city government responded to it first with measures to end the violence, and then with the establishment of an intergroup

[22] Further analysis reveals, too, that those people of higher status appointed to the committee participated less in its work. See Chapter 3.

[23] La Guardia to Johnson, Hendrickson, Tobias, Campion, and Granger, March 1, 1944, box 714.

[24] Others have noted this. See, for example, Morris Janowitz, *Social Control of Escalated Riots* (Chicago: University of Chicago Center for Policy Study, 1968).

committee. The latter action was responsive to vocal minority demands that antedated the violence itself, mainly from black groups but also from Jewish organizations especially concerned with racism in the World War II era.

Contradictions are evident in the original conceptions of the committee's role in city government. Blacks had long been shut out of the city's political and administrative processes. John Morsell documents the black leaders' long struggle even to capture control of their own local political clubs in the 1920's and 1930's, and Theodore Lowi points out the dearth of blacks in high city administrative posts even into the 1950's.[25] Minority leaders knew that "the power of all political participants must be exercised through some formal governmental agency" [26] and therefore sought—and thought they had obtained in the Unity Committee—an organization that would give them a voice *within the formal governmental structure.*

The mayor's original conception, on the other hand, was of a high-level research organization *independent of city government.* It was for that purpose that he designed the structure of the agency. His own appointments to the committee, however, contained within them the seeds of the defeat of his notion. The members of the new committee were locally oriented and were representative of the city's different ethnic groups with their diverse demands and political desires. The new committeemen's conceptions of their proper roles were to prove to be closer to the ideals of the minority groups than to those of the mayor who had appointed them.

[25] John Morsell, "The Political Behavior of Negroes in New York City" (Ph.D. diss., Columbia University, 1950), p. 51, and Theodore Lowi, *At the Pleasure of the Mayor* (Glencoe: The Free Press, 1964), p. 42.

[26] Lowi, p. 228.

3

The Unity Committee, 1943-1955:
The Formative Years

The Unity Committee in action was radically different both from the mayor's conception of it and from the ideal organization envisioned by civil rights pressure groups. Some of these differences between administrative conception and administrative reality were implicit in the organization's original structure, some were the result of political necessity, and others were rooted in the dominant race-relations ideology of the era in which it functioned.

The Unity Committee's structure was dictated by the demands of interest groups and by the mayor's view that it would function as a research agency. By opting for this form of organization, Mayor La Guardia built tensions into the committee that would become crucial when differing ideas of its role in the city were to clash. The new appointees, selected as group representatives, came to the committee with primary loyalties to the organizations and groups from which they were selected, and not to the committee itself. Since the group's mandate was unclear, or at least was understood differently by the different people who were responsible for bringing it into being, the committee members were not given a clearly defined common goal toward which to work. Each one, instead, attempted to define the organization's goals in relation to his own prior understandings and organizational commitments. At the very least this could make the body slow moving and inefficient. At worst, it could render it totally ineffective.

The social and political functions that the Mayor's Committee on Unity actually performed in New York City during its twelve-year history cannot easily be categorized, perhaps because the organization's leaders themselves were never entirely sure of even its

38

manifest role within the city government. Nevertheless, in retrospect, an attempt at categorization is necessary both for comparing the committee's work to that of later organizations acting under different circumstances in the city and for understanding the establishment of "race relations" as a legitimate governmental concern in New York.

Analysis reveals four basic areas of action for the Unity Committee. It became the institutionalized focus for individual and group complaints about discrimination in New York. It provided the mayor with an agency with which he could investigate racial and ethnic *causes célèbres* and thus offered the city administration a convenient way of seeming to act to meet racial problems while at the same time delaying action. It attempted to define the objectives of the city in race and minority relations and to influence and direct city policies in these areas. Finally, it attempted to justify its own existence by glorifying its achievements and planning extensive and impractical programs. In doing this the committee was essentially asserting, albeit hesitatingly, the legitimacy of minority-group affairs as a concern for city government.

The first two functions illustrate the committee's apologist role, by far the dominant one for it during the 1943–1955 period. Its job in this area was to "handle" complaints,[1] minimize the racial aspects of problems in the city, and generally protect the mayor from involvement in and political injury from racial issues. The third and fourth functions, minor during this period, illustrate the committee's advocate role. Here the agency attempted to act as a spokesman for minorities and especially blacks within the city government and in the city at large.

Leadership and Philosophy

During the short history of the Unity Committee the executive directorship was held by three people: Dr. Dan Dodson, Mr. Mil-

---

[1] The committee acted to handle complaints in the same way that patrolmen in some cities are expected to "handle" their beats, with a minimum of disruption. See James Q. Wilson, *Varieties of Police Behavior* (Cambridge: Harvard University Press, 1968).

ton Stewart, and Mrs. Edith Alexander. Their tenure corresponded roughly with that of the three chairmen: Charles E. Hughes, Jr., Franklin D. Roosevelt, Jr., and Arthur Wallander.

Dodson was a sociologist active in the New York University Human Relations Center and one of the early professionals in the field of intergroup relations. An active scholar in his field, he, with Hughes, involved the committee in some controversial matters—the integration of baseball and the integration of higher education in New York State, for example—but viewed the organization primarily as an instrument responsive to the mayor, the task of which was to calm racial tensions with as little publicity as possible. The technique of these early leaders was to minimize the racial nature of outbreaks, to deny that problems were racial, and often to castigate the newspapers for reporting them as such.[2] The objective seemed to be, above all else, to keep things quiet. Though committed to La Guardia's research philosophy for the committee, Dodson and Hughes did take the first reluctant steps in using the staff to respond to individual complaints of discrimination. This tendency was reinforced by the referral of several complaints of this type to the committee by the mayor's office.

Stewart's tenure was brief. He came in as Roosevelt's assistant and left when his boss won a congressional seat and went to Washington. Roosevelt's impulse seemed at first to be to invigorate the committee. He talked, in a letter to Mayor William O'Dwyer, of a "blueprint of the Committee's proposed program" and in committee meetings expressed impatience at the slow progress of the proposed statement on segregation.[3] Initially, Roosevelt's presence sparked the organization, and Edith Alexander, associate executive director at this time, spoke of him at a meeting of the West Side Committee on Civil Rights as a great new leader.[4] Soon, however, it became apparent that Roosevelt and Stewart were simply using the com-

[2] See, for example, the committee's treatment of the "Franklin K. Lane High School Incident," discussed below, p. 54.

[3] Roosevelt to O'Dwyer, April 1, 1949, files of the committee, Municipal Archives, box 1215. All documentary citations in this chapter are from the city archives.

[4] Speech to the West Side Committee on Civil Rights, n.d., box 718.

mittee as a platform from which to wage a congressional campaign. They left for Washington under a cloud of suspicion, never publicly expressed, that committee resources had been illegitimately used for campaign purposes.[5]

The early departure of Roosevelt and Stewart left the Unity Committee leaderless. Judge Edward Lazansky, a longtime member, consented to serve as chairman while a new chairman was being sought by the mayor, and with him Edith Alexander stepped into the acting executive directorship. Mrs. Alexander, the backbone of the Unity Committee's staff from the agency's inception, epitomized the committee in its later years. A graduate of Columbia University's School of General Studies, she had obtained a master's degree in 1928 from New York University while working for the Phillip A. Payton real estate company in Harlem. During the 1930's Mrs. Alexander obtained extensive governmental experience in the city Department of Welfare, where, after twelve years' service, she rose to the position of director of the community relations division. Her appointment to the Unity Committee as associate executive director was a natural one for a woman of her experience and commitments.

Because of her connections with the Democratic party in Harlem and with the Urban League, Mrs. Alexander spoke with authority to and for the leaders of the city's black community. Committee members respected her competence and sincerity, and when the committee was left leaderless some pushed for her permanent appointment. A letter from a committee member to the acting chairman illustrates that this promotion to the top staff job in name (and in salary) to correspond with what had been Mrs. Alexander's actual work for quite some time was not *pro forma:* "I think that it is a piece of imposition to assume that Mrs. Alexander would accept the position of acting director without first consulting her. Secondly, I feel that she has been carrying the burden of the Director of this committee long enough without proper status or remuneration. . . . I sincerely do not believe that the fact that she is a woman and a Negro should be held against her. You know, and

[5] Committee minutes, June 29, 1949, and Sept. 27, 1949, box 1215.

every member of the committee knows that she is the backbone of the committee and should have been made the director . . . long ago." [6]

Though she was the first black executive director, Mrs. Alexander did not define the objectives of the committee any differently than had her predecessors. She was, through long training, committed to the "gradualist" and educational approach to intergroup relations. She worked well under Lazansky and under his successor, Arthur Wallander, a former police commissioner and vice president of Consolidated Edison, who was appointed by Mayor Vincent Impellitteri. Under Alexander and Wallander the committee continued its established concern with individual case work and branched out into a consideration of more general discriminatory practices in city government and in New York generally. Quieting emergency situations remained an important function of the agency, but new emphasis was given to long-term education of New Yorkers in tolerance. Under Mrs. Alexander, the New York committee also became involved in the national movement for the professionalization of the intergroup relations field.

Staff

The most important element within the institutional structure of the Unity Committee was the agency staff. It prepared the minutes, wrote the reports, investigated the cases, and generally defined the alternatives from which the committee selected courses of action. The staff was the committee as it functioned daily, and thus its successes, failures, and problems proved a measure of the record of the committee as a whole.

In his original plans, Mayor La Guardia had envisioned a moderately sized professional staff for the committee, capable of doing original research on the causes of racial problems. Fund-raising difficulties, however, placed severe limitations on these plans. At first, the committee was provided with an executive director, an associate executive director, two associate directors, and a small contingent of clerical people. As time passed and funds became more limited, staff resigned and these positions were often vacant.

[6] John Singleton to Lazansky, July 12, 1949, *ibid.*

Associate directors usually engaged in investigations of alleged discriminatory activity, in "constructive dialog" with organizations suspected of discriminatory practices, and in reporting the activities of the agency's subcommittees to the full committee. They were aided in their first two tasks by subcommittee members, whose status as mayoral appointees lent more legitimacy to their efforts (eventually, as the staff diminished, subcommittees took over these jobs entirely). Staff jobs with the committee did not pay well, and after a time even the most dedicated people were forced to give them up. Jobs with the committee were attractive only to individuals for whom the job market was restricted, like black college graduate Harold Hunton, or for those like Irving Goldaber, a graduate student in sociology, who had a special professional interest in the committee's work.[7]

The bureaucracy of the Unity Committee, in short, did not exhibit the normal expansive tendencies that one expects from government bureaus. In fact, its story is one of a struggle for survival. As the agency grew older, instead of augmenting itself the staff declined in numbers, and staff positions became more difficult, not easier, to fill. The explanation for this can be found in the quasi-governmental status of the committee, and especially in its financing difficulties, which in turn reflected a lack of support from the mayor's office. By 1950, the staff of the committee had been reduced to an executive director, one full- and one part-time associate, one secretary, one stenographer, and one part-time typist. The committee would not have been able to maintain even this staff if the city had not provided salary lines, purloined from other departments, for the executive director and stenographer. Independent funding had left the committee's staff, in the end, neither independent nor funded.

Because of the problems of funding and staff turnover, Mrs. Alexander became the greatest single influence in the committee's work. She participated ex officio on the full committee and on all subcommittees, and much of the preparation for these fell upon her shoulders.

Though they attended committee meetings, the occupants of

[7] Interview with Irving Goldaber, former committee employee, Jan. 13, 1969.

lower staff positions were far less important in giving direction to the organization's activities than was the executive director. Positions at the assistant and associate director level were maintained in strict racial and ethnic balance (i.e., when the "Jewish spot" was vacant, a Jew would be sought for it, and it would not be filled with a black).

The Committee Members

The Unity Committee as a whole functioned mainly in reaction to the initiatives of the leadership (both volunteer and staff) and within the limits set by staff work. Meetings were held monthly, except during the summer, and generally attracted about half the membership (but never more than two-thirds).[8] Though the leadership and staff provided the framework, the committee, unlike later human rights organizations in the city, functioned as the decision-making center for the agency. Because of lack of staff, the committee found it necessary to carry its work forward through *ad hoc* subcommittees created to deal with particular problems, in addition to the usual standing committees. As the number of staff declined and the financial difficulties increased, the subcommittees proliferated. By 1950, nine subcommittees were in operation (YMCA, city services, publicity and press relations, discrimination in resort advertisements, Stork Club controversy, Curtis Williams case, finance, and membership), and five new ones (housing, education, community councils, discrimination in public accommodations, and press treatment of minority-group news) were being proposed.[9]

The reliance upon the voluntary membership for "staff work" added to the demands placed upon the time of members by the monthly meetings, and even this minimal participation, as will become evident, was a burden for many. Consequently, matters were dealt with slowly, and there was a constant effort by active members to diminish the burden by increasing the size of the committee.

Though the mayor retained the formal power to appoint mem-

---

[8] See Chart 1.   [9] Committee minutes, Sept 27, 1950, box 1215.

bership, the Unity Committee, because of its internal dynamics and the lack of continuing mayoral attention, became largely a self-perpetuating entity. O'Dwyer and Impellitteri appointed new members only upon the suggestion of the committee, and there is no record of even the exercise of a mayoral veto on suggested appointees.

New people gained consideration by being sponsored before the membership subcommittee, an ethnically balanced body, by a sitting member. The subcommittee then forwarded its recommendations to the full committee. From there they were sent to the mayor. Standards for membership were rather vague. There was an attempt to maintain a racial, ethnic, and geographic balance (at one time, for example, the committee sought a "Staten Island member") and to maintain the representative nature of the organization by adding members from newly emergent ethnic groups in the city. Beyond this, prospective members had to show an "interest in the committee's work" and understand that it was a "working body." [10]

Though the committee could propose new members, it could not remove those who did not conscientiously perform their duties. Consequently, unless they resigned, nonworking members remained on the committee. The committee had little more luck with new appointees than with old members. Less than half of these were active in the agency after appointment. Thus, though the membership grew from eighteen in 1943 to thirty-five in 1953, the percentage of the total membership that was active declined during this period. Membership policies merely added size to the agency; they did little to add to its ability to act.

Constituency

Because of its structural difficulties and lack of visibility, the Unity Committee was an important organization only for those groups that had either an intrinsic interest in the subject matter of the agency's work or limited access to the other decision-making

[10] Report of the membership subcommittee, n.d., box 1215. Manuel Cabranes, a "Puerto Rican representative," was added, for example, in 1950.

arenas in the city government. For New York during this period, the two groups that fit this description were the city's two most self-conscious minorities, the Jews and the blacks.

Jewish groups were attracted to the committee because of a long-standing human rights commitment bolstered by the experience of the war, but also because of rivalries among themselves. Appointment by the mayor of a member of the American Jewish Congress, the American Jewish Committee, or the Anti-Defamation League to the Unity Committee would symbolize to the constituencies of these groups that the city recognized that particular group as the legitimate spokesman for Jewish interests in New York. For the Jewish groups, access to government was much less important than symbolic recognition because access had already been obtained to decision-making arenas of much more substantive importance.

For blacks, on the other hand, access was the crucial issue for they were still, at this juncture, excluded from the other arenas. The great hope of this group was to create an agency within the city government that would be responsive to their needs and from which they could influence other governmental decisions to some degree.

The interest of these two ethnic groups can be measured in two ways from the available evidence. First, one can obtain some indication of interest in the committee by discerning what groups attempted to influence appointments to it. Second, records of attendance at committee meetings may be used as an indicator of the seriousness with which unpaid committeemen took their appointments.[11] It will be assumed in employing this indicator that frequent attendance meant that the member regarded the committee as a meaningful organization, one whose course was worth influencing through a commitment of time and effort.

Influencing Appointments

In this area it is evident that the greatest amount of concern was expressed by Jewish and black groups. Jewish groups had often

[11] Attendance records are taken from minutes of committee meetings, boxes 714–718.

taken the lead in opposing racial and religious prejudice in the city, and committee vacancies were often the cause of internecine warfare among them. In 1947, for example, in a letter to Mayor O'Dwyer, Rabbi Stephen Wise of the American Jewish Congress complained about the lack of representation of his group on the committee. He claimed that the Jewish membership in the Unity Committee was blocking liberal legislation and that it was "unrepresentative of the character of the current Jewish constituency of the Committee." The Rabbi further suggested that the appontment of Shad Polier, a vice president of the Congress, would "redress the balance" on the Unity Committee.[12]

Concern of the Jewish groups seemed often dictated as much by their struggle to gain the upper hand in their constituency, the Jewish community in the city, as by their desire to further the Unity Committee's work. They were interested in visible signs of the city's recognition of their legitimacy as Jewish spokesmen, and in this regard the Unity Committee was useful. This is evident in a letter to the mayor from the president of the American Jewish Congress, Israel Goldstein, in which Goldstein recommended a replacement for a Jewish committee member who had held the Congress' "seat" on the Unity Committee. Unfortunately for this organization, Mayor Impellitteri, perhaps not as wise in the ways of Jewish pressure organizations as La Guardia had been, had already filled the post.[13]

Black groups, besides trying to influence the membership of the committee, were also concerned with its leadship. This tendency, combined with the lesser propensity of the black groups to differ among themselves (at least publicly, when dealing with the mayor), illustrates a greater concern in these organizations for the substantive work of the Unity Committee.

Thus, although in 1949 they did not expect the chairman of the Unity Committee to be a black, several NAACP chapters attempted to exercise veto power over the mayor's choice for this post. They objected to the appointment of former police commissioner Arthur

[12] Wise to O'Dwyer, June 17, 1949, box 1215.
[13] Goldstein to Impellitteri, Sept. 3, 1952, box 6633.

Wallander because, in the words of Charles Carrington, president of the Jamaica chapter, this was

> another in a long series of gratuitous insults inflicted by you on the Negro citizens of New York City. . . . Mr. Wallander, as police commissioner, condoned numerous assaults on Negro citizens by brutal police officers, which has left some of them maimed for life. . . . The majority of the complaints coming before the committee have to do with allegations of police brutality and your appointment of the ex-police head creates doubt in the minds of the fair minded citizenry of New York City as to the intrinsic value of your Committee on Unity. Indeed, it destroys confidence in the committee.[14]

No evidence exists that indicates organized efforts by members of other ethnic groups (Irish, Italian, Puerto Rican, and others) to gain committee representation, and the attempts of black and Jewish groups to influence appointments were largely unsuccessful. The important factor, however, is not the success or failure of these two groups but their effort. They were the only groups that chose to expend resources in trying to influence the composition of the Unity Committee. They were the only ones to define this arena of conflict as even a marginally important one in city affairs.

Attendance

A second available indicator of interest in the Unity Committee is the attendance records kept in the minutes of the organization's meetings. These, for 1949–1952, indicate that attendance was best among original appointees to the committee who had established a continuing commitment to the organization, and with few exceptions these were the black and Jewish members. The blacks and Jews stayed on the committee longer and attended meetings more regularly.

Chart 1 illustrates that eight people fall into the first quartile when ranked according to their attendance at Unity Committee meetings during their time as members of the committee (i.e., these eight attended 75 per cent or more of the committee meetings held while they were members). Of these, the records of two, Franklin

14 Carrington to Impellitteri, n.d., box 1213.

D. Roosevelt, Jr., and Arthur Wallander, can be explained by their formal position in the organization; the fact that each had held the chairmanship caused them to attend regularly. Of the remaining six, one, a 1951 appointee, was Jewish, and the rest were black.

Chart 1. Minority group attendance at Unity Committee meetings as an indicator of interest, 1949–1952 (analysis by quartiles)

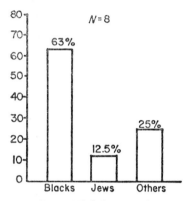

Quartile I—High interest (members attending 75 per cent or more of the meetings)

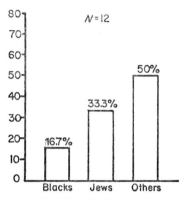

Quartile II—Moderate interest (members attending 50–75 per cent of the meetings)

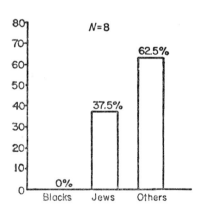

Quartile III—Low interest (members attending 25–50 per cent of the meetings)

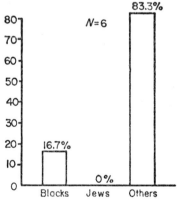

Quartile IV—No interest (members attending less than 25 per cent of the meetings)

The second quartile (those members attending between 50 and 75 per cent of the meetings) contains twelve committee members. Of these, four were Jewish and two black. This category also contains several members who were original La Guardia appointees and who seemed to have established an organizational commitment to the Unity Committee during their tenure. This quartile is somewhat distended by the presence in it of two late appointees who were active on the committee for a short time but then seemingly lost interest in the organization and resigned. The only Puerto Rican member, Manuel Cabranes, is also in this group.

The third and fourth quartiles offer further evidence about the hypothesis of disproportionate black and Jewish interest in the committee. There are no Jewish members in the lowest participation group (0–25 per cent attendance) and only one black, a lawyer who resigned after less than a year's service. No black members are found in the third quartile (25–50 per cent attendance), and three of the eight in this group were Jewish. These three were longtime members of the committee and, though not regular attenders of agency meetings, were active in the subcommittee structure of the organization. Two were subcommittee chairmen, and one headed two subcommittees.[15]

Of the twenty most active members of the Unity Committee for the period between 1949 and 1952, seven were black (35 per cent) and five Jewish (25 per cent). Other ethnic groups, of course, did have active representatives on the committee—40 per cent remain to be accounted for—but it is nevertheless true that a disproportionate amount of attention to the agency came from members of the city's black and Jewish communities. Further evidence for this emerges when one examines the change in the membership of the committee over time. In 1944 blacks and Jews together made up one-third of the Unity Committee's membership; by 1952 the figure was 49 per cent.[16]

[15] List of subcommittee membership, Feb. 10, 1949, box 718. Black members who seem from Chart 1 to have low participation rates are not included in the analysis because their terms of service ended just at the beginning of 1949.

[16] It is interesting to note that the percentage of blacks and Jews in the two most active quartiles is higher by 10 per cent than this 1952 figure

Attendance and membership records, like documentary evidence of attempts to influence mayoral appointments, offer a clue to different groups' conceptions of the relative importance of the Unity Committee. To blacks, whose participation in the city's political process was minimal at this time, appointment to the Unity Committee seemed most significant and most valued. The committee was one of this group's few points of entrée into the administrative process of the city at a (seemingly) policy-making level. Work on the committee had a disproportionate value for Jewish members as well, but participation was not as complete or as valued as it was for blacks. Interest of Jewish members was sustained because of great sensitivity to problems of discrimination and of human rights, but also, as we have seen from other evidence, because of pressure to be "represented" by private Jewish agencies.

Social and Political Functions

The Unity Committee performed four major functions. It became the focus for individual complaints of discrimination in the city, it investigated racial *causes célèbres* for the mayor, it attempted to influence the city's policies toward minorities, and it struggled to maintain itself. In performing these functions over time, the committee legitimized race relations as a proper area of policy concern in New York and established the committee structure as the proper one for governmental action in this policy area.

Individual and Group Complaints

There was at first some question about whether the Unity Committee would deal with individual complaints of discrimination as part of its work, primarily because of the ambiguity of the organization's mandate. Chairman Hughes, for example, adopting La Guardia's view of the committee as a research body, was predisposed to avoid this function. He answered a complaint about discrimination in a Coney Island bathhouse by saying: "It is not the function of the Mayor's committee to deal with individual cases of such violations, nor has it the resources to do so, but we are

_____

for their percentage of the committee membership. This further supports the thesis of their disproportionate activity.

interested in knowing about them as they add to the factual information which the committee is collecting as to discriminatory practices of various sorts in the city." [17]

It soon became evident, however, that the Hughes view was not to prevail. Handling complaints seemed a natural function for the organization to a majority of the committee members, to the staff, and to the mayor's office. Individual complaints came to the staff both directly and by referral from city hall. Their subject matter was varied. They included allegations of discrimination in public places, in businesses that served the public, in housing, in employment, in the provision of city services, in education, and in the administration of city government.[18]

Serious complaints of discrimination were made primarily by black New Yorkers, and a procedure for handling them was soon regularized. Previously, there had been few blacks in high political posts in the city administration, and the task of dealing with "Negro questions" fell to them.[19] Now these matters were referred by the mayor's office instead to the Unity Committee staff.

The committee usually proceeded by investigating the complaint and attempting to conciliate the grievance. As a mayor's committee it had no statutory or coercive power. If the alleged discrimination was within the jurisdiction of the State Commission Against Discrimination, created in 1945, the matter was referred to that commission for action. This cooperation occasionally brought results. In the instance of a complaint that came to the Unity Committee about discrimination on southbound Pennsylvania Railroad trains, for example, the matter was referred to the state agency, and through the use of its influence, the railroad's policy was altered.[20]

Over time, a complaint procedure for racial problems began to become institutionalized in the city. By 1949, J. Raymond Jones, a leading black figure in the Manhattan Democratic party, when

[17] Hughes to Wright, n.d., box 714.

[18] These are collected in the files of the committee, box 1215.

[19] Theodore Lowi, *At the Pleasure of the Mayor* (Glencoe: The Free Press, 1964), p. 43.

[20] Unity Committee, "Report on Discrimination on Southbound Trains in Pennsylvania Station" (New York: The Committee, 1949).

contacted by the mayor's secretary on the matter of a complaint about the living conditions in a neighborhood in Harlem, could say that this was not his province and that the matter was one for the Unity Committee. A regular administrative channel for these kinds of problems had been developed, and by 1952 Jones himself was using it to lodge complaints.[21]

This channel was a convenient referral system for the mayor's office; it provided evidence that the administration was "doing something" about minority problems. Far from being almost irrelevant to the committee's work, as Hughes had suggested, these complaints became a central concern for the organization. Though never numerous, they structured the committee's daily work and defined what its larger projects were to be.

This is evident from the minutes of the organization and from its claims of achievement. A 1951 investigation of automobile insurance company policy toward potential black policy owners grew out of complaints filed with the committee by individuals living in black neighborhoods who could not obtain insurance. Investigations of bank mortgage policies were similarly impelled. A prolonged dialogue with the YMCA about the membership policies of its Brooklyn branches was begun after an individual complained of being denied membership because of his race.[22]

The fact that a governmental structure came into being to deal with complaints of discrimination, and that these complaints sometimes resulted in larger investigations, hardly means that the committee was effective in its efforts. It was a governmental agency only partially, and it had no regulatory power. Because of its structure, its ethos, and its amorphous position in city government, it could often be ignored with impunity, and was. Nevertheless, the administrative implications of the experience of these early years go beyond the substantive results. The committee was taking the first hesitant few steps and thus was providing a framework for the

[21] Memo, Jones to John D. Tierney, March 31, 1949; memo, Tierney to Roosevelt, n.d.; memo, Jones to Alexander, n.d.; box 6630.

[22] A running record of these cases can be found in the minutes of the committee, 1949–1952, box 1215.

treatment of discrimination as a governmental problem in New York City.

Dealing with *Causes Célèbres*

The Committee on Unity was of some value to the mayor's office as a place to which individual complaints of discrimination could be referred, but it was of even more utility in the handling of crisis situations. When racial differences in the city flared up and were publicized, the mayor often called upon the committee to investigate. In this way, he could respond to the situation immediately without committing himself to any policy promises. While the committee investigated, the situation was given a chance to cool down. By the time he received the committee's report, there was often no necessity for the mayor to act.

Committee members enjoyed these crisis assignments because they gave the organization a measure of visibility and placed them, for a time, in the center of city affairs. Reports that emerged from these investigations generally indicated, at least from the mayor's point of view, the sagacity of referral of these matters to the committee. They tended to minimize the racial nature of the particular clash and to lay the blame for its initiation and continuation on other than racial causes. It is evident from these reports that, as an instrument of the mayor, the committee gave first priority to its tension control function (that is, denying that a problem was racial in origin) and lesser priorities to other functions (such as getting to the causes of clashes between racial groups). In particularly explosive incidents the impulse was to keep the peace; the investigation of "discrimination" required a slower pace and a more peaceful context.

Several examples serve to illustrate the committee's orientation. In their report on an incident at Franklin K. Lane High School in 1951, for example, the committee found that "no direct racial antagonisms were involved" in after-school fights between white and black youths. The irresponsible daily press, the committee reported, had exacerbated, with exaggeration, error, and misrepresentation in its reporting, differences between individuals that were not essentially racial. Conferences were held with representatives of the newspapers in order to correct this situation, and the Board of Education was advised on the shortcomings of its public-relations staff.[23]

For its efforts in the Lane situation, the committee received praise from the mayor's office. Executive secretary William J. Donoghue wrote to chairman Wallander: "I think that the mayor can write to you regarding the report of the findings in the Franklin K. Lane incident and express his appreciation to you and the committee for the painstaking efforts which they made to get to the cause of the disturbances and to commend them for the recommendations they made, which, if followed certainly should go a long ways towards the desires and efforts of all of us to eliminate racial tensions or at least to hold them to an irreducible minimum." [24] The mayor had reason to be thankful. The committee had helped him to deal with a difficult problem without any demands upon his political resources and without committing him to any action.

In cases of alleged discrimination against prominent individuals, the committee's reluctance to attribute discord to racial factors was equally evident. In October 1951, Josephine Baker, an expatriate black singer visiting New York, experienced considerable delay in getting served at the Stork Club, an exclusive New York nightspot. She attributed the delay to the prejudices of the club's southern-born owner, Sherman Billingsley. Miss Baker's indignation at her treatment was considerable, and she expressed it in the daily press. The matter was soon a *cause célèbre,* and the mayor asked the Unity Committee to investigate.

The committee asked Billingsley for a statement of policy but could elicit no more than his assertion that "it is our policy to cater to a clientele made up of the people of the world." Even in the face of this obvious evasion, the committee in the end found no discrimination in this case. Its recommendations for action were equally equivocating. Places of public accommodation, said the

[23] Unity Committee, "Report to the Mayor on the Franklin K. Lane High School Incident" (New York: The Committee, 1949).

[24] Donoghue to Wallander, March 13, 1951, box 1215.

committee report, should take it upon themselves to "exercise vigilance" in order to "avoid misunderstandings" that might give rise to the "slightest suspicion that they had practiced discrimination." By the time the report appeared the committee had already done its work; the issue had lost its visibility.[25]

This "safety-valve" function of the committee is also evident in its relations with other city departments. In response to complaints from minority-group leaders, the committee began, in July 1948, with the approval of Mayor O'Dwyer, a survey of city services in congested areas. This activity, chairman Wallander explained to the mayor, was valuable because it "allowed community agencies to express themselves." [26] Intermittently, for a period of almost three years, a subcommittee of the Unity Committee traveled from borough to borough taking testimony on the performance of various city agencies (such as the Board of Education, the Health Department, the Housing Authority). Representatives of "responsible community groups," especially clergymen, were invited to testify, and complaints were referred to the relevant departments for comments, replies, and action.

The subcommittee's final reports, twelve in number, were submitted to Mayor Impellitteri on October 3, 1953.[27] Here, as before, racial tensions were minimized. There were, to be sure, "minor shortcomings" in the services of city departments in minority areas, but these could be attributed to overwork, not to discrimination. For the most part, said the reports, city departments displayed "keen judgment" and "administrative flexibility" in serving all areas of the city while plagued with a shortage of personnel and equipment. False accusations of discrimination, thought the sub-

[25] Unity Committee, "Final Report to Mayor Vincent R. Impellitteri on the Stork Club Controversy" (New York: The Committee, 1951).

[26] Wallander to Impellitteri, Sept. 3, 1953 (accompanying the "Report to the Mayor on City Services in Congested Areas"), box 1215.

[27] Unity Committee, "Report to the Mayor on City Services in Congested Areas," #1, Dept. of Hospitals, Aug. 31, 1953; #2, Housing Dept., Sept. 3, 1953; #3, Police Dept., Oct. 2, 1953; #4, Parks Dept.; Health Dept.; #6, City Planning Commission; #7, Housing Authority; #8, Dept. of Traffic; #9, Transportation Department, all Oct. 23, 1953; #10, Dept. of Sanitation, Oct. 27, 1953; #11, Dept. of Welfare, Oct. 28, 1953; and # 12, Fire Department, Nov. 5, 1953; box 1215.

committee, grew out of "tensions" based upon "ignorance." In fact, some agencies, notably Housing Authority, were pursuing policies that positively promoted integration. "We can say," the subcommittee concluded, "that we found no evidence of knowing discrimination on the part of the City Departments concerned."

Chairman Wallander went even further in his letter of transmittal to the mayor. "We noted," he said, ". . . an absence of any feeling on the part of those attending [the hearings] . . . that there had been discriminatory treatment because of race, religion or other extraneous condition."[28] Again the committee had served the mayor by providing an outlet for grievances without requiring the substance of action. Impellitteri was pleased. He circulated the report, with a few words of praise, to the Police, Fire, Welfare, Housing, and Sanitation departments, and to the Board of Education.

Influencing the Administration's Minority Policies

It has become apparent that the Unity Committee served as a useful tool for the mayor in handling minority problems. The relations between the committee and the mayor, however, were somewhat reciprocal. While the mayor employed the committee as a resource he vested in it some legitimacy and allowed it, to some degree, to influence his minority policies.

In order to maintain the committee as a useful device, the mayor from time to time had to raise money for it (to assure its continued existence), appear at its luncheons, and praise its work. Each mayor did this as he came into office, or at some time during his term. This requirement to provide support for the committee gave a succession of mayors an available platform from which to make positive statements on civil rights issues. Given the marginality of these issues during this period, the very existence of the committee thus defined an "arena of action" for the mayor that perhaps otherwise would not have become manifest.[29]

[28] Wallander to Impellitteri, Sept. 3, 1953, box 1215.
[29] For an extensive discussion of "defining the arena of conflict" see E. E. Schattschneider, *The Semisovereign People* (New York: Holt, Rinehart, & Winston, 1960).

Mayor Impellitteri, for example, pledged in a speech to the committee "total access in housing" for minority-group members in the city and "full elimination of customs that controvert the law." He said further: "It is a basic and deep conviction with me that interracial and interfaith understanding are essential to good government. I shall continue to rely upon this committee to advise me on matters dealing with intergroup relations on such incidents as may jeopardize the peace and tranquillity of our city. I pledge for your support the full resources of the Mayor and all departments directly responsible to him. . . . I want to assure each and every one of you of my full support in the work that you are doing. Feel free to call upon me at any time." [30] Though it is evident—from the budget problems mentioned above, for example—that the mayor's actions belied his words in this pledge, it is quite possible that without the availability of the committee platform even the rhetoric would have been lacking.

In fact, during the late 1940's and early 1950's the committee staff provided the city administration with a major channel into the black community. During the Impellitteri administration, Edith Alexander wrote letters and speeches for the mayor and represented him at Urban League conferences. In addition, she served Deputy Mayor Charles Horowitz as a contact for information on consumer merchant affairs in Harlem. In return, Mrs. Alexander was able to use her staff position to influence administration policy and to draw upon significant political figures for support for the committee's work.

At a more concrete level, the Unity Committee's plans, programs, and position papers occasionally nudged the administration into public stances. The progress toward a statement on segregation chronicled below was tortuous, but eventually the statement was endorsed by the administration.

The provision of the level of support for the committee outlined above entailed minimal costs for the mayor. During this period, though some reciprocity was evident, the Unity Committee made few demands upon the administration and rarely acted as an advo-

---

[30] Committee press release, June 20, 1951, box 6632.

cate for minority positions within the city. The proper role for the agency, most members believed, was to protect the mayor, not add to his problems.

Keeping the Committee Alive

Much of the day-to-day effort of the staff of the Unity Committee was spent in the simple task of maintaining the organization and in justifying its existence. There are many indications of this preoccupation. Though experience repeatedly showed that the organization's resources were limited and that it was doing all that it could when it dealt in some fashion with immediate problems, plans continued to be drawn on a relatively grand scale. Though achievements were minimal, the implications of what was achieved were overdrawn to burnish the committee's image. Though the visibility of the organization remained low, quantitative figures (the number of letters mailed and received, for example) were issued in order to prove that there was an attentive public for the committee's work. Heavily dependent upon volunteer members, the committee was continually faced with the necessity of sustaining itself by "proving" that it had done or was about to do good and essential (if little-known) work.[31]

Grandiose Plans

The standard for large-scale and optimistic planning was set by the Unity Committee's first executive director, Dan Dodson. In the first program he drafted for the committee in 1944, Dodson envisioned six major action areas: employment, housing, education, health, law enforcement, and research. More specific concerns were indicated in each of these areas. In education, for example, segregation was to be attacked, stereotypes in teacher's minds destroyed,

[31] An interesting analogy can be drawn between the performance of this function by the committee staff and similar activity by the staff of national lobby organizations. See Lester Milbrath, *The Washington Lobbyists* (Chicago: Rand-McNally, 1963). The function of committee rhetoric is also similar to that of rhetoric in an election campaign, noticed by Paul Lazarsfeld *et al.*, *The People's Choice* (New York: Columbia University Press, 1948).

and schools "related to the needs of the community." [32] In law enforcement, said Dodson, the committee had to help "educate" the community to trust the police, and the police to trust the community.

Five years later, committee leaders were still thinking of the organization's purposes in a broad manner, although experience by then had shown that it could deal successfully only with particular kinds of problems in particular contexts. In a statement of committee purposes presented to the mayor a short while after he became chairman, Franklin Delano Roosevelt, Jr., wrote of plans in the fields of education and public relations, and spoke of programs for grievance processing, research, segregation, cooperation with private agencies, coordination of public agencies, and tension reduction.[33]

Plans in specific areas were as ambitious in scope as was the program itself. In public relations, for example, Roosevelt envisioned an annual conference attended by the mayor, city officials, and private-agency heads; a regular monthly newsletter with a planned circulation of several thousand; and advisory councils of clergy, businessmen, and social scientists. This attempt to "establish the committee with opinion leaders" would be supplemented with a campaign directed at the general public through regular news releases, pictorial displays, pamphlets, speakers, radio programs, ceremonies, and public hearings. All this was to be achieved without any increase in committee resources or any change in basic organization.

The committee again planned for the future in 1951, this time at a half-day conference called specifically for this purpose. The conference call hints at the reinforcement function of the planning activity and, incidentally, points out the total failure of the Roosevelt public-relations program: "Many of us who serve on the Mayor's Committee on Unity have, on occasion, been at a loss for

[32] Dan Dodson, "Mayor's Committee on Unity: Purposes and Program" (New York: The Committee, 1944).

[33] Roosevelt to O'Dwyer, "Statement of Programs," April 1, 1949, p. 3, box 718.

the *specific* reply, when asked a question about our functions—
what we do, what we are for, and how we operate." [34] Unlike previous conferences, this meeting was directed at the organization's
problems, and it could have been useful if it had led to any changes
in the committee's operations. In fact, there is no evidence of such
changes. After a Saturday morning of discussion, business as usual
resumed at the committee on Monday.

The committee's annual reports, published only for 1951 and
1953, exhibit a similar tendency to deal with the agency's work
in grand and highly impractical terms. Objectives for 1951, for
example, include investigation of real-estate financing and city
services in the black community (these had been going on inter-
minably), stimulation of neighborhood organization, educational
research in cooperation with the Board of Education, development
of an intergroup relations library, sponsoring the annual conference of the national Intergroup Relations Organization, cooperating with city and private agencies, and, again, better public relations.

Exaggeration of Achievements

When some of the realities of committee achievements are compared directly to the rhetoric of planning, the supportive function
of the rhetoric becomes more clear. The committee's plans for
1951, for example, were formulated during a financial crisis that
threatened the organization's very existence, yet there is no allu-
sion to this crisis in the plans. Claimed achievements jibed only
minimally with planned programs. By 1950, committee literature
claimed nine major achievements for the organization: the Benjamin Franklin High School report, the Discrimination in Higher
Education report, referral of discrimination on the Pennsylvania
Railroad to the state commission, its role in helping to integrate
baseball, its efforts for the public market in Harlem, the city services report, a report on the desecration of houses of worship, the
Timone report (an investigation of alleged anti-semitism of a

[34] Benjamin Namm to Fellow Members, Dec. 3, 1951, box 6632.

Board of Education appointee), and its role in improving Harlem consumer relations.[35]

From this list it is obvious that in no instance could the committee claim that its work had caused the kind of large-scale substantive change in city policy in which its plans indicated that it was interested. Investigations by the committee into the private sector of city life (insurance, housing, and so on) likewise rarely produced policy changes. Most of the organization's claimed achievements emerged not as products of the planning program but as by-products of special investigation mandated by the mayor. Even in these areas, the change effected in the pattern of relations between the races in the city was minimal.

The dichotomy between the Unity Committee's program planning and its operations is also evident if one examines the way in which the work of the organization was ordered. The broad-based committee structure, established in accord with stated goals, tended to diffuse the agency's focus and fragment staff efforts. Extravagant definitions of goals contributed to a basic failure to recognize organizational limits. Standing policy subcommittees did exist, such as the program subcommittee, but work was more likely to be carried forward by *ad hoc* groups dealing with specific problems (e.g., car insurance, the statement on segregation, YMCA discrimination). The organization planned broadly but functioned by meeting particular problems on a day-to-day basis. Planning was not integrated into the other functions of the agency; it was functional in and of itself.

The rhetoric of ambitious planning helped the Unity Committee to maintain itself, to convince its own members that "the work of the committee . . . was its own reward." [36] In doing this the committee was, in effect, asserting the legitimacy of intergroup relations as an area of concern for city government. In a final assessment of the value of the Unity Committee, its success in maintain-

[35] Mayor's Committee on Unity, "Annual Report" (New York: The Committee, 1951), pp. 1–3.

[36] Fannie Hurst to Impellitteri (accompanying 1953 annual report), p. 1, box 6632.

ing itself in the face of great organizational problems until a more soundly based substitute could be established is perhaps the organization's greatest single achievement.

The Organization and Functioning of the Unity Committee: Two Examples

The structural problems and the decision processes of the Unity Committee are evident from an examination of two short but crucial incidents in its history. In both situations the agency's relationship with the office of the mayor is clearly highlighted. Further, these incidents illustrate the effect of this relationship and of the committee's organization upon its internal functioning.

Committee Financing: Structural Weakness

The key structural problem of the Committee on Unity was the method by which it was financed. La Guardia sought private financing in order to assure independence and nonpartisanship on the committee. In doing this, however, he deprived the committee of the legitimacy that it would have had as a full-scale city agency with annual funding through the city budget, and he was left in the end with an organization that lacked consistent long-term support from private sources. From the first the Unity Committee was a stepchild, and an anemic one at that.

La Guardia's objective was to raise funds and obtain pledges from diverse sources so that he could provide the committee with a budget of $50,000 a year for a minimum of three years. He appealed for support to foundations, banks, corporations, and wealthy private individuals, but failed to reach his goal.[37] Even with a pledge from the New York Foundation of $25,000 a year for three years, the size of which compromised the mayor's scruples about too much dependence on one source of income, the committee was limited to an annual budget of $35,000 for the first two years. Relative security was maintained during the second

[37] Totals raised: 1944, $24,425; 1945, $37,866; 1946, $32,795; 1947, $28,500; 1948, $38,360; 1949, $33,500; 1950, $7,450 (budget memo, April 6, 1951, box 6632).

two years through an extension of the New York Foundation's support and through the contribution of two salaried positions by the city, but a redirection of the foundation's resources in the summer of 1948 left the committee in the midst of a financial crisis.

An appeal by executive director Dodson to the mayor's office produced a fund-raising letter signed by Mayor O'Dwyer and circulated among his friends, businesses, and "political sources." This effort netted $9,000 and provided a short-term solution. Examination reveals that under the Democratic successor to La Guardia the source of the committee's financial support switched from foundations, philanthropists, and good-government groups to construction and road contractors who were probably more interested in doing the mayor a favor than in sustaining the committee.[38] This, in four short years, was the fate of La Guardia's attempt at apolitical financing.

The committee's continuing income dropped off further in 1950, and the crisis was exacerbated because the mayor's office, preoccupied with the changeover from O'Dwyer to Impellitteri, could not be called upon for aid. The budget was cut drastically but still could not be funded. Most of the efforts of committee members and staff were now not directed at substantive programs but at simply trying to assure the organization's survival. A budget committee was formed, but the Unity Committee could not remain viable on the income from luncheons and small gifts.

By June 1951 the committee had cut its budget to the absolute minimum of staff and salaries and still could not meet its payroll. There was even a deficit of $382.68, a large part of which was salaries owed the secretarial staff. In anticipation of this problem, negotiations had been proceeding between chairman Wallander and Deputy Mayor Horowitz. The committee wanted the city to provide personnel and maintenance money so that it could carry

[38] Letters of appeal may be found in the files of the mayor, box 6632. It is ironic that at this critical juncture the committee was saved by a group that was to be one of the principal targets, as discriminatory, of the later City Commission on Human Rights.

on its work. Horowitz offered $15,000 from the mayor's relief fund but made no continuing commitment beyond the positions provided in 1944.[39] The committee was thus reduced to the level of one of the mayor's good works; its right to survive, under this arrangement, would be reviewable annually.

The failure of the city administration to offer wholehearted support for their efforts affected the Unity Committee in several ways. First, the members were forced to realize that their budget problem would be a continuing one, one that would constantly be diverting the organization's attention from other matters. Second, it was evident that the committee's rather anonymous and undefined position, within and yet outside city government, would continue indefinitely. Third, and perhaps most crucially, the very ethos of the organization was shaken. If the mayor's office did not find the agency important enough to give it continuing financing, how could its members go on believing it played a crucial role in fostering racial harmony in the city? How could they be expected to go on giving time and effort to the organization? They could not, and eventually the dedication of all but a few began to flag.

The Statement on Segregation: The Committee Decides

The Unity Committee's attempts to draft a "Statement on Segregation" provoked divisions within its ranks and consequently raised to a level of visibility the agency's relationship with the mayor and its internal functioning during the late 1940's.

Early in 1947, the Right Reverend Monsignor Raymond Campion, an original La Guardia appointee to the Unity Committee, sought a formal policy statement from the organization declaring that segregation was against "natural moral law." "Improvements in . . . the Negroes' condition without a fair and frank recognition of their rights," said Campion in a letter to Mayor O'Dwyer, "simply confirms in us a false policy of racism." "Segregation,"

---

[39] Memo, Alexander to Wallander, July 16, 1951; memo, Wallander to Horowitz, May 12, 1951; memo, Wallander to Impellitteri, Oct. 18, 1951; minutes, Sept. 20, 1950, and Oct. 24, 1950; memo, Wallander to Members, Oct. 5, 1950; box 718.

he continued, "strikes against the natural right of all men to essential equality. Segregation on the sole basis of race is humiliating to the Negro because it strikes at his dignity as a human person." [40]

Campion's appeal to the mayor was occasioned by the opposition to his draft document by chairman Hughes and the majority of the committee. Hughes disliked the term "natural moral law," perhaps because of his training as a lawyer, but more likely because of his conception of the proper role for the committee in the city. He claimed to favor some sort of policy statement but seemed reluctant to have the committee commit the city administration to any course of action in this area of policy.

The monsignor kept the pressure on the administration by submitting his resignation to the mayor, ostensibly because of the "increasing pressure of duties" but more likely because "the committee never took a positive stand on the question of segregation of Negroes. Because of this, much of its work seemed futile." [41] O'Dwyer, sensing the bad publicity that could emerge from a resignation from the Unity Committee under clouds of disunity, persuaded Campion to stay on.

Protracted discussion continued in the committee on the wording of the proposed statement on segregation. Campion, differing with the administration on another issue six months later, issued a blast to the press and resigned.[42]

M. T. Brunetti then emerged as the new champion on the committee for a strong statement. In July 1948 he wrote to Mayor O'Dwyer urging a "definitive stand," a "pronouncement by a representative group of white people condemning segregation." This, Brunetti said, "should pave the way for a termination of this evil." [43] Still, the mayor failed to act.

Draft after draft was proposed and amended. One, for example, was offered by the newly constituted subcommittee on the state-

[40] Campion to O'Dwyer, June 7, 1947, box 1215.
[41] Campion to Hughes and O'Dwyer, May 23, 1947, *ibid.*
[42] Campion to O'Dwyer, Dec. 23, 1947, *ibid.*
[43] Brunetti to O'Dwyer, July 23, 1948, *ibid.*

ment on segregation, chaired by Michael M. Nisselson, to the general membership in the meeting of February 1949. It began with a quotation from the Preamble of the Declaration of Independence and continued by calling for "equal opportunity," stressing the high cost of segregation to human dignity, pointing out the international implications of this practice, and showing the necessity for immediate action.

This version was apparently returned to the subcommittee for more work, because on March 16 they offered a new document to the full committee. This one stressed the immorality of segregation ("an outrage to the moral traditions of our country, our state, and our city") and its economic and social costs. In addition, this draft attempted to identify housing discrimination as the cause of segregation and cited both federal and state constitutions to offer authoritative statements of value that condemned the practice. It ended with an appeal; "Segregation finds no sanction in the laws; it should find none in our lives." [44] After due consideration, this too was sent back to the subcommittee for reworking. The minutes reported that "the consensus of opinion was that the redraft should not state conclusions, but should be a frontal assault on the evil of segregation." [45]

The identities of the contending groups on the committee are unclear from the record—that is, it is difficult to divide the members into categories like "pragmatists," "legalists," or "moralists" —but what is clear is that the new chairman, Roosevelt, was getting impatient. He considered the segregation statement to be part of the "basic philosophy" of the committee, a philosophy that he wanted the organization to define. Finally, under his prodding, the mayor's office sanctioned the statement.[46]

With this green light from the administration, the draft of May 16 was officially adopted by the committee. It was much like the others. It stressed the fact that segregation was against both the democratic and Christian traditions, and that discrimination was a

[44] Minutes of the committee, Feb. 28, 1949, *ibid.*

[45] Minutes of the committee, May 16, 1949, *ibid.*

[46] O'Dwyer to Roosevelt, April 7, 1949, *ibid.*

"moral travesty." It ended with a promise of action: "Segregation destroys the unity of the American people. The Mayor's Committee on Unity will bend every effort for its extinction." [47]

The committee's work was finished on the project, but the annual summer recess prevented the taking of any final action. Finally, on November 23, 1949, almost three years after the debate was initiated, the statement was sent to the mayor for his signature.[48]

The episode of the statement on segregation is interesting because it reveals the nature of the committee's ethos, its role in city government, and the extent of that government's involvement in race relations in the late 1940's. It is clear from this case study that the committee had difficulty in reaching policy decisions. Its structure, a large membership representing many different groups with concomitant differences in points of view and endless deliberation on these differences, and its voluntary nature, which meant infrequent meetings, indifferent attendance, and marginal commitment from many members, were part of the cause of this difficulty. Fundamentally, however, the problem was rooted in the committee's conception of its role within the city government.

A semiofficial agency, the committee functioned largely to protect the mayor, to be his apologist in the area of race relations in the city. With this role defined, most committee members felt a commitment to the administration that precluded action on anything even faintly resembling policy without mayoral approval. Thus the Unity Committee suffered some of the disadvantages of being part of the official city bureaucracy but, as is evident from its financial difficulties, few of the advantages. The locus of effective decision making at the agency was neither in the voluntary committee structure nor in the full-time staff; it was in the mayor's office. Despite structural difficulties, the organization could act with some dispatch when approval from the mayor was at hand.

[47] Unity Committee, "Statement on Segregation" (New York: The Committee, 1949), *ibid.*

[48] It was recorded as approved by the mayor and released to the press on March 22, 1950.

The nature of the issue that occasioned almost three years of debate is also interesting. It was not a question of action, but one of ideological commitment. The committee contemplated no steps beyond the simple passage of the declaration. Nevertheless, decision was difficult.

The identity of the major actors in this case is also revealing. The lead was taken mainly by whites. Of those members representing groups most interested in influencing committee membership decisions and high on the attendance scale, only Jews were active on this issue. Black members did not assume a leadership role in the debate. The evidence of other cases is simply too skimpy to support general conclusions about the participation of black representatives in the debates of the Unity Committee, but it is certainly true that their hesitancy in this case simply served to contribute to delay and indecision.

Significance

Several factors in the experience of the Unity Committee emerge as important in assessing its impact upon both its successor organization and upon city government in general. First, the establishment of the committee as a continuing organization that spanned the life of several administrations marked minority relations as a legitimate area of concern for city government. Staking out this claim was a necessary first step for further action, and a step that some local jurisdictions in the United States are still experiencing great difficulties in taking.

Second, the experience of the Unity Committee established the representative committee as the proper and legitimate administrative form in the city for dealing with racial problems. This form, with all its potential and demonstrated structural difficulties, was perpetuated in the legislation establishing the statutory commission, and thus further legitimized.

Third, the history of the organization begins to illustrate the inherent contradictions in the role or political functions of the official human rights agency. Such an agency faces what I have labeled the advocate-apologist dilemma. How strong an advocate of minority interests can such an agency be? How much must it protect the interests of the key politicial actors in the city and thus act in ways basically dysfunctional for the minorities? This early organization, acting in a new policy area for city government, was a creature of the mayor and acted largely as an apologist for him. Some tentative steps toward advocacy were taken, however, and the question remained: Would the balance be struck differently by a more independent statutory agency?

Fourth and finally, the Unity Committee defined the "proper approach" to racial problems in the city, an approach that most political actors found congenial because it disrupted few of the ongoing social, political, and economic processes. This philosophy, education in human relations and conciliation of racial problems, was the inheritance of the new statutory committee and a powerful guiding force in its first years, even after the commission received regulatory and enforcement powers.

4

The Commission on Intergroup Relations, 1955–1960: The Conciliation Years

By the early 1950's, important parts of the constituency of the Unity Committee were becoming increasingly critical of its work. Reports of the achievements of several statutory race relations agencies by the Chicago-based American Council on Race Relations were being read in the New York City civil rights community,[1] and these organizations functioned at a level of activity that the Unity Committee, with its structural and financial problems, could not match. Disenchantment with the work of the committee was especially evident during the early 1950's among the strategically placed staff of some of its most important constituency groups, the Jewish civil rights organizations.

This attitude was evident, for example, in a memo from Morris Sass of the Anti-Defamation League's New York regional office to J. Harold Saks, a higher official of that organization. Saks had asked about the advisability of a thousand-dollar allocation by the ADL to the financially distressed Unity Committee. Sass replied negatively because, he said, "Nearly all the agencies concerned with human relations programs and intergroup relations in the New York City area are dissatisfied with the work of the Mayor's Committee." [2]

Acting upon this dissatisfaction, four of the key Jewish organizations in the city—the American Jewish Congress, the American

[1] See, for example, "The Proceedings of the Institute on Race Relations and Community Organization," mimeographed (Chicago: American Council on Race Relations, University of Chicago, 1945).

[2] Memo, Sass to Saks, n.d., files of Morris Sass, Anti-Defamation League of B'nai B'rith.

Jewish Committee, the Anti-Defamation League, and the Brooklyn Jewish Community Council—decided to work for an official human relations agency for the city to be modeled after those already in operation in several other cities. Mobilized by a rash of complaints about police brutality in 1951, several staff people in these agencies (especially Mr. Sass, Will Maslow of the American Jewish Congress, and Arthur J. S. Rosenbaum of the Brooklyn organization) decided to seek support for this effort among other groups.[3]

A meeting was called, to which all the city civil rights and civil liberties groups that might possibly have been interested in the establishment of a statutory human rights commission were invited. About fifty organizations sent representatives, but fewer were ready to commit themselves. Only fourteen groups of the fifty represented at the meeting decided to join in the sponsoring of the proposed "Ad Hoc Committee for the Establishment of a Statutory Mayor's Committee on Intergroup Relations for the City of New York." [4]

In addition to the groups already mentioned, the Americans for Democratic Action and the American Civil Liberties Union had been involved in the project, in varying degrees, from the start. Others that joined included the American Association of University Women, the Ethical Culture Society, the Jewish Labor Committee, the League for Industrial Democracy, the New York City Congregational Churches, the United Parents Association, the New York State Committee on Discrimination in Housing, and the Community Church Social Action Committee. Key black groups—the NAACP, CORE, and the Urban League—were conspicuous by their absence.[5]

The new *ad hoc* group organized itself in anticipation of the 1953 election year. It constituted itself as a permanent organiza-

---

[3] Interview with Morris Sass, Fall 1968.

[4] Minutes of the *ad hoc* committee, June 19, 1952, files of Morris Sass, ADL.

[5] List compiled by Morris Sass, 1953, files of Morris Sass, ADL. See Edward Banfield and James Q. Wilson, *City Politics* (New York: Vintage, 1963), p. 257, on the strategy of the formation of *ad hoc* groups.

tion, the New York Council for Civil Liberties and Civil Rights, formalized its structure (Rosenbaum and Sass became the principal officers), established a steering committee, and set out two basic organizational objectives.[6] First, through an appeal to labor, veteran, good-government, Christian, black, Puerto Rican, and other groups, the new council hoped to broaden its membership base so that it could appear a legitimate spokesman on this issue for all interested groups in the city. Second, it hoped to formulate a framework for action, a strategy through which the proposed human rights commission could become a reality.[7]

The first objective was never achieved. At the council's height it had only twenty-one member organizations, and several significant groups (i.e., the Catholic Interracial Council, the Council of Churches, the Urban League, and CORE) never joined the effort. This failure was not crippling, however, because the council retained the important illusion of being inclusive.

The second objective, the formulation of a strategy, was more important, and here the new organization was considerably more successful. The strategy that emerged was two-pronged. The council prepared a case for the establishment of a commission on the merits of the issue alone, but it also sought, through manuevering during the campaign, to make the need for such an agency a campaign issue and to get all the candidates to commit themselves positively on it.

The case on the merits was fairly straightforward. It had been in preparation for some time at the Anti-Defamation League and had even been sent to Edith Alexander for comment late in 1951.[8] The thirty-three-page report consisted of an assessment of the work of statutory committees on human rights in other cities, a critical analysis of the Unity Committee, and a "model statute" providing for the establishment of the commission.[9]

[6] Minutes of the council, July 19, 1953, files of Morris Sass, ADL.

[7] *Ibid.*

[8] Sass to Alexander, Nov. 9, 1951, files of Morris Sass, ADL. The Unity Committee was effectively neutralized and did not oppose the plan.

[9] "Report of the New York Council for Civil Liberties and Civil Rights Concerning a New York City Mayor's Commission on Intergroup Rela-

In the report the Unity Committee was indicted for "inconsistency," a weakness that was viewed as endemic to any voluntary organization. The committee, its critics noted, had done some good work under Hughes in its early years, but later both the extent and the intensity of its effort had decreased. In order to meet this problem, the report proposed to replace the voluntary agency with "a New York City Mayor's Committee on Intergroup Relations of eleven members with the power to investigate complaints and to initiate its own investigations, to hold hearings, to issue subpoenas, and take testimony under oath, and with the duties of issuing publications and reports, and coordinating and cooperating with official departments and private human relations agencies."

The new committee was to act in six major policy areas, areas in which the Unity Committee had been found by the report to be deficient. First, it would provide in-service training for police and other city employees in daily contact with minority-group members. Second, it would take the lead in seeking antidiscrimination legislation for the city. Third, it would "provide a consultative service for individuals and groups who are interested in participating in intergroup relations work . . . and . . . be prepared to investigate tension situations and individual complaints of discriminatory practices." The fourth project of the committee would be large-scale research for "planning and prevention" of intergroup tensions. Fifth, the organization would "launch a large scale information campaign in the intergroup relations field." Finally, it would cooperate with and integrate the work of private agencies.

The overall objective to be achieved by the creation of this new agency was the establishment of "a statutory committee responsive to community pressure." By "community," the organizations in the *ad hoc* council meant themselves. They envisioned advisory committees, composed of people selected from among their membership, being convened and continually consulted by the new committee. The mayor's committee was to be the focal point for the work of its creators. In order to assure this, the representative

tions," mimeographed (New York: The Council, n.d.). The following several paragraphs are based on this report.

committee structure, used by La Guardia in the Unity Committee, was retained by the advocates of the new agency. The difficulties of the Unity Committee, the council claimed, were rooted in its voluntary nature. Structural difficulties were not mentioned.

The political tactic used by the council to pursue its goal was as ingenious as it was simple. Using its report to show the need for the proposed committee, the council contacted every candidate for elective office in the city from the mayoralty on down and asked each for a written statement of his position on the issue. All candidates—Democratic, Republican and American Labor—endorsed the idea.[10] The council seemed victorious, but the real fight had not yet begun.

Origins of the Commission on Intergroup Relations

After the election, Mayor Wagner, in his first "state of the city" message, reaffirmed his campaign commitment to "a permanent well staffed agency . . . in the area of Human Rights." "The matter of intergroup relations," he said, "is far too important to be assigned to an informal and temporary agency." [11] The mayor was thus committed to some sort of human rights agency; there were differences of opinion, however, both within and outside the administration, on exactly what form this organization should take.

Three proposals were made in the city council. One, sponsored by Brooklyn borough president Abe Stark, suggested that a city council investigating committee be established to study the need for such an agency. This was an obvious attempt at delay and was sent to the rules committee, from which it never emerged. The other two proposals, both in the form of bills, were introduced by council president Joseph T. Sharkey. Bill No. 1, introduced on January 19, 1954, as the first legislative measure to be placed before the council in that year, was the original Council for Civil Liberties and Civil Rights model statute. Bill No. 117, introduced

---

[10] The letters from the candidates to the council may be found in the files of Morris Sass, ADL.

[11] *New York Times,* Feb. 3, 1954, p. 16, col. 4.

on March 9, 1954, was the administration measure. It used the council bill as a base but modified it considerably to limit the proposed commission's power and increase the mayor's control over it. Several examples will illustrate how this was done.[12]

The council bill called for the commission to:

receive and investigate complaints and to initiate its own investigations of . . . discrimination against any person, group of persons, organization or corporation, whether practiced by private persons, corporations, associations, or other organizations or by city officials or city agencies. . . .

. . . hold both public and private hearings, to subpoena witnesses and compel their attendance, administer oaths, take the testimony of any person under oath and in connection therewith to require the production of any evidence relating to any matter under investigation or in question before the commission.

So far as practicable, the services of all other city departments and agencies shall be made available by their respective heads to the commission for the carrying out of the functions herein stated. Information in the possession of any department or agency shall be furnished to the commission when it is requested.

The administration bill read:

receive and investigate [complaints] . . . whether practiced by private persons, associations, corporations, or, *when authorized by the Mayor,* by city officials and city agencies. . . .

. . . hold hearings, compel the attendance of witnesses, administer oaths, take the testimony of any person under oath and in connection therewith to require the production of any evidence relating to any matter under investigation or in question before the commission. *No public hearing shall be held without the written approval of the Mayor.*

So far as is practicable, *and subject to the approval of the Mayor,* the services of all other city departments and agencies shall be made available to the commission for the carrying out of the functions herein stated. The head of any department or agency shall, *subject to the written approval of the Mayor,* furnish information in the possession of such department when it is requested.

[12] Marked-up copies of both measures may be found in the files of Morris Sass, ADL. Emphasis is mine.

The administration's bill also proposed procedural restrictions on the new commission that were absent from the council proposal: Commission hearings would require the presence of three commissioners, whereas the draft of the civil rights groups required only one. Witnesses would be allowed the right to counsel. The judgment about whether the new commission needed legal counsel assigned from the corporation counsel's office was left to the head of the latter rather than the former agency. All these changes were designed to make the proceedings of the intergroup relations agency more subject to outside control and more judicial, and thus less expeditious.

Furthermore, language in the original measure that closely tied the proposed commission to its constituent agencies was removed from the administration proposal, as was language which gave the voluntary commissioners (the appointment of whom the civil rights groups hoped to dominate) administrative control over the agency. Under the draft of the mayor's office, appointments to the commission were not required to be "broadly representative of the religious, racial, and ethnic groups in the community." The power "to create such advisory committees and sub-committees as in its judgment will aid in effecting the purpose of this local law and to empower them to study the problems of prejudice, bigotry, discrimination and disorder occasioned thereby" was removed from the administration draft. The authorization to "accept contributions from other sources" was likewise deleted. Finally, the commissioners were left with the power, in this draft, to appoint the executive director of the proposed agency, but without the authority to select "such additional personnel as [they] may deem necessary and to fix their compensation within the limits of the funds made available to the commission."

The thrust, then, of the effort of the mayor's office was to create an agency but to limit its powers and ties to private civil rights groups and to make it more directly responsible to the mayor. In this, the era of Joseph McCarthy on the national scene, the great fear was that an agency with open-ended investigative powers could become a monster. As Henry Epstein, an assistant to the mayor, noted in a city council hearing on the bill, with the powers given it in the original draft of the civil rights groups the commission could "bedevil every department, crucify the Mayor, and utterly destroy the governmental function of the city." "The measure," he went on, "was destruction of orderly government." [13] To the mayor and to Epstein, their version seemed a reasonable beginning. "One step at a time," they said, "is sound policy." [14]

The agencies that had proposed the original bill were not as sanguine about the revisions as were the administrators at City Hall. They felt that the mayor's proposal "completely destroyed the aims and objectives sought" through the establishment of a statutory commission, that the resulting organization would be much like the Unity Committee, and that, in sum, they had been "sold down the river" by the mayor.[15] An interoffice analysis of the administration bill summed up what was wrong with it from the point of view of the civil rights groups.

This triumvirate of provisions endows the Mayor with unique powers over a Commission that was originally designed to be an independent body. In case of discrimination by city officials alone, the Mayor can exercise the following choices without let or hindrance. He can, in the first place, refuse to allow the complaint to be officially received or investigated, and can forbid the Commission from initiating its own investigation into discrimination. If he decides to allow such an investigation, he can refuse a public hearing, thus keeping the proceedings effectively hidden from the public and from civic agencies. If the commission makes a report he doesn't wish to have see the light of day he can simply refuse to make it public. All rests with the Mayor. The commission and its work rest in his vest pocket.[16]

The agencies had some valid objections, but they were also upset for other reasons. They had sought to create an agency "outside politics," an agency largely responsive to their control and their priorities, and with the powers they thought it should have. They had done all the work and now the mayor was indicating

[13] *New York Post,* Jan. 20, 1955, p. 18.
[14] Epstein to Rosenbaum, n.d., files of Morris Sass, ADL.
[15] Sheinberg to Sass, March 23, 195(?), files of Morris Sass, ADL.
[16] *Ibid.*

that he, not the city civil rights groups, was going to set the priorities in this area of policy.

Two alternatives lay open to the agencies. They could reject the commission outright on the mayor's terms and fight for all or nothing, or they could seek a compromise. They met to decide upon tactics. Problems were immediate; the twenty-one groups could not agree on a common position.[17] Finally, they agreed to disagree. Individual agencies would act separately for the bill, and the council would be used to seek conferences with Wagner, Sharkey, and Epstein (who was on the board of the Anti-Defamation League and spoken of in memos as "our deputy mayor"), to call a press conference to attack the mayor's proposal, and to circulate an analysis of the two bills among the city council members.

In April a committee of the Council for Civil Liberties and Civil Rights met with Epstein at City Hall. He stood firm on most of the administration's changes but did react favorably to minor adjustments on the matters of hiring staff, releasing commission reports to the public after a two- or three-month silent period, and appointing "technical advisory councils." This, however, was as high in the administration as the council could reach. The mayor would not see its delegate committee.[18]

The division among the civil rights groups proved decisive for the ultimate political outcome. In the face of the administration's reluctance to make further concessions, most of the agencies expressed a willingness to "accept the bill as is for a trial run." [19] Of the twenty-one members of the council, only three—the American Jewish Congress, the American Civil Liberties Union, and the NAACP—remained intransigent and attacked the mayor in the press for reneging on his campaign pledge.[20] At the final public city council hearings no speaker for the agency bill committed himself against the administration bill, which passed, largely unchanged, early in 1955.[21]

[17] Minutes of the council, April 12, 1954, files of Morris Sass, ADL.

[18] Sass to Epstein, April 15, 1954, files of Morris Sass, ADL.   [19] *Ibid.*

[20] *New York Times,* June 3, 1954.

[21] Sass memo, Jan. 20, 1955, files of Morris Sass, ADL, and *New York Post,* Jan. 20, 1955, p. 18.

Transition

The Unity Committee continued to function while the city council debated the form of the legislation that would create its successor organization. The chairman wrote to the mayor late in 1954 to assure him that committee members would continue to serve until the new agency was constituted.[22] Wagner accepted these assurances but delegated few tasks to the committee. Mrs. Alexander devoted most of her time to the emerging National Association of Intergroup Relations Officials (NAIRO) and to chronicling, in a final report, the Unity Committee's achievements.

In fact, the committee leadership and staff participated remarkably little in the debate over the nature of their successor organization. In July 1955, after the passage of the basic legislation, chairman Wallander and Mrs. Alexander transmitted a few ideas about the proper role for the new commission to the city administrator's office. They stressed the need for close cooperation between the commission and the mayor. This, they said, would help the agency avoid the pitfall of "personal self-glorification" and would "keep groups from pressuring the city for their own ends."[23] Programs, they advised, should emphasize education, research, and cooperation with other city agencies. In order to smooth the transition, Alexander and Wallander recommended that some Unity Committee members be retained in the new organization and that a joint meeting between the incoming and outgoing groups be arranged. The proper level of financing, both agreed, would be $50,000 per year.

The leaders of the old committee could only envision the new organization in the context of their own experience. For them, the commission would be best if it were the committee, reconstituted by the removal of its nonworking members and relieved of financial difficulties. It is therefore not surprising that their direct

[22] Wallander to Wagner, Dec. 1, 1954, files of the Committee, Municipal Archives, box 1969. All references to documents in this chapter are in the Municipal Archives unless otherwise indicated.

[23] Robert J. Mateson, confidential report to Luther Gulick on the Unity Committee, July 1, 1955, Wagner Collection, box 1499.

influence upon the new agency was minimal. The legacy of the Unity Committee for the commission was more subtle, and thus more lasting. It was rooted in the committee's philosophy and methods, the pattern of behavior that it had established in the political system of the city.

To be sure, the Unity Committee's financial and staff problems were mitigated in the new organization, and new constituency relationships were developed, but the agency's role in city government remained the same. Like the old committee, the new Commission on Intergroup Relations approached race relations with methods of conciliation and compromise, convinced that the basic problem was simply to educate the population of the city in tolerance. Like the old committee the new agency functioned largely as a protective device for the political leadership in the city, helping it to deal with racial issues without major expenditures of time or resources.

The establishment of the Commission on Intergroup Relations (COIR) was an indication that concern about racial inequalities had reached a new level of political importance in New York City in the mid-1950's. In this, developments in New York paralleled national trends. This concern was exceeded by a more basic concern that the agency not be given powers that could upset the political status quo in the city. The mayor recognized the need for such an agency, and he promised that he would create it, but he was equally convinced that its functioning should be closely controlled.

Philosophy and Goals

The philosophy and goals of the COIR were directly descendant from those of the Unity Committee and were outlined for the agency in the mayor's office. Bargaining and education were the commission's acknowledged tools and an integrated society in the city its major objective. In a draft program for the commission in 1955, mayoral assistant Stanley Lowell outlined these functions for the COIR: (1) high-level negotiation, (2) policy making, (3) keeping city hall informed, (4) fact finding, (5) inservice training, (6) coordination of resources, (7) public information, (8) investigation, (9) recommendation of legislation and executive orders, and (10) publishing findings.[24] Most of the tasks on this list are passive. The commission was not expected by the Wagner administration to take many initiatives or to perform functions, like law enforcement, that might have been felt as "coercive" by some in the city.

The agency's own outline of its "purposes and program," drafted in 1956, indicates that its staff and leadership accepted the role offered by the mayor's office.[25] In their view, the COIR was to act as "a city agency through which the City of New York officially may encourage and bring about mutual understanding and respect among all groups in the city." They would seek to do this by being a "catalytic agent and coordinator," cooperating with other agencies and groups, suggesting programs to them, and perhaps aiding them in carrying these programs out.

Speaking in 1962, Alfred J. Marrow, chairman of the COIR for much of the early period, reaffirmed that conciliatory methods had been the "most useful and successful" tools for the commission during his tenure. These he listed as "(1) participation, (2) negotiation, (3) use of mass media, (4) appeal to law, (5) education." Though "appeal to law" seems to indicate something of an "enforcement" orientation, for Marrow it meant "tak[ing] advantage of the law-abiding nature of the overriding majority of the population and thus help[ing] stimulate a change in prejudicial attitudes." [26]

From this short summary it is evident that the methods and goals of the COIR in the mid- and late 1950's were much the same as those of the Unity Committee in the late 1940's. Underlying these was a conviction that justice was possible through slow

[24] Stanley Lowell, draft program, March 1, 1955, his files, box 1490.

[25] Anon., "Outline of the Commission on Intergroup Relations Purposes and Program," May 31, 1956, files of COIR, box 6633.

[26] Alfred Marrow, *Changing Patterns of Prejudice* (Philadelphia: Chilton, 1962), pp. 243–244. Implicit in this analysis is a contrast between "conciliation" and "enforcement" as styles for the agency. The enforcement orientation was adapted in the 1960's and will be discussed in a later chapter.

change and established processes, and that discrimination could be conquered if its victims could only wait.

Leadership and Organization

Ironically and perhaps prophetically, the Commission on Intergroup Relations began its life on the basis of two principles of public administration that were increasingly coming into disrepute among political scientists by the mid-1950's: the idea of the separability of politics from administration and the corollary notion that "politics" could and should be removed from certain public endeavors. In conception, the dichotomy was very simple. The unpaid COIR commissioners, meeting periodically, would make agency policy under the direction of the chairman, and the staff, guided by the executive director, would carry it out. In execution, however, simplicity was lost.

The Chairman and the Commissioners

The first chairman, Herbert Bayard Swope, had assumed the post reluctantly, after a three-hour conversation with the mayor, and was happy to leave the initiatives to his executive director, Frank Horne. With the cooperation of Lowell in the mayor's office, Horne, who had been brought in from Washington, D.C., to fill the executive directorship, was able to assemble a staff (racially and ethnically balanced in the manner of the Unity Committee), establish a set of operating procedures, and draw up an initial budget for the agency.[27]

In accordance with his agreement with the mayor, Swope resigned after a year and the chairmanship was assumed by the former vice-chairman, Alfred Marrow. With this change, the relationship between the chairman and the executive director was redefined. Marrow possessed a unique combination of credentials. He had earned a doctorate in psychology, was a student and friend of Kurt Lewin, and was deeply involved in human relations research. He had witten a book on intergroup relations, *Living with-*

---

[27] There were, at first, three blacks, two Jews, and one Puerto Rican on the professional staff.

out Hate, and considered himself an expert in this field. At the same time he was the president of a large manufacturing corporation.[28] Marrow in the chairmanship was a potential danger to executive director Horne; he had, because of his business, a good deal of time to devote to an unpaid position and, because of his education and research, would not find it necessary to defer to Horne's expertise.

Under Swope the sole work of the commissioners had been to convene monthly to hear the reports of the executive director; under Marrow a subcommittee structure was established. Three major standing subcommittees, planning and program, education and city departments, and Puerto Rican affairs, were appointed, and their reports to the full commission paralleled those of the executive director.[29]

As time passed, more of the power of the full commission gravitated into the hands of the chairman. As an unpaid volunteer, appointed to represent a particular group in the city, each commissioner had a different degree of interest in what the commission was doing, and their interests also differed in kind. Several members viewed their role as simply to connect the agency with one group in the city and took little interest in overall policy matters.

As commission functions grew, increasingly greater demands came to be made on the time of commissioners. For example, a provision of the city fair housing ordinance provided that hearings under the new law be presided over by three commissioners. In reaction to this some commissioners resisted all demands upon their time. One remarked: "We wasted a lot of time on the commission. You had to be careful because the more time you gave the more time they wanted." [30] In avoiding service, commissioners who took this view relinquished any power they might have exercised in the organization.

[28] Alfred Marrow, *Living without Hate* (New York: Harpers, 1951).
[29] Alfred Marrow, "Report of the Chairman," June 27, 1956, files of COIR, box 6633.
[30] Interviewee wishes to remain anonymous.

Active commissioners recall spending as much as a quarter of their time on agency business. When they did become active in policy areas, however, their activities were confined to a limited sphere (service on subcommittees or on panels hearing individual complaints of housing discrimination). The majority of commissioners, even when interested, were unable to get an overall perspective on the workings of the commission. Only the chairman was in a position that offered such a view. He was an ex officio member of all subcommittees and by virtue of formal position could enter into all areas of commission business.[31]

In short, Robert Michels' iron law of oligarchy was operating in the commission during this period,[32] and this operation coincided with the tenure of a chairman who sought to draw the power of the organization to himself, if only because he was convinced that he knew best how to use it. The increased importance of the chairman in relation to the commission and the executive director can roughly be measured by the visibility of the two men and the organization in the media, as indicated by the number of appearances of each of these in the *New York Times Index*. From 1955 to 1959, the visibility of the commission and of the executive director as measured by this index declined, and that of the chairman increased.[33] By 1959 the unpaid chairman was clearly the public spokesman for the commission; the executive director's name rarely appeared in the press.

This confluence of events was not a happy one for Frank Horne, the executive director; a power center was developing from which his control of the COIR's daily operations could be challenged. Since power had not been usurped, however, and since the changes that did occur stemmed from dynamics of the

[31] Interview with Marrow, Feb. 5, 1969.

[32] "It is indisputable that the oligarchical and bureaucratic tendency of party organization is a matter of technical necessity. It is the inevitable product of the very principle of organization" (Robert Michels, *Political Parties: A Sociological Study of the Oligarchical Tendencies of Modern Bureaucracy* [New York: Dover, 1959], p. 35).

[33] See Table 2.

organizational structure of the agency itself, Horne could do little more than meet the challenge when it arose.

The Executive Director and Staff

Informal adjustment in the commission's decision-making processes was paralleled by large-scale changes at the staff level in the agency. In size alone growth was tremendous; 1955–60 was the only period in the history of the commission when its budget grew faster than that of the city government as a whole.[34] In 1956–57 the COIR's budget was $120,000 and it employed twelve people. By 1959–60 the budget had more than doubled to $370,525 and the staff had expanded to fifty-three employees. Much of this change was due to the city's vesting in the commission the responsibility for administering the Sharkey-Brown-Isaacs fair housing act, passed in 1958. Between fiscal 1958 and fiscal 1959, almost $200,000 was added to the commission's budget and thirty-three people to its payroll.

This expansion in the scope of the organization's activities and augmentation of its responsibilities led to internal changes. With the increase in size, decision making could not be intimate; a large staff could not meet together as frequently or know each other as well. With the assignment of new responsibilities, resources had to be redistributed, emphases redefined, and energies redirected— and all this just a few years after the agency was established. It is not surprising that critics viewed the COIR as always getting ready to do something but never acting, and felt that what it did accomplish was not commensurate with the resources committed to it.[35]

Difficulties were compounded because the rapid growth occurred while the original definition of the agency's functions was still ambiguous. In fact, the COIR's assigned task defied proper definition. In contrast to the main task of the city Fire Department, for example, the main task of the COIR (i.e., "promoting good

[34] See Table 12.   [35] Interview with Earl Brown, summer 1968.

intergroup relations") was vague in the extreme. Furthermore, the ambiguity extended to the staff job descriptions. The skills of the fireman are relatively clear cut compared to those needed by the "intergroup relations officer."

Within the context of rapid growth and functional ambiguity, pressures grew for the appointment of personnel for reasons other than professional competence (which was, after all, undefined). The creation of the commission entailed not only the establishment of new jobs, but new kinds of jobs. Hiring in new categories was not as bound by civil-service tradition and regulation as in already titled positions. Increasingly, positions on the commission staff were sought as rewards for politically loyal minority-group Democrats.[36] These appointment practices did not necessarily produce an incompetent staff, but they did produce a staff whose primary interest was not in the commission's work and whose loyalty was to the party and not to the commission.

All appointments, of course, were not made on a patronage basis, but the executive director did not act vigorously to forestall this challenge to his control of agency personnel policy. Similarly, Horne did not run a tight ship administratively. He had never administered a large organization himself but had served in an advisory capacity to men who had. He was at ease as executive director when the commission remained small, but as it grew he made errors of omission. One expert who studied the commission in the late 1950's recalled: "In a purely technical sense there were many instances of poor management during the period when Frank Horne was Executive Director. Some staff were poorly supervised, some of the record systems were inadequate, and there were inadequate policies on such things as overtime. Horne's forte was policy analysis and program conception and, at his best, he was a near genius." [37]

The stage was thus set for a clash. The responsibilities of the

[36] Interview with Earl Brown and others.
[37] Henry Cohen to the author, April 25, 1973.

agency grew, but it seemed to be inefficient and poorly administered. The incumbent chairman sought to expand his control. The
position of the executive director was being undermined.

Constituency

The constituency of the Commission on Intergroup Relations in
the late 1950's was composed of three basic elements: organized
civil rights groups, community organizations, and individual complainants. In addition, the commission attempted to pay special attention to the city's Puerto Rican minority.

Since it was they that had forced the mayor to commit himself
to the establishment of the COIR, the city's private civil rights
groups believed that they were entitled to a continuing role in the
direction of the commission. Stanley Lowell, the assistant to the
mayor with responsibility for this area of policy, basically agreed
with this premise. After the legislation establishing the commission
had been passed, he requested from these organizations recommendations for the position of commissioner.[38] Though a twelve-
man commission was planned at first, enough appointments were
made to satisfy everyone. It is perhaps more than a coincidence
that fourteen organizations were asked for suggestions and exactly
that number of commissioners was finally appointed (excluding
the chairman).

The commission, like the Unity Committee before it, was carefully balanced; an attempt was made to obtain representation from
all the city's racial and ethnic groups and even some economic
and academic interests. Worksheets of Lowell and Henry E.
Epstein, another mayoral assistant, illustrated this attempt at balance. Names are listed with race or religion appended ("John
Davis, Negro") and are grouped according to these identifying
characteristics ("recommendations for the Commission on Intergroup Relations [Jewish]").[39] Notes indicate that the mayor's aides
thought that the commission "must include an AFL-CIO man"

[38] Lowell to various agencies, June, 21, 1955, files of Stanley Lowell, box
1490.
[39] Lowell to Epstein, n.d., files of Stanley Lowell, *ibid.*

and that the New York University Human Relations Center should be represented.[40]

This attempt to gather together a representative commission was praised by members of the agency's organized constituency. This proved, said one leading civil rights advocate in the city, that the "commission would be independent of partisan political control." [41] In fact, his veiled hope was that the commission would make policy in the agency, and that the groups would control the commission. Constituency control was seemingly further solidified with the selection of the chairman and the executive director for the COIR. The first chairman, Swope, served reluctantly. Frank Horne, though a City College graduate and greatly respected in the local black community, needed time to become acclimated to his new environment. The situation of both allowed the organized constituency represented on the commission the opportunity to direct the fortunes of the agency.[42]

Exactly which civil rights groups constituted the active and interested constituency of the commission? This can be measured by determining which organizations supported the agency from the inception of the commission idea in June 1952 to the final selection of the commissioners by the mayor in December 1956.

As is evident from Table 1, the majority of the consistent long-range support for the agency came from liberal Jewish groups. These groups had the largest hand in creating the commission and seeing it through its first days. Most members of the original commission had specific support from at least one of the organizations represented on the table. Those who did not were Michel Cieplinski, head of the national Democratic party's minorities division, and the two union representatives, Vincent Lacapria and Charles Kerrigan. As time passed, positions on the committee came to be regarded as the seats of the groups that had first captured them.

[40] Epstein to Wagner, May 18, 1955, box 1969.

[41] Harriet Boonen, "Study of the Passage of the Sharkey-Brown-Isaacs Law in NYC" (M.A. essay, Columbia University, 1960), quoting Morris Sass, p. 18.

[42] In fact, as we have seen, most commissioners did not avail themselves of this opportunity.

Table 1. The constituency of the Commission on
Intergroup Relations, 1953–1956

Group	Supported commission idea (1953) *	Consulted by mayor on appointments (1955) †	Provided commissioner (1955) ‡	Consulted by commission on program (1956) §
American Association of University Women	x			
American Civil Liberties Union	x			
American Jewish Committee	x	x	x	x
American Jewish Congress	x	x	x	x
Americans for Democratic Action	x			
Anti-Defamation League of B'nai B'rith	x	x	x	x
Brooklyn Jewish Community Council, Inc.	x			
Catholic Interracial Council		x	x	x
Citizens Union		x		
Committee on Civil Rights in East Manhattan				x
Commonwealth of Puerto Rico, Migration Division		x		
Community Church Social Action Committee	x			
Council of Spanish American Organizations of Greater New York		x	x	x
Ethical Culture Society	x			
Jewish Labor Committee	x	x	x	x
Jewish War Veterans		x		
League for Industrial Democracy	x			
NAACP		x	x	
National Conference of Christians and Jews				x
New York City Congregational Churches	x			
New York State Committee on Discrimination in Housing	x	x		
Protestant Council of the City of New York		x	x	x
United Neighborhood Houses of New York				x
United Parents Association	x			
Urban League of Greater New York		x	x	x
Women's City Club of New York		x		

* Source: files of Morris Sass, Anti-Defamation League of B'nai B'rith.
† Source: files of the mayor, Municipal Archives, box 1490.
‡ Source: New York Times, Dec. 1, 1955, p. 30, col. 5. This categorization depends upon public identification of the commissioner with the group in the Times story. Other groups that may have provided a commissioner are not accounted for here.
§ Source: Horne to Marrow, June 22, 1956, Municipal Archives, box 6633.

As vacancies occurred, they were filled by nominees from these agencies.

During the crucial first days of the commission, the period in which initial policy directions were established, the organized constituency of the COIR played a predominant role. Leaders of the new agency sought to consult with the "outstanding professional agencies" in order to "gain their opinion on how the Commission on Intergroup Relations could better act on Public Law 55." Commission staff envisioned these conferences as "a first step in the web of program involvement which COIR will face these agencies with in the future." "We believe and hope," said one staff member in a memo to the chairman, "that private agencies will be involved in every aspect of COIR's activities from the planning to the execution stage." [43]

It was natural that the COIR staff turn to these organizations for program support; they were the agency's main, and perhaps only, source of solid support in the political system of the city. Behind this attempt at cementing relationships, however, was a further thought. Just as the constituency groups attempted to direct the agency, the COIR staff was attempting to use these groups to its own ends. The staff envisioned the commission as a possible place from which the resources of all the civil rights groups in the city could be coordinated and directed, hopefully by the staff itself.

The staff was aware of organized constituency attempts to control the organization. They were willing to consult all groups, collectively and individually, on the agency's program and to allow them some leeway in defining program areas for the COIR, but, in the end, the staff resisted the formal establishment of group representatives, despite the fact that, in an earlier concession, the mayor had indicated that he would not object to such an action. The commission, thought the staff, was representative enough of these interests.[44]

[43] Memo, Wellington Beal to Horne, May 31, 1956, files of COIR, box 6633.

[44] Memo, Paul Klein, n.d., 1956, files of COIR, *ibid.*

After the replacement of Swope by Marrow in the chairmanship of the COIR in September 1956, the relationship of the committee to its organized constituency became even closer. Whereas Swope had been an "ethnic neutral," Marrow was the "American Jewish Congress man" on the commission, and his closest associates were the "representatives" of the other major Jewish groups. Under Marrow the COIR continued the policy of "consult[ing] and cooperat[ing] with private organizations." [45] Marrow, to be sure, was not simply a conduit for the ideas of these private agencies, but his approach to human rights problems did basically converge with that of the milieu from which he was recruited.

Community Organizations

In order to augment its close and continuing relationship with citywide civil rights organizations, the COIR decided early to try to expand its constituency by reaching out to the neighborhood level in the city. Many of these initiatives were taken partly at the suggestion of the citywide groups and were clearly within the legislative mandate of the agency. The commission had much to gain from fostering indigenous organization in minority neighborhoods. Besides the obvious value of such efforts for its statutory functions—promoting intergroup harmony and anticipating and preventing "tension situations"—the promotion and support of neighborhood groups allow the agency to "win acceptance" among the people it sought most to serve, the Negro and Puerto Rican minorities in the city. Observing the COIR in this area of activity only, Clarence J. Davies noted: "its primary function was actually to serve as a pressure group to defend minorities." [46]

In an early memo, commission staffer Wellington Beal urged that the commission seek the "real leaders" in ghetto neighborhoods and have these men and women "sit with the commission and express their problems as they see them and tell how they think the

---

[45] COIR, *Annual Report, 1958* (New York: The Commission, 1959), p. 1.

[46] Clarence J. Davies, III, *Neighborhood Groups and Urban Renewal* (New York: Columbia University Press, 1966), p. 62.

commission can be of help." [47] Later the COIR acted in this area by encouraging the creation of local organizations for the improvement of race relations in changing neighborhoods. Where local groups were formed staff was made available for consultation by them. In both the Seaside-Hammels and West Side Urban Renewal Area housing controversies, for example, the COIR provided staff aid for *ad hoc* local groups.

In fact, the establishment and support of local groups was difficult except in crisis situations. The commission sought to act as a catalyst and to have neighborhood organizations emerge from a "felt need" of the community, but this need simply did not make itself felt in the normal course of events. In the 1958 report of the commission, for example, many instances of community action by the agency are cited, but these were all responses to "tension situations." [48] The commission was not successful in promoting or sustaining an outgoing network of broad-based neighborhood organizations in critical areas that could deal with local problems, with some aid from COIR staff, as they arose.

As the commission acted to meet new problems, the local organizations promoted to deal with old ones faded away; without an immediate crisis they could not sustain themselves. The agency's failure to establish a network of neighborhood organizations is evidenced by the fact that its leaders, again and again throughout the late 1950's, kept calling for such a network and illustrating the need for it.[49] Late in this period, when the commission attempted to establish a "tension control unit" with contacts throughout the city, it could not rely upon indigenous neighborhood organizations, but instead had to draw for local information upon the outlying units of other city agencies.[50] Eventually, attempts at community

[47] Beal memo, *op. cit.* at n. 43.

[48] Anon., "Proposed Structure of the Community Approach," n.d., files of COIR, box 6633. See also COIR, *Annual Report, 1958*, p. 16.

[49] Text of speech by Frank Horne, Jan. 13, 1958; press release, n.d., 1960, files of COIR, box 6633; and COIR pamphlet, *How to Set up an Intergroup Relations Committee in Your Neighborhood* (New York: The Commission, 1960).

[50] *New York Times,* Sept. 21, 1959, p. 1, col. 1.

organization degenerated into a series of conferences, clinics, workshops, and forums for leadership training and education in tolerance.

Individuals

The Commission on Intergroup Relations, as the successor to the Unity Committee, inherited that organization's responsibility for dealing with individual complaints of discrimination. The commission staff was especially concerned with situations that could burgeon into major intergroup confrontations, but it did establish a regular complaint procedure with which to deal with less visible complaints.[51] The procedure was largely based upon closed hearings and conciliation of differences, but it gave the commission considerable power to initiate investigations of discriminatory activity.

With the passage of the Sharkey-Brown-Isaacs fair housing act in 1958, internal commission procedures in individual cases were superseded by those prescribed by the city council. Studies of individual complainants under this law (and these comprised the vast majority of the individual cases that came to the commission) revealed that most were black and middle-class. Of 791 housing discrimination complaints filed between April 1958 and December 1960, 85 per cent were initiated by blacks and 9 per cent by Puerto Ricans. Of the complainants, only 10 per cent had less than a high school education, and 31 per cent were college graduates. More than three quarters of the commission's individual complaints originated with people who held professional or white-collar jobs, and 39 per cent of the complainants earned more than $100 a week.[52]

The striking factor that emerges from an overview of the commission's constituency in this early period is the contrast between the nature of the organizations that supported it and the clientele

[51] Paul Klein, "Report on the Hill Case," May 12, 1956; memo, Beal to Walker, Nov. 21, 1957; files of COIR, box 6633.

[52] *COIR Reporter*, Vol. 3, no. 1 (Spring 1960), and "Fact Sheet on COIR Operations under Local Law #80, April 1, 1958, to Dec. 30, 1960," files of COIR, box 6633.

it served. On one level, the agency had strong ties with the professional civil rights organizations, mostly white and Jewish, that had helped create it and that were integrated into the agency through the commission structure. On another level, the commission attempted to create for itself, without too much success, a constituency of indigenous neighborhood organizations in minority neighborhoods. Finally, at a third level, the agency actually provided services for middle-class blacks who approached it with complaints of discrimination.

Relations with Other City Agencies

With the attainment of a legislative mandate from the city, the staff of the new Commission on Intergroup Relations was convinced that the agency had achieved the legitimacy that had eluded their semiofficial predecessor organization and that a closer working relationship with other city agencies could therefore be established. The staff considered such relationships with several departments (police, welfare, housing) to be essential to its work and sought to solidify them almost immediately after the commission began to function.

Despite the commission's official status, however, these efforts faced substantial difficulties. Besides the agency's youth and its leadership's lack of informal contacts throughout the bureaucracy that would have eased the path toward cooperation, the basic organizational design of the commission worked against this endeavor. Whereas most city agencies were organized by function, the COIR was organized to serve a constituency, and its vague mandate allowed it to cross functional lines. Every city agency dealt with minorities either externally (by providing them services, regulating their conduct, and so on) or within the organization itself (as employees).

The result of its organizational premise was that though it did not have a single discrete function for which it alone was responsible, the commission seemingly could, in pursuance of its mandate, enter the functional area of almost any other city department. Even when this type of organization is necessary and legitimate, it is obvious that it can raise bureaucratic suspicions, which in turn mitigate against interagency cooperation.

Struggling against this fact of organizational life, the COIR staff attempted to establish cordial relations with the city bureaucracy. With a plan analogous to the one it developed for cooperation with private agencies, the commission sought to make itself the clearinghouse for the intergroup relations activities of all city departments. In June 1956, executive director Horne and chairman Swope asked the mayor to call a meeting of the heads of the major city departments in order to stress to them that the COIR was "part of the official city family," that "its investigations were confidential," and that it sought to cooperate with the other agencies of city government. The mayor rejected this idea but agreed to circulate a memo to department heads requesting that they cooperate with the commission. The reaction to the memo, reported the commission, "was immediate and genuine, with the officials of the city warmly welcoming any cooperative action that would help eliminate discrimination." [53]

After the success of this general approach, individual commission staff members sought meetings with officials at specific agencies to discuss specific projects. In several areas of policy the commission sought roles in the agencies' decision-making processes. Seats were requested for the executive director, for example, on the Housing Authority, the Planning Commission, and the Mayor's Committee on Slum Clearance, and an official role was sought for the agency in the grievance procedure of the Department of Labor in cases where discrimination was claimed.

As part of the drive for cooperation the commission sought to get each city department to create, with COIR guidance, an in-service intergroup relations training program in order to "prevent problems growing out of the necessity to integrate." [54] To the Youth Board the COIR suggested cooperative programming.

[53] Memo, Horne to Swope, June 6, 1956; memo, Wagner to Department Heads, Aug. 22, 1956, both in files of COIR, box 6633; COIR, *Annual Report, 1956* (New York: The Commission, 1957), p. 6.
[54] Memo, unsigned, May 31, 1956, files of COIR, box 6633.

Within the sphere of the Board of Education it desired a voice in planning for integrating the city's schools. Again with the Labor Department, cooperation was sought in enforcing a little-known clause in city contracts that prohibited discrimination by contractors on any work done for the city. With all agencies, the commission sought to open lines of communication and begin cooperative action.

Some of these initial projects were successful. The COIR was admitted into the employment grievance procedure, was invited by the Board of Education to cooperate with its Commission on Integration, and even received backing from other departments in seeking an appropriation from the city council for a special census of the city's minority population.[55] More often, however, commission initiatives were met with an expression of concern for minority problems but with little action leading to substantive changes. In the especially crucial Police Department, for example, staff member Sid Frigand found that "Commissioners Kennedy and Arm [were] especially sensitive to problems of tension resulting from intergroup antagonisms or hostility." They met regularly, he noted, with community leaders and had established civilian grievance machinery. Frigand therefore suggested that the commission "augment or supplement police efforts." [56] In other meetings such issues as recruitment of police from among minority groups, Spanish-police relations, and in-service training for police in intergroup relations were discussed.[57] Discussions led to further discussions, however, and not, by 1960, to substantial changes in police recruitment or enforcement policies.

This was the pattern for the late 1950's. In the areas of housing and education, the commission entered the periphery of the decision-making process. In other areas, such as tension control and the coordination of city agency work in the neighborhoods, the commission's entrance was resisted and limited by agencies jealous

55 Memo, Klein to Horne, Aug 1, 1956, *ibid.;* COIR, *Annual Report, 1956,* p. 5.
56 Memo, Frigand to Horne, June 7, 1956, files of COIR, box 6633.
57 Minutes, "Meeting with the Police Department," Nov. 3, 1956, *ibid.*

of their own prerogatives. Although it was consulted on some issues, in no single area was the new agency becoming central to the process of governing the city.

Relations with State Agencies

The prior existence of the State Commission Against Discrimination (SCAD), established in 1945, further compounded the difficulties that the city commission was having in defining its proper role in city affairs. Primarily concerned with employment discrimination, SCAD's powers exceeded those of the city commission in many substantive areas, and in these it pre-empted any activity by the COIR.

The state commission resisted relinquishing any of its prerogatives to the local agency. In an early meeting between the representatives of the two groups, "COIR's representatives were told emphatically that there would be no relinquishing of SCAD's jurisdiction in order to enable the City Commission to handle discrimination complaints arising from city employees." [58] Dr. Horne resisted this interpretation, but his defense in the area of city employment was tenuous (at least until the commission was included in the grievance procedure as noted above), and in other areas no basis for jurisdiction could be found. Consequently, cases that did come to the city agency were referred to the state; in other less contentious areas of operation (such as community relations) some cooperation between the two commissions was planned.

Only when New York City passed an antidiscrimination ordinance more inclusive than the state legislation then in force could the COIR gain concessions on jurisdiction from the state agency. In 1958, after the passage of the Sharkey-Brown-Isaacs Act, chairmen Marrow of the COIR and Charles Abrams of the SCAD agreed in a unique formal signed compact that: (1) either agency would accept complaints and refer them to the proper agency for handling, (2) all supporting evidence would be sent to the agency that was to act, and (3) all housing complaints not covered by

[58] Memo, Beal to Horne, July 27, 1956, *ibid.*

state law would be referred to the city.[59] This formal compact was the beginning, as a later chairman of the city agency noted, of an unwritten agreement between the two agencies to "keep out of each other's business." [60]

Action in Substantive Areas

The legislation in which the city council provided for the creation of the Commission on Intergroup Relations gave the new agency relatively little policy direction. It provided that the commission work with federal, state, and city agencies to develop courses of instruction on effective intergroup relations techniques; enlist the cooperation of groups; study problems of prejudice, intolerance, bigotry, and disorder engendered by these problems; and receive complaints and investigate (a) racial, religious, and ethnic group tensions, prejudice, intolerance, and bigotry, and (b) discrimination outside city agencies and within these agencies after consultation with the Mayor.[61]

This rather vague delimitation of powers allowed the commission latitude in choosing the specific areas within which it would act. In the late 1950's, both before and after the passage of fair housing legislation for the city, the commission expended most of its efforts in the area of housing. In addition, during the school integration and bussing controversies of 1957 and 1958 the agency gave a good deal of attention to education. Employment was its third area of priority; though the commission early discovered the usefulness of the antidiscrimination clause in city contracts for fighting employment discrimination, efforts in this area were not stressed during this period.

Finally, all action in various policy areas was wedded to the commission's ultimate concern for tension control. All substantive work of the agency must be considered in the light of this major task—the minimization of the occurrence, visibility, and effect of

---

[59] Jay Anders Higbee, *Development and Administration of the New York State Law Against Discrimination* (University, Ala.: University of Alabama Press, 1966), p. 85.

[60] Interview with Stanley Lowell, summer 1968.

[61] Local Law No. 55, 1955, Section B1-5.0.

racial clashes in the city. Implicit in the omnipresence of the tension-control function for the COIR is a role conflict for the agency, a conflict that was emergent in the work of the earlier Unity Committee. Although the impulse of the agency was to act as an advocate for minority groups in the areas of housing, education, and employment within the city's political process, this advocacy had the effect of exacerbating and making more visible political conflict along racial lines in New York and thus compromised the COIR's most important "political" function, tension control.

Different actors in the civil rights arena—the agency's organized constituency, minority groups, the agency's staff, and the mayor's office—had different expectations from the COIR and placed conflicting demands upon it: The commission was required to function simultaneously as advocate and apologist. The reconciliation of these two roles was difficult but possible during the period in the late 1950's when racial issues had relatively low visibility in the city, and when the expectations of most constituency groups coincided. As these issues became increasingly more central, as advocates outside the agency began to take more extreme positions, and as constituency expectations began to diverge from one another, the maintenance of both roles became impossible.

Housing

The tensions inherent in the COIR's multiplicity of roles were most easily overcome, during the 1955–1960 period, in the area of housing integration. Here the agency could advocate minority positions both within the city government and in the city at large, and thus please its constituency, while avoiding direct political difficulties. The agency's advocacy was simply channeled by the city council and the mayor's office, through legislation and control of the purse strings, into relatively "harmless" directions politically.

It was natural that a preponderance of the new commission's effort be in the area of housing, for it was in this policy area that the new executive director had all of his experience.[62] An early

[62] Horne had been an adviser on race relations at the Housing and Home Finance Agency in Washington and had apparently lost his job for partisan

convocation of city civil rights groups reinforced the commission's predisposition to emphasize housing problems when it noted that experts in the city "generally agreed" that "housing is the root of the problem" of racial discrimination.[63] If housing could be integrated, integrated education would follow, and people who lived together could not object to working together.

Acting upon these convictions, Horne had in hand by mid-June of 1956 an "Open Cities Program," drafted for the commission by Corienne Morrow, an assistant he had brought with him from Washington. The objective of the program was to change substantially, within five years, segregated residential patterns in New York City.

The plan, cast in the mold of COIR's philosophy of conciliation and cooperation, was thorough. Housing vacancies would be listed comprehensively in a central location, and machinery would be established, in cooperation with private civil rights groups, to inform minority families of openings and, in the case of one-family houses, available financing. Systematic referral and follow-up procedures were outlined. Negotiations were to begin with apartment owners in order to open housing to minorities, and with bankers to convince them to allow qualified blacks mortgage aid for home buying. In white neighborhoods "myths and misconceptions" about the effects of integration were to be dispelled through an educative program and by making commission services available during periods of transition. All public and private resources would be marshaled and coordinated by the COIR in this comprehensive effort.[64]

The plan faltered, however, on the two rocks of financing and group participation. The city would support the planning of the program, for which the Board of Estimate allocated $10,000, but would not provide the $100,000 per year for five years necessary to put it into effect. Support, furthermore, could not be obtained

---

political reasons. See Charles Abrams, "Segregation, Housing, and the Horne Case," *The Reporter,* 13 (Oct. 6, 1955), 30–33.

[63] COIR, *Annual Report, 1956,* p. 3.

[64] Corienne Morrow, "Outline of Scope of Cooperation Open City Plan," Nov. 27, 1956, files of COIR, box 6633.

from private foundations. Civil rights group consultants thought the plan meritorious but would not commit the necessary staff for a sufficient time to make it operational. Confronted with these difficulties, the Open City plan, when finally launched by the commission, was more a rhetorical than an operative reality.[65] Advocacy was limited by lack of resources.

Advocacy was more successful when it coincided with the commission's role as protector of the mayor's interests. Early in 1956, for example, executive director Horne warned the mayor against completing a contract to build the Alexander Hamilton houses at 144th Street and Seventh Avenue in Harlem. This development was opposed by the State Commission Against Discrimination and the Urban League as one that would contribute to further housing segregation. Proceeding with it, Horne wrote, would lead to "a protest that would heighten tensions and embarrass the city." [66] In this instance the commission was able to act both to protect the mayor's interests and to support the position of its constituency groups at the same time.[67]

Though the commission's ambitions in the area of housing were large in 1956 and 1957, its involvement was restricted by higher level political actors. The passage of the Sharkey-Brown-Isaacs Act in 1958 qualitatively changed the role of the agency in the housing integration area.[68] The legislation, largely the work of black city councilman Earl Brown, was the first in the United States to outlaw racial discrimination in privately owned housing.

[65] "Open City" became the theme of the commission's housing program, a program that thenceforth was pursued through pamphleteering, radio and television publicity, and periodic conferences with the economic interests that controlled the city's housing market. See two COIR pamphlets *Fair Play in Housing for Everyone* (1958) and *Blueprint for an Open City* (n.d.), files of COIR, box 6633.

[66] Memos, Horne to Wagner, April 11 and April 27, 1956, *ibid.*

[67] The commission took a similar stance, that of protecting the mayor, in a controversy over the relocation of Lower East Side residents in connection with a planned project (memo, Morrow to I. Mitchell Felt, June 22, 1956, files of COIR, box 6633). When the two roles did not coincide, the agency was less successful; see Davies, p. 62.

[68] Betty Bender, "Administrative Action against Residential Discrimination in New York City" (M.A. essay, Columbia University, 1962).

It prohibited discrimination in multiple dwellings and in housing developments of ten or more units and established an elaborate complaint procedure to enforce this prohibition.

Brown and other civil rights advocates wanted violations of the fair housing law to be tried in criminal court under the full glare of what they hoped would be adverse publicity. Others favored an attempt at conciliation between landlord and prospective tenant and shied away from criminal penalties. Inclusion of the commission in the law and the establishment of an elaborate conciliation procedure was the ultimate compromise result.[69]

The procedure provided that the commission staff, upon receipt of a complaint, make a preliminary determination of "probable cause" that discrimination had occurred. If probable cause was found, the alleged discriminator was to be called to the office of the commission for a conciliation conference. If the issue could not be solved through conciliation, it was then taken to a hearing presided over by three commissioners. A determination of discrimination here could then be appealed to another voluntary unpaid body appointed by the mayor, the Fair Housing Practices Panel. From there, appeals were possible through the regular civil court system. Until this final point, all hearings and appeals were, by law, confidential proceedings.

The COIR was thus given its first real substantive powers in order to lessen the effects of a civil rights measure; it was rewarded with the task of administering a procedure designed to guarantee that the impact of open housing legislation in the city would be gradual and minimal.

The passage of this legislation had other implication for the commission. As the COIR assumed the new administrative responsibilities delegated to it by the Sharkey-Brown-Isaacs Act, the agency altered its basic conceptions about how to deal with housing discrimination in the city. The large-scale plans for social change of 1956 were abandoned in favor of schemes for the more efficient processing of individual complaints. After the passage of the bill, commission activity in housing was measured in terms

[69] Interview with Earl Brown, summer 1968.

of the legislation. The number of cases heard and the number settled became the criteria of success for the agency.

This changed focus was encouraged by a commissioned private study by Ernst Dichter of the Institute for Motivational Research which indicated that the new legislation could lead to large-scale social change. Dichter noted that "New York City property owners and managers are far more ready to accept the inevitability of integrated housing than they publicly admit," and that "a combination of toughness and understanding [in enforcing the law] can achieve integrated housing in six or seven years." [70]

It is not surprising, then, that by 1960 most of the COIR's plans in the housing area were defined by its responsibility for administering the Sharkey-Brown-Isaacs Act. Agency staff thought in terms of extending the coverage of the legislation, improving the law procedurally, and making it better known. Other plans in housing, periodically presented as new, were simply leftovers from the ill-fated Open City program (area surveys and conferences with landlords and prospective mortgagers, for example) and were distinctly secondary in the agency's set of priorities in this policy area. The city's political leaders, in giving the COIR the responsibility for administering this legislation, had effectively redirected the agency's efforts and had, albeit inadvertently, minimized the agency's role as advocate of minority-group positions in housing in the city.[71]

Education

In the school integration struggle, as in housing, the COIR was able to avoid the potential conflict among the various roles required of it during the late 1950's. It did this by pressing the Board of Education for integration within the bureaucratic structure while at the same time seeking, through education and community organization, to moderate tensions that arose in the neighborhoods in which schools were being integrated.

[70] COIR press release, June 23, 1959, files of COIR, box 6633.

[71] COIR, *Annual Report, 1960* (New York: The Commission, 1961), p. 18. It is interesting that the agency's advocate stances in the area of housing originated with its community-relations staff and not with those directly charged with the responsibility for housing.

The Board of Education was one of the first city departments to agree to cooperate with the Commission on Intergroup Relations when the agency was first established. Early in 1956, anticipating the new commission's interest, the board invited it to sit with its newly constituted Commission on Integration. In cooperating with the board, the COIR's objectives were threefold: It sought action against *de facto* segregation in the schools of the city, a revision of school curriculums, and the establishment of in-service training in human relations for teachers in minority areas.[72]

After several meetings with the board on particular problems, however, the commission staff found that, despite its rhetorical commitment to integration, the establishment at 110 Livingston Street was hardly oriented toward action on the question. The specific matter of the integration of Junior High School 258 serves as an example.

In this case the commission attempted to act as an arbitrator among the Harlem Parents' Committee, the NAACP, and the Board of Education. The scenario is familiar. The parents were up in arms about a new school built in an area zoned in such a way that segregation would be perpetuated. The NAACP threatened litigation, an action that chairman Horne feared would "embarrass the city." A meeting was arranged between representatives of the COIR and several members of the Board of Education. The commission members presented the problem, and board members responded by pointing out the "technical difficulties" involved in integrating the city's schools. At one point, in fact, chairman Horne felt constrained to remind the board that integration was, after all, their official and declared policy. In subsequent meetings and memos, COIR staff members and commissioners presented zoning and pupil transfer plans, but board representatives resisted change as "not practical at this juncture." In the end, nothing was done.[73]

In other situations, the commission was faced with similar pas-

[72] Staff program paper, May 31, 1956, and minutes of a staff conference, Dec. 11, 1956, files of COIR, box 6633.

[73] Memo, Horne to Commissioners Mary L. Riley and Pearson Neaman, July 27, 1956; memos, Paul Klein to Horne, Aug. 1 and Aug. 3, 1956; report of meeting, Aug. 30, 1956; *ibid.*

sive resistance by the board. Recommendations for the transfer of experienced teachers to "special-service schools," for example, were similarly demonstrated by the board to be "unworkable." [74] Despite these setbacks, the COIR chose to continue to work within the system rather than to take criticism of the Board of Education to a larger public. In fact, the commission took pride in its cooperation with the board, perhaps because it experienced so much difficulty in gaining cooperation from other city agencies.

In its annual report for 1958, COIR noted that it had "worked closely with the Board of Education on integration" and cited in a 1960 leaflet the aid that it had given the board in planning and effecting the open enrollment policy.[75] As we have seen, cooperation with the board did not preclude internal recommendations on site selection, zoning, and other integration techniques, but it did prevent criticism in the larger political system of the slow pace and partial nature of that agency's integration measures.

Within the larger political system, much of the commission's activity in education in the late 1950's focused upon the anticipation and prevention of the development of potentially explosive situations from attempts at integration. For example, COIR helped to prepare white, black, and Puerto Rican parents for the city's first mass transfer of students from a black to a white school in 1959, and in 1960 paved the way for a rezoning that integrated an East Side school in Manhattan.[76] In both cases, the main concern of the commission was the avoidance of violent protest and its attendant political consequences.

The COIR's duality of roles, in fact, gave it some unique advantages in the school integration struggle. Because of its advocacy within the bureaucracy, minority leaders came to believe that they could trust the agency, while at the same time its refusal to carry criticism to the public led city agencies to perceive its approach as "balanced." Consequently, for a time in the late 1950's and early

---

[74] Marrow, *Changing Patterns of Prejudice*, pp. 151–154.

[75] COIR, *Annual Report, 1958*, p. 6, and COIR pamphlet, *A Progress Report on Human Rights in New York City* (1960).

[76] Marrow, *Changing Patterns of Prejudice*, pp. 149 ff., 156.

1960's the COIR provided a forum in which the Board of Education and its critics could hammer out differences.

Thus, in 1960, the Reverend Milton Galamison, of the Parents' Workshop for Equality in the New York City Schools, who had threatened a boycott and "sit-out" of segregated schools in Brooklyn, was able to gain concessions on interzone transfers and open enrollment from board chairman Charles H. Silver and superintendent of schools John J. Theobold at a meeting held under the auspices of the commission.[77] COIR was able to bring both sides together to talk to each other and provide a forum for compromise.

In education, the commission avoided the potential conflict in its roles by strictly limiting advocacy to behind-the-scenes maneuvers, by stressing its responsibility to avoid racial disorders in the city, and by maintaining cordial relations with all parties engaged in the various school integration controversies. It was able to minimize its advocate role in this way and still maintain its ties with minority-group leaders because of their basic belief that the COIR was sympathetic to their cause.

Employment

Though an obvious area of activity for the commission, discrimination in employment received relatively little attention from the agency in the late 1950's for several reasons. First, and most obviously, the state had pre-empted the field; New York was one of the first states to establish a "little FEPC," and its State Commission Against Discrimination was active all over the state in receiving individual complaints of employment discrimination. Second, the city commission's resources were limited and already committed in other areas, and this prevented a concerted effort against employment discrimination. Third, and perhaps most important, investigation of employment discrimination, especially in the private sector of the economy, involved union-employer relationships and had great political implications. The mayor's rela-

[77] *Ibid.*, p. 158.

tionship with labor unions in the city was a close one, and therefore a concerted effort in the area of employment discrimination would require the commission to abandon its apologist role. This it was not yet ready to do.

The city commission's main concern with employment discrimination during this period was therefore limited to establishing a procedure for dealing with incidents of discrimination within the city government itself. Soon after it began functioning late in 1956, the commission attempted to establish itself as the agency with the jurisdiction to investigate such complaints. Amendments to the mayor's grievance procedure were drafted in the commission's offices, and conferences were held with the Department of Labor and with the city administrator's office "in order to integrate COIR into the grievance procedure." [78]

Finally, in August 1957, with an election in the offing, the mayor crowned the commission's efforts with an executive order "prohibiting discrimination by city departments and agencies because of race, religion and national origin" and establishing a procedure through which allegations of discrimination were to be heard by the commission.[79] This procedure was used. In 1958, for example, twenty-three cases were brought to the offices of the commission and settled, mainly through conciliation procedures.[80]

In the area of contract compliance—the process of ensuring that contractors who did business with the city did not discriminate in their employment practices on the basis of race or religion—the commission received less support from the mayor than they had in their effort to fight such discrimination within the government. Though city contracts had included clauses prohibiting such discrimination for many years, an investigation by the Corporation

[78] Memo, Beal to Horne, Dec. 4, 1956, files of COIR, box 6633.

[79] Executive Order No. 41, April 22, 1957; COIR press release, June 7, 1957, files of COIR, box 6633. A secret poll prepared for the mayor by Louis Harris in October 1957 showed him to be weak among minority voters.

[80] Memo, Beal to Arthur D. Walker (mayor's office), n.d., files of COIR, box 6633.

Counsel's office, made at the behest of the commission, revealed that there was no recorded instance of this prohibition having been enforced.[81]

Acting upon this information, the commission sought a declaration of policy from the mayor. After several staff conferences within the commission, tentative policy suggestions for the administration were outlined. Under this plan each department would be responsible for enforcing the nondiscrimination clauses of the contracts within its jurisdiction, but at the same time all would work closely with the commission. A copy of each contract and a form recording the name of the contractor and subcontractors, the unions involved in the project, the nature of the work, and the source of the workers would be filed with the commission. The COIR would be given the power to spot check for violations of the clause, to investigate, and to seek compliance.[82] Conciliatory methods would be used first; if these failed, executive action and possibly legislation would be recommended.

The mayor failed to act upon the commission's initiatives in this area and, as with original agency plans in the area of housing, without mayoral backing there was little that the COIR could do. In 1958 the commission talked to city departments, large contractors, unions, and community groups about a modified plan for "voluntary contract compliance." [83] Under this scheme some departments would amend their standard contract forms, departments would agree to file copies of contracts with the COIR, and commission literature would be included in contract solicitations. This plan too had little success.

From the commission's early experiences in the employment policy area a great lesson emerges, a lesson learned and passed on by Edith Alexander even before the statutory commission began to function. The strong support of the mayor was necessary for the success of the COIR in any area of policy. When the mayor could be convinced to act, as in the case of discrimination within

[81] Memo, Beal to Horne, Aug. 2, 1956, *ibid.*
[82] Memo, Beal to Horne, Nov. 13, 1956, *ibid.*
[83] *Memo,* Sept. 21, 1956 (unsigned), *ibid.*

the city government, the commission was successful; when he could not be convinced, the commission was left powerless. In light of this reality, it is no wonder that during this early period the commission gave greater priority to its relationship with the mayor than to its role as advocate for minority groups.

Tension Control

The COIR's tension-control function was most visible when the agency became involved in racial and ethnic *causes célèbres*.[84] When Catholic organizations complained of anti-Catholic remarks in a college newspaper, COIR stepped in. When white and black high school students clashed, the commission brought together city officials, educators, and the youths themselves to seek a solution. When a wave of anti-Semitic outbreaks hit the city, the agency provided a place to which the matter could be referred, a way in which city officials could "do something." Similarly, when the son of New York's most prominent black citizen was denied membership in the West Side Tennis Club, COIR was the agency through which the city could defuse the problem.

More basically, however, tension control was the underlying function of the commission in all its areas of activity. In its work in housing, education, and employment the anticipation of the emergence of racial conflict and the maintenance of conflict at a manageable level was the agency's rationale for being included in the decision-making process. In engaging in tension control the commission was acting in a way functional for its minority constituency. By "putting out fires" for the mayor, the COIR was helping him to meet minority problems with rhetoric, and with a minimum of commitment of actual resources.

Crisis in the Commission

A complex of personality differences and political circumstances brought the organizational problems of the Commission on Inter-

[84] This account is based upon Marrow, *Changing Patterns of Prejudice*, pp. 47, 67–68, 73, 85.

group Relations to a head in late 1959. During his term as chairman, Alfred Marrow had become progressively more disenchanted with the work of the staff of the commission, and, in fact, there was more than a kernel of truth to his objections. The executive director was a poor administrator, and some of the staff (especially among the political appointees) were not totally committed to the work of the agency. Marrow, moreover, believed that he, as chairman, was publicly responsible for the work of the commission and that, in the light of the agency's administrative shortcomings, it was incumbent upon him to take over the daily management of the agency in order to properly meet this responsibility. As a corporation president and a social scientist, furthermore, he believed that he was eminently qualified for this task.

Marrow, however, never completely understood all the reasons for the commission's difficulties. He placed all the blame on the executive director and staff and failed to realize that many of the problems were inherent in the agency's organizational structure and in the ill-defined nature of its mandate. As a businessman, Marrow was accustomed to the board of directors–chief administrative officer arrangement. It did not occur to him to question it as a form of governmental organization, especially since his power base in the organization was among the commissioners.

Furthermore, Marrow failed completely to understand the political role that the commission played in city government, a role that, as we have seen, the organization performed quite well in the late 1950's. The chairman's academic training was in the human-relations school of organization theory, and not in public administration or politics. He was not a political man. Henry Cohen, a deputy city administrator who studied the commission in 1960 recalled: "Marrow was both a social scientist and corporate executive. Both his thinking processes and management style were more precise and refined than Horne's. There is always a no-man's land between what constitutes executive (professional) responsibility and what constitutes trusteeship (lay leadership) responsibility. Given their differences of background and style, it was almost inevitable that there would be conflict between the two, particularly in a field which so often gets nebulous, such as human rights and intergroup relations." [85]

Once he decided to act, Marrow employed several tactics in order to gain complete control of the agency. At the commission level, Marrow's major objective was to limit the number of effective actors. He did this by having the commission create an executive committee, the membership of which fell by default into the hands of the most active commissioners, the representatives of the American Jewish Congress, the American Jewish Committee, and the Anti-Defamation League.[86] The executive director was excluded from the meetings of this committee, and Marrow sought to have it delegate to him, as chairman, full power to act in its name. The ultimate result of this maneuvering was a resolution passed in March 1960 by the executive committee and sent to Deputy Mayor Paul O'Keefe which "delegated to the chairman the full authority of the commission over all operations of the staff, subject to periodic reports by the chairman to the commission." [87] This resolution attempted, in effect, to make the voluntary chairman the chief executive officer of the agency.

While assuring himself of the support of the commission, or at least of the executive committee, Marrow began more and more to intervene in the administration of the agency. He was constantly present. He attempted to fire staff and to hire consultants outside the commission's normal channels, without regard to budgetary limitations. He acted for the commission and at least once retained outside consultants for a study without the knowledge of the executive director or the staff. He required daily written reports from the staff of their activities. In short, the chairman sought to bypass the executive director and control the staff—and, occasionally, even to bypass the staff. In the words of the deputy director, Irving Goldaber: "within the past month or two Dr. Marrow has continued to

[85] Cohen to the author, April 23, 1973.

[86] Memo, Horne to Lyle Fitch (city administrator), Aug. 24, 1960, files of the city administrator, box 4123.

[87] Memo, Marrow to Commissioners, April 12, 1960; memo, Fitch to Wagner, July 26, 1960; *ibid.*

operate on the program activities of the commission. Clearly, he has planned program items and directed the staff on their implementation. In some instances, he has gone ahead with programing without any consultation with staff." [88]

In attempting to make the agency more efficient, Marrow only succeeded in disrupting it further. Finally he took an action that dramatized the issue. Just before Christmas in 1959 he attempted to remove from the staff two black women, Corienne Morrow, Frank Horne's associate from Washington, and Dr. Rheta Arter, research director of the agency. Black political leaders immediately defined the issue racially. J. Raymond Jones and Earl Brown both protested to the mayor, claiming that there was a conflict between blacks and Jews on the commission and that Marrow was trying to remove the militant blacks.[89]

Although they were not entirely sure about the merits of his position, Jewish group leaders felt constrained to support the chairman. With the advice and aid of Will Maslow of the American Jewish Congress, Marrow began to marshal behind-the-scenes support in both the black and white liberal communities for his actions. Claiming that "if every time a Negro employee was to be fired Negro politicians automatically rushed to the defense of the employee, it would be impossible to maintain an efficient staff in any government agency," the chairman, for a time, had some success with his appeal. This position, which masked the real issues involved in the COIR dispute, drew endorsements from such prominent blacks as Kenneth Clark, Gardner Taylor, and Lester Granger.[90]

Faced with the growing polarization on this issue, the mayor sought to restore the status quo. He asked Marrow to reinstate the employees involved and directed the city administrator's office

[88] Will Maslow to Isaac Tobin, Feb. 8, 1960, Mr. Maslow's files, American Jewish Congress; memo, n.d., Goldaber to "files"; memo, Fitch to Wagner, July 26, 1960, both box 4123.

[89] Memo, Maslow to Tobin, Polier, Pfeffer, and Levine, Dec. 18, 1959, files of Mr. Maslow.

[90] Memo, Maslow to Tobin, Dec. 18, 1959, files of Mr. Maslow.

to do a complete administrative survey of the commission. Delay, he hoped, would help to cool off the conflict.[91]

When the city administrator's office entered the conflict the situation stabilized at a high level of tension. Marrow continued to attempt to run the agency from the offices of his textile firm. The commission staff circulated a petition for his removal but abandoned a plan for mass resignation in anticipation of the city administrator's report. In the *Amsterdam News* columnist Jimmy Booker, who apparently had informants at the commission, periodically reported on the anti-Marrow sentiments of black staff members and uptown political leaders.[92]

Of all the actors involved in the crisis at the commission, Frank Horne had the greatest reason to welcome the proposed investigation by the city administrator. The restoration of sound administrative practices at the agency would uphold his position as the COIR's operating head, a position that was progressively being undermined by Marrow's incursions. For Horne, acting city administrator Lyle Fitch and his deputy, Henry Cohen, were not a threat, but were potential allies against the chairman.

The Fitch report, based upon an exhaustive examination of agency records, interviews with personnel, a survey of interest groups, and a comparison of the New York City commission with those of several other major cities, was secretly submitted to the mayor on March 4, 1960. Although Frank Horne was criticized for weak leadership and poor administrative practices, his position was generally vindicated. The city administrator placed the blame for the "confused situation in the intergroup relations agency" upon "the failure to organize the commission properly and to define the respective roles of the commission members, the commission chairman, and the staff." "The agency," the report continued, "never organized itself on a sound basis. This failure is the chief cause of its present difficulties. It succumbed to all the inherent dangers of

[91] *Ibid.* and *New York Times,* Dec. 17, 1959, p. 45, col. 7. Delay, as we have seen from the work of the commission, was one of the mayor's chief traits and one he was reputed to have learned from his father.

[92] Jimmy Booker, "Uptown Lowdown," *Amsterdam News,* Dec. 12, 1960, p. 11.

the commission form of organization. We find confusion of authority. There is no clear definition of purpose and objectives. The staff is demoralized." [93]

Difficulties at the COIR, as recorded by the city administrator's investigators, were legion. The chairman and individual commissioners often bypassed the executive director and issued directives to the staff. The staff, as a result, was confused and resentful. The executive director was not strong enough in directing the staff, defining functions, and resisting illegitimate initiatives. No means existed to evaluate the effectiveness of the staff. The agency never planned ahead; it always waited for a crisis before acting.

In the commission itself, bylaws were lacking and standing committees languished. There was little coordination among commissioners and between commissioners and staff. The commission rarely held the chairman accountable or made policy, but was content to accept *faits accomplis* from him. The hearings procedure (and the requirement that three commissioners be present for each case) placed a great burden upon the lawyer members of the commission and caused inordinate delays in administering the law.

The Fitch report was especially critical of the internal organization of the staff, and criticism took the form of traditional public-administration analysis. Twenty-five professionals and an equal number of clerical people were spread thin over five divisions with little distinction between line and staff functions and much overlapping among divisions. Consolidation of functions and the elimination of at least one division was necessary, the city administrator believed, if the resulting friction in the agency was to be eliminated.

In order to deal with this great catalog of problems, Fitch recommended extensive changes in the commission. First and foremost, the city administrator sought to define and delimit the role of the commissioners. They were to engage in making policy and in reviewing staff activities but were not to concern themselves with the formulation of specific programs or with the day-to-day operations of the agency. These functions would be reserved to the

[93] Fitch report, March 4, 1960, files of the city administrator, box 4123. The next several paragraphs rely on this report.

executive director, who would also serve as a link between the commission and the staff, and would, alone, direct the staff. Commissioners would be called upon to handle specific tasks only in "sensitive situations."

Fitch called for a total reorganization within the agency. Hearing officers and full-time counsel, he said, should be added to the commission's staff to relieve the burden that the housing hearings placed upon the time of the voluntary commissioners; when the latter were called upon to serve, Fitch added, they should at least receive expenses. To relieve the burden on the executive director Fitch proposed a deputy director for administration whose job would be to direct some staff activities, including the new division of agency services. The divisions of public relations and research, as before, would remain under the executive director's immediate control.

A final recommendation was aimed at meeting problems of staff turnover and salaries. A new civil service title, assistant intergroup relations officer, was to be created. Though the salary proposed for this title was low ($4,850 annually), the education and experience requirements were considerably less than those formally required of intergroup relations officers, and Fitch hoped that through this device new young staff could be recruited for the commission. In addition, a $300 raise in the starting salary of the intergroup relations officer (from $5,750 to $6,050) was recommended.

The Fitch report was a political document.[94] Given the circumstances at the commission, and the ethos of the city administrator's office,[95] the conclusions that the report reached were almost inevitable. Marrow and his allies on the commission sought to meet with the city administrator to temper the tone and conclusions of

[94] Ample evidence for this exists in the mayor's insistence that it was simply an efficiency study of the agency and his refusal to make it public. Copies were so difficult to obtain that one interviewee doubted the fact of the report's availability seven years later.

[95] For a discussion of this office see Demetrios Caraley, *New York City's Deputy Mayor–City Administrator* (New York: Citizens Budget Commission, 1966).

his forthcoming report in late February and early March.[96] Horne, on the other hand, resisted changes in the report, saying that he was confident that the judgment of the "trained analysts" of the city administrator's office was valid. When Henry Cohen of Fitch's staff sounded Horne out on possible changes, the executive director replied, "When I agreed to criticisms it was with no notion that the report was subject to revisions by me or the chairman. . . . When you suggested the possibility of 'softening up' some of the wording, I expressed my reservations regarding any changes." [97] As has been illustrated, Horne's resistance was largely successful. Now, with the backing of the report, he sought to regain control of the commission.

In a memo addressed to the chairman and other commissioners, Horne indicated that he was at work making administrative adjustments in accordance with the Fitch report proposals and in response to an earlier commission request that he draft a set of operating rules for the agency.[98] Six documents, the executive director said, were in preparation; a set of bylaws and regulations for the commission, plans for a staff reorganization, employment and termination procedures, administrative rules, a procedure for staff reporting to the executive director, and a clearance procedure for the release of statements to the press.

These documents were submitted to the commission in the middle of April and adhered quite closely to the city administrator's recommendations. Under the bylaws, for example, eight commissioners were to constitute a quorum, and no binding decisions on policy were to be made for the COIR by the commissioners in executive session. The executive director was given the right to vote in commission meetings (and therefore could not be excluded), to prepare the agenda, and to act for the commission in emergencies after polling the membership. Staff was to be consulted on com-

96 Memo, Pearson Neaman to Henry Cohen proposing a Feb. 29 meeting, n.d., files of the city administrator, box 4123.

97 Memo, Horne to Cohen, n.d., *ibid.*

98 Horne to Commissioners, March 25, 1960, *ibid.*

mission decisions but was to be directed solely by the executive director. Similarly, memos on personnel policy, the reporting system of the agency, and procedures of initiating, processing, and approving press releases and public statements stressed the central role of the executive director. The chairman, for example, was permitted to make policy announcements, but all press releases had to be cleared with the executive director.[99]

Despite the fact that Horne's proposed changes now had the imprimatur of the city administrator's office, Marrow continued to attempt to control the commission. He pressed for policy decisions in meetings of the executive committee, and persisted in excluding the executive director from these meetings. In a public hearing at the city council the chairman stressed the need for new personnel for the COIR, to be hired outside of Fitch's organizational guidelines, at the same time that the executive director was struggling to limit the budget in response to a mayoral directive and to find, somewhere, money to raise the salaries of longtime staff members.[100]

Furthermore, Marrow sought to continue to direct the staff through "daily activity reports," contrary to the Fitch recommendations, and to act unilaterally in the issuance of press releases in the name of the commission. Now, however, Horne had an ally; he faithfully reported all of the chairman's activities to the city administrator's office.

In order to neutralize this alliance, Marrow submitted to the office of the city administrator minutes of committee meetings which made him seem to be acting much more in response to commission initiatives than he actually was. In fact, as time passed, Marrow came more and more to treat the Fitch report as a temporary setback. When executive director Horne was stricken with a heart attack, Marrow took advantage of the situation to lower the necessary quorum for commission meetings from eight to six and then to establish a policy-making executive committee of three members. He dispensed with the executive director's order of busi-

---

[99] All of these were released on April 18, 1960, and are in box 4123.
[100] Memo, Horne to Fitch, March 24, 1960, *ibid.*

ness, consulted less with the staff, sought to control staff appointments and to hire consultants, and generally asserted executive control.

Before his illness, Horne had attempted to enlist the city administrator to "umpire" his proposed reforms in order to assure that Marrow acted within their constraints.[101] When Horne was incapacitated in May, the mayor instructed Fitch to "keep a close watch over that agency and to consult daily with the staff." [102] Through May and June, Fitch became increasingly more distressed with Marrow's actions; finally, late in July, he wrote to the mayor:

> There is a considerable amount of resentment against the chairman in certain quarters, particularly in the Negro community. Virtually all segments of the Negro community—political, civic, social, press—are committed to getting rid of the chairman and there is no likelihood that this attitude will change. He is held responsible for crushing Frank Horne, first emotionally and psychologically and then physically. The Negro community will never forgive Al Marrow for this. As long as he is chairman they will view the Commission on Intergroup Relations with suspicion, and your positive image in intergroup relations will be tarnished.[103]

Fitch was convinced that Marrow had to be removed and replaced with a chairman acceptable to the black community and that, in addition, several other commissioners had to go before the commission could be revitalized. Furthermore, black leaders were pressuring the mayor directly to remove Marrow.

With Horne in the hospital, Marrow designated Irving Goldaber, a senior staff member, to supervise the staff, and called a commission meeting on May 16 to decide upon a course of action. The conflict increasingly began to focus upon the filling of the new position of deputy executive director, for during Horne's convalescence the man in this job would control the agency's daily operations.[104] For this post Marrow and his allies championed Cur-

101 Memo, Horne to Fitch, March 29, 1960, *ibid.*

102 Memo, Wagner to Fitch, n.d., *ibid.*

103 Memo, Fitch to Wagner, July 26, 1960, *ibid.*

104 Memo, Marrow to Lester Walton, Aug. 29, 1960; letter, William Dean Embree to Wagner, Sept. 2, 1960; *ibid.*

tis Roosevelt, FDR's grandson. Some support from civil rights groups was forthcoming for this appointment, though surprisingly not from Jewish groups. They had their own candidate, Philip I. Metzler.

Horne resisted Marrow's initiatives. In a letter to the chairman written from his hospital bed he indicated that, though he had nothing against Roosevelt, the man lacked governmental experience and a knowledge of the field. Other things had to be considered and political leaders consulted before an appointment could be made.[105]

In anticipation of this position, Marrow had earlier proposed an amendment to the recently adopted bylaws of the commission. Section five stated that vacancies in the commission staff were to be filled by the executive director, with the approval of the commission. Marrow sought a provision that the commission, in the event of the absence or disability of the executive director, could appoint a deputy or a two-man committee of commissioners to run the agency. To this Frank Horne was unalterably opposed. He was, he said, available to recruit a deputy, and would not be by-passed.[106]

In light of previous events, black sentiments, and the conclusions of the city administrator, Marrow was pressing forward on dangerous ground. His position with the agency was eroded even further as the result of a political error. On June 5, Marrow had charged on the NBC-TV program "Citizen's Searchlight" that there was considerable discrimination against nonwhite United Nations delegates in fashionable East Side restaurants. Blacks were not denied entry, Marrow said, but were often kept waiting, given bad tables, and served cold food.[107]

This story made national headlines, was carried prominently in all the New York metropolitan dailies, and even produced a condemnatory editorial in Monday's *Times*.[108] Mayor Wagner was furious, especially when the Committee on Civil Rights in East Man-

[105] Letter, Horne to Marrow, Aug. 16, 1960; letter, Marrow to Horne, Aug. 11, 1960; *ibid.*

[106] Horne to Marrow, *ibid.*

[107] *New York Times,* June 6, 1960, p. 1, col 2.

[108] *Ibid.,* June 7, 1960, p. 34, col. 2.

hattan, in a letter published in the *Times,* denied having made the studies upon which Marrow had ostensibly based his accusations and claimed that his charges were basically unsound. In a letter to Marrow, Wagner called the publicity "unfortunate" and unnecessary and asked for substantiation or a retraction.[109] Marrow attempted to substantiate, but he had little evidence beyond that which he had already presented. No retraction, however, was forthcoming.

Matters came to a head in August. Frank Horne wrote to Lyle Fitch suggesting that the COIR had to be revitalized if it was to function viably during the 1960's, when issues of race in the city would be more intense. In a rambling note, Horne suggested further that more black and Puerto Rican commissioners were needed at the agency. Then he got to the point. With conditions the way they were, he could no longer serve with Marrow. Either Marrow had to go, or he would go.[110]

Fitch was already convinced that Marrow had to be eliminated if the good will of the black community was to be retained. In the forthcoming election year, with the Democratic party organization aligned against him, the mayor could not afford to let this matter cost him political capital. Furthermore, Marrow had made public errors; instead of protecting the mayor from racial issues and keeping him out of squabbles, he had embarrassed and involved him.

All of this happened largely behind the scenes. When a *New York Times* reporter noticed on September 2 that the terms of fourteen of the fifteen COIR commissioners had expired, Deputy Mayor O'Keefe dismissed this fact as simply the result of an oversight. "The commission," he said, "has done a very good job in a difficult field," and "in the next two weeks we will formalize things." Seven days later, chairman Marrow's resignation was front-page news.[111]

Marrow, in fact, had reluctantly agreed to resign in a conversa-

[109] *Ibid.,* June 9, 1960, p. 67, col. 4; Wagner to Marrow, June 9, 1960, files of the city administrator, box 4123.

[110] Memo, Horne to Fitch, Aug. 11, 1960, box 4123.

[111] *New York Times,* Sept. 2, 1960, p. 21, col. 4, and Sept. 9, 1960, p. 1, col. 1.

tion with Stanley Lowell, who convinced him that in light of the circumstances the step would be best for the agency, the mayor, and himself. Lowell, who had left the government in 1958, took on this task as a favor to Wagner when communications between Marrow and Fitch on this matter broke down. Later Marrow apparently had second thoughts and attempted to marshal fellow commissioners to fight the resignation drafted in the mayor's office. In a note to them he said: "The Mayor never discussed this matter with me. The letter of resignation that was reported in the press was never written by me, nor did I know of its existence until I read it in the *New York Times*." [112]

Apparently, however, by September 11 the former chairman had accepted his fate. On the television show "Direct Line" he indicated that he had left the commission because of loose administration and poor staff in the agency, and because, he implied, the mayor was not committed to commission goals.[113] With him left many of the commissioners who had supported Marrow's efforts to control the COIR; the executive director emerged victorious.

What may one learn from the crisis in the commission and the changes it engendered? An examination of the dynamics of the situation reveals several things. Marrow, the aggressive protagonist, was dissatisfied with the commission because its measurable costs (recorded in the city expense budget) did not justify its measurable outputs. Its staff, untrained as Marrow was in the human-relations school of management, seemed to him wholly incapable of performing the tasks the agency ought to be doing. The commission in its internal operations was clearly inefficient, nor did it produce any substantial degree of "equality" in any of the substantive areas in which it acted. In short, as a businessman and a psychologist, Marrow believed that he could do a better job of running the agency, and as commission chairman he thought that he had the responsibility to act on this belief.

Marrow's method of seeking change in the agency, however, il-

---

[112] Marrow to Commissioners, Sept. 9, 1960, files of the city administrator, box 4123.

[113] *New York Times,* Sept. 2, 1960, p. 23, col. 1.

lustrated that he understood neither the delicate balance of its constituency relationships nor its political role. Though the commission's organized constituency was Jewish, the agency served the city's black and Puerto Rican minorities. Marrow's initiatives, and Horne's responses, separated the traditional sponsor groups of the COIR from its clientele. Despite Marrow's excesses, Jewish groups felt constrained to support him. In return, Horne and the city's black politicians defined the struggle at the commission in racial terms. The ironic result was racial tension in the Commission on Intergroup Relations.

Horne understood the essentially political nature of the administrative process better than Marrow did and consequently was able to gather support for his position within the administration. Horne's appeal to "good administrative practices" found a ready ear in the city administrator's office, and his implied threat of black dissatisfaction if he was not supported (confirmed by Fitch) was effective in an election year in which the mayor was taking on his own party's regular organization.

Marrow, on the other hand, did not understand the political role of the COIR, its apologist function. During the late 1950's the commission worked largely to protect the mayor from criticism and from involvement in clashes between minority groups. When Marrow, by his actions both within and outside the agency, compromised this function and instead of solving problems for the mayor began creating them, he brought on his own removal.

The conflict in the commission places in high relief the structural weaknesses of the agency. The original vague mandate of the COIR laid the groundwork for the dispute, for it created a condition in which variable conceptions of what the commission should do were almost inevitable and also made possible many of the administrative practices that upset the chairman (for example, partisan political appointment of staff). The commission–executive director structure, furthermore, provided the context which made the struggle possible. Though personality and circumstance played a great role in exacerbating the crisis at the COIR, the crisis could not have arisen if the commission had not provided the voluntary chairman with a power base from which to act. The voluntary commission functioned as a source of tension in the agency, a place which, even after the struggle was over, retained the potential to undermine the executive direction of the COIR.

Finally, the crisis provided the opportunity for a new departure. New administrative guidelines had been produced, and one of the protagonists had been removed from the scene.[114] Perhaps a new chairman, one with political influence who was acceptable to both the black and Jewish constituencies, could bind the agency's wounds and direct it to meaningful substantive achievements within the constraints of the city's political realities.

[114] The crisis also illustrates the change in black political influence in the city from the days of the Unity Committee.

5

The Commission on Human Rights, 1961–1965: From Conciliation to Affirmative Action

The change in the chairmanship of the City Commission on Intergroup Relations in 1960 paralleled and in part reflected a basic change in the national civil rights struggle. On the national scene, and especially in the South, discriminatory social mores were beginning to be challenged by nonviolent direct action. Sit-ins and freedom rides, it was hoped, would produce results where discussions, accommodation, and legal action had failed. Though the means had changed, however, commitment to the overriding goal, an integrated society, remained unshaken.

Leadership

In this changing national context, the new chairman, Stanley Lowell, came to the city commission reluctantly but with a deep commitment to the civil rights struggle. At the time of the crisis in the COIR, Lowell, who had been a longtime political associate of Mayor Wagner, was preparing to leave his position as deputy mayor for private law practice. Wagner prevailed upon him to accept the chairmanship because he was one of the few men in the city who commanded the full respect of both Jewish and black leaders. Faced with an election year in which his future was far from certain, the mayor realized that the appointment of Lowell, recently one of his closest advisers, would serve as a gesture of commitment to the minority community and would be a positive step toward rebuilding the commission.

When offered the post in the mayor's office, Lowell attempted to resist. The appointment was especially embarrassing to him because it was he who had interceded for Wagner with Marrow. When Wagner insisted, however, he finally agreed to serve. As was expected, the news of the mayor's action was well received in both the Jewish and black constituencies of the agency. Praise for the new chairman was expressed to the press by representatives of the Anti-Defamation League, the American Jewish Congress, the NAACP, the Urban League, and Harlem political interests.[1]

Lowell brought to the commission a different concept of the proper role for the organization, or at least a different emphasis, from that of the previous chairman. For Lowell, the commission's primary job in the city was to pave the way for action by the mayor on civil rights issues, and thus move the administration in favorable directions.[2] This conception was based upon the new chairman's belief that the "mayor's heart was in the right place" on civil rights questions, and that he would act positively on them if only his built-in set of priorities could be affected.

This was a position of advocacy of minority rights within the city government, but Lowell's advocacy was tempered by other values. First, as a lawyer and a civil libertarian, he believed that in advocating the rights of one group in the city, the rights of other groups or individuals should not be compromised. Second, as a longtime member of the Wagner administration, the new chairman felt an intense loyalty to the mayor. He believed that, as part of the administration, the chairman of the COIR, the commissioners, and the executive director should work for change within the city government but should not covertly criticize the administration in the press in order to pressure the mayor. If a commissioner could not live with the policies of the administration, he could resign his position and then, Lowell believed, ethically pursue his protest. In sum, as a politician Lowell saw the commission as an agent for progress and change; at the same time he viewed it as a mayoral agency with final policy decisions in the hands of the mayor.

[1] *New York Times,* Sept. 10, 1960, p. 14, col. 2., and *Amsterdam News,* Sept. 10, 1960, p. 1.

[2] Interview with Lowell, summer 1968. This account of Lowell's philosophy is based upon this interview.

To add to his greater commitment to advocacy of minority-group positions within the city government, Lowell brought a new set of priorities to the commission. For Lowell, employment discrimination was the key substantive area in which the COIR had to act if the pattern of discrimination in the city was to be destroyed. This evil, the new chairman believed, was the "basis for the pyramid of discrimination." [3] If the economic problems of minority workers could be solved, Lowell thought, solutions to housing, education, and other problems would follow.

Previously the commission had been primarily concerned with housing; it was obvious that under Lowell this would change, although statutory commitments would remain. The change was foreshadowed in the agency's 1961 annual report. Dealing with employment discrimination had been "primarily a state function," the report noted, but its "Goals for 1962" stressed the importance of combating employment discrimination with the techniques of "education, conciliation, and enforcement." [4]

This envisioned change in role and policy orientation for the COIR, combined with the fact of Frank Horne's unsteady health and diminished vitality, pointed to the need for a new executive director for the agency. The replacement of Marrow offered the political opportunity for such a change (the agency's black constituency had had their victory), and Lowell's unpaid status pointed to its necessity, for a full-time executive was needed at the helm. After a waiting period necessitated by the highly charged nature of the Marrow-Horne struggle and the intrusion of an election year, the mayor was ready to act.

First Lowell was formally reappointed to serve in the "new" administration. He then convinced Frank Horne that it would be in the best interests of both the agency and himself if he stepped down and a more vigorous executive director was appointed. As recompense and in recognition of his service, a consultantship in

---

[3] COIR press release, Nov. 3, 1961, quoting testimony before the Education and Welfare Committee of the U.S. House of Representatives. (New York: The Commission, 1962).

[4] COIR *Annual Report,* 1961, pp. 22, 53.

human relations at the Housing and Redevelopment Board, which carried with it the same salary as the commission executive directorship but fewer administrative duties, was created for Horne.[5]

For the vacant executive directorship the commission considered several people but finally settled upon Madison Jones. Jones, an expert in race relations and a trained administrator, was the director of intergroup relations at the New York City Housing Authority. When approached by the Mayor, he was reluctant to take the job, but as a member of the administration Jones could not directly turn Wagner down. He decided to deal with the problem by asking for an exorbitant salary and by refusing to serve unless his terms were met; when the mayor agreed to his request ($20,000 a year, another job for Frank Horne, and total executive control of the agency), Jones was left with the post.[6]

Philosophy and Goals

The change in the top leadership of the commission at first caused no change in the agency's basic approach to minority problems, for Lowell and Jones had been schooled similarly to their predecessors. Nevertheless, the new leaders, men of the 1950's rather than the 1930's and 1940's, brought with them a flexibility that allowed them to change the commission's direction as conditions within the city changed. Thus, in reviewing 1960, the commission assessed its approach as "fact finding, consulting, and cooperating" and saw itself as a "symbol of the city's deep commitment, an educational instrument, a catalyst." [7] In 1962, Madison Jones said this about his new job: "The big thing is to change habit. . . . I found that the same thing worked in housing if you went to everyone in the community and got them to try out new habits. As I see this new job of mine we have to get public opinion on our side so we don't have to use punitive measures. We've got the right climate; we've got the tools—and we're going

[5] *New York Times,* Jan. 13, 1962, p. 31, col. 3, and interview with Earl Brown, summer 1968.

[6] Interview with Jones, Jan. 20, 1969.

[7] COIR *Annual Report, 1960* (New York: The Commission, 1961), p. 1.

to do the job." [8] The key words again were "conciliation," "education," and "restraint." By 1964, however, this had changed. In that year the commission documented "a deep shift in rationale." The central words became "affirmative action" for integration, and the commission saw itself as "marching out to meet the enemy." [9]

This shift in rhetoric was paralleled by a shift in goals. In 1961 the objectives of the commission were "equal privileges and responsibility for all in housing, schools, and employment." [10] By late 1963 chairman Lowell was calling for "preferential treatment" in hiring for members of minority groups and suggesting that "color consciousness" rather than "color blindness" was necessary for dealing with minorities fairly.[11] During 1964 and 1965 conciliation and persuasion remained prime tools of the commission (and were used in seeking agreements with large employers and builders), but the organization was becoming less and less reluctant to use the enforcement powers that it had gained in the early 1960's. In fact, the threat of the use of enforcement powers made efforts at conciliation more credible to those businesses approached by the commission.

In order to dramatize the commission's change in philosophy and goals, the chairman sought a change in the name of the agency from the Commission on Intergroup Relations to the City Commission on Human Rights (CCHR). This he achieved in February 1962, in one of the first pieces of commission-related legislation to pass the city council after he took office.

Organizational Flux

In coming to the commission after the Marrow-Horne affray, Stanley Lowell's prime organizational task was to re-establish a working relationship between the voluntary commissioners and the staff of the agency so that the commission could be molded into an efficient operating unit. Secondarily, of course, the new chairman

[8] *New York Post,* April 10, 1962.

[9] City Commission on Human Rights *Annual Report, 1964* (New York: The Commission, 1965) p. 2.

[10] COIR *Annual Report, 1961,* p. 2.

[11] *New York Times,* Oct. 28, 1963, p. 1, col. 2.

sought to restructure the agency so that it would emphasize the new set of priorities that he brought to it. Lowell was only partially successful in both objectives, for he was hampered by the basic organizational problems of the commission, problems that could not be solved by a change in leadership or a staff reorganization.

One of the characteristics that had marked the Commission on Intergroup Relations from the beginning was uncertain organization, and this was never more apparent than in the early 1960's. Noting this fact in an interview, one highly placed agency official observed that "organizational changes were being considered on the day of my arrival at the agency, and other changes were on my desk on the day I left." This observation was confirmed by former deputy director Irving Goldaber, who noted that "the only constant in the organization of the commission was change."

The uncertainty about how the commission should be organized was the result of several factors. Since the commission's objectives were rather general and the exact scope and extent of its powers undefined, it was difficult to know how it could pursue these objectives and employ these powers. This uncertainty led to the vague feeling that if the commission were reorganized it could "do better." Charges of waste and inefficiency, leveled by Marrow and others earlier, had added to this feeling and contributed to the attempts to deal with the problems of the agency through reorganization. In addition, reorganization was a convenient device through which the commission's new leadership could redefine its priorities, make their weight felt, and get the agency off to a new start.

Lowell's first major reorganization plan, put into effect early in 1962, was thus aimed at getting the commission more actively into the vital area of employment discrimination and at strengthening the enforcement orientation of the agency. Two new divisions were created, one for business and employment and one for enforcement, and the functions of the division of housing and relocation and that of compliance and investigation were combined into a division of housing and compliance. These three new subunits, when added to the unchanged divisions of community relations, research, and public relations, gave the commission six operating subdivisions, and seven when the division for administrative services was added.[12] In their effort to involve the commission in the area of employment discrimination the leaders of the agency, instead of consolidating the CCHR's subunits as was recommended by the Fitch report, helped further their proliferation.

Throughout the early 1960's, the money and personnel made available to the CCHR by the city remained relatively constant. Between 1961 and 1965 the budget of the commission increased at a slower rate than that of the city as a whole (in two years it declined),[13] while at the same time reorganization increased the number of subunits at the agency. Furthermore, legally mandated responsibilities, like the enforcement of the city fair housing law, absorbed a good part of the available agency resources (twelve of thirty professional staff were assigned to the housing subunit in 1963, not to mention others in other subdivisions concerned with this task). The consequence of the expansion of the number of subunits and the limited nature of agency resources was that, though the agency was minimally active in many areas, its impact in any one area was also minimal.

This problem was accentuated by the tendency of commission divisions to further subdivide. In the community relations division in 1962–1963, for example, there was a tension control unit (two people), a minority services unit (two people), a neighborhood services unit (two people), and an education unit (two people).[14] An additional subdivision, a nationalities unit, was created in 1963. By failing to focus its efforts in particular policy areas, the commission was, through reorganization, minimizing its own effectiveness.

In 1963 the leadership of the CCHR considered another re-

[12] *CCHR News,* vol. 4, no. 4 (1962). The most complete collection of COIR and CCHR newsletters and press releases may be found at the library of the State Division of Human Rights in New York City.

[13] See Table 12.

[14] Betty Binder, "Administrative Action against Residential Discrimination in New York City" (M.A. essay, Columbia University, 1962), p. 69.

organization, but this one was aimed at the commissioners rather than the staff. When he came to the commission, Lowell reorganized its subcommittee structure to correspond with his changes at the staff level; as time passed, however, the chairman became increasingly aware of the problems of the commission structure, and of the burden that his own unpaid post placed upon him, and began to consult with civil rights groups about possible changes in the top-level organization of the CCHR.

Three basic alternatives were considered: (1) a full-time chairman, and six full-time commissioners, all paid (similar to the top structure of the State Commission Against Discrimination); (2) a city department-type organization, with a commissioner and four or five deputies; (3) retention of the existing structure, with an expanded staff "trained in law." [15] Ultimately, the third alternative was chosen; apparently, to the commission and its organized constituency, the advantages of the commission structure outweighed its faults. [16]

The Chairman and the Commissioners

The original careful racial and ethnic balance devised by Lowell when he was a mayoral assistant was maintained through a process of reappointment and selective new appointments of commissioners. Though tenure on the commission was formally limited to three years, the mayor only made new appointments to replace members who had resigned or died in office. In fact, during the later years of his term Wagner sometimes even neglected to fill vacancies, and sitting commissioners often continued to serve without formal reappointment. [17]

When appointments were made, it was generally with the understanding that certain civil rights groups in the city were entitled to "seats" on the commission. Thus Murray Gross of the Jewish Labor Committee replaced Charles Zimmerman on the commission and Brendon Sexton was appointed to fill one of the "labor"

[15] *New York Times,* July 1, 1963, p. 16, col. 3.

[16] CCHR, *Annual Report, 1963* (New York: The Commission, 1964), p. 8.

[17] *New York Times,* June 13, 1965, p. 79, col. 4.

seats formerly held by Charles Kerrigan. The balance altered slightly from time to time (generally in the direction of increasing the number of female, Jewish, and black commission members), but the fundamental principle of "representativeness" remained intact.[18]

Within the commission, Lowell attempted to establish an ongoing subcommittee structure to parallel the structure put into operation at the staff level. Each commissioner served on one or more of the six subcommittees which met at intervals between the monthly commission meetings. After the staff bitterness about the previous chairman had subsided, subcommittee members were able to work closely with staff members in substantive policy areas. Policy positions were worked out cooperatively and ultimately presented to the full commission for its sanction at the monthly meetings. Staff members under Lowell attended commission meetings and served at them in an advisory capacity, as they had not done under Marrow.

Though the commission as a whole was the ostensible policy-making body for the agency, as it was legally mandated to be, Lowell and Jones increasingly became the effective decision makers. Lowell found it relatively easy to control commission meetings. First, he had all the advantages inherent in controlling the chair. Second, attendance was generally rather low (it ranged from about half to two-thirds of the commissioners). Third, Lowell was more informed about the work of the commission than were his colleagues (he spent more time at the job, and because of his position got an overview of the agency) and was more willing than they to attempt to direct its activities. Fourth, he had had a very close relationship with the mayor, an important asset. Finally, he was willing to take exceedingly (for the time) liberal positions, and therefore, though he was from the "Jewish group," his civil rights commitment could not be questioned by minority members.[19]

18 Several interviewees confirmed that this principle was at work during the 1961–1965 period.

19 Interview with Lowell. Lowell estimated that he spent about one-third of his time while a voluntary unpaid chairman on commission business.

Lowell, in addition, was the "public member" of the commission and therefore commanded more media exposure than the other members (and more, for that matter, than the executive director). His visibility in the *New York Times,* for example, exceeded that of both the commission as an organization and of Jones during this period (see Table 2). This predominance in the public eye gave the chairman an advantage in commission decision making over his colleagues.

Table 2. Relative visibility of the commission, the chairman, and the executive director in the *New York Times,* 1955–1971 (in number of citations in the annual *Times Index*)

Year	Executive director	Chairman	Commission
1955	1	4	8
1956	3	6	8
1957	5	3	4
1958	4	7	3
1959	5	11	3
1960	0	18	8
1961	4	16	7
1962	5	22	11
1963	5	38	9
1964	7	16	2
1965	5	41	16
1966	4	92	12
1967	0	54	7
1968	0	53	2
1969	2	39	22
1970	1	42	6
1971	0	52	1

Source: New York Times Index, 1955–1971.

Estimates of most other commissioners were "one day a week," or one-fifth of their working time. Attendance figures are from Henry J. Stern, "Freedom When?: A Report on the City Commission on Human Rights Prepared for the Task Force on Economic Development of New York City," typescript, 1965, p. 1. This report was prepared during the Lindsay campaign and is on file at the mayor's office.

In fact, as chairman, Lowell sometimes found it necessary to make or modify decisions before the commission could be consulted. Lowell's visibility to the public also gave him a relative advantage over the executive director in decision making. Relations between Lowell and Jones were generally good. Jones never had the difficulties that Horne had had in participating in commission meetings, and he was supported by the commission in his administrative control of the staff. In return, Jones rarely took unilateral action. Nevertheless there was, from time to time, tension between the two men, and this is admitted by both. This tension centered around such things as publicity, the question of who could legitimately take credit for commission achievements, and public actions taken by one and not cleared with the other. Though these difficulties were eventually worked out, they do show that the Marrow-Horne controversy was more than the result of a clash of personalities.

Aside from the monthly policy meetings, the main task of the voluntary commissioners was to preside over hearings that arose under the complaint procedure established to administer the fair housing law. Complaints that could not be resolved by the staff were heard by a panel of two commissioners, which then either rejected the complaint or recommended action to the full commission.

It was here that the most glaring weaknesses of the commission structure became apparent. About two complaints a week reached the hearing level.[20] Though volunteer commissioners claimed that they gave at least one day a week to commission business, it was almost always difficult for the executive director to find two commissioners free at once to sit on hearing panels as the cases reached this level.[21] A disproportionate amount of the work therefore fell upon the shoulders of the commissioners who were willing to serve, and the ardor of most of these soon cooled under the burden. This was especially true of the lawyer-commissioners, who, because of the quasi-judicial nature of the housing hearings, were in special demand. As a result of these difficulties, the al-

[20] Binder, p. 75.   [21] Interview with Morris Plowscowe, Dec., 1968.

ready tortuous complaint procedure was delayed even further, and the unavailability of commissioners often helped to deny effective relief to victims of housing discrimination.

A further result was that black groups in the constituency of the commission became increasingly upset about what they considered to be the indifferent administration of the fair housing law. In mid-1963, the *Amsterdam News* ran an exposé series on the CCHR. It claimed that "the New York City Commission on Human Rights is saying very little or almost nothing on the color problem" and that there was a "tension torn rivalry on the commission, . . . the composition [of which] makes it almost impossible for effective action by the staff." "Official requests of the commission," reporter Jimmy Booker pointed out, "were often ignored at city hall," and commissioners (including the chairman) "are often too busy with their private affairs to hold housing hearings." In a later article, leaders of the city's black politicial community (Gardner Taylor, Percy Sutton, J. Raymond Jones, George Fowler, Hubert T. Delany) were quoted on the inadequacies of the commission and on how these reflected upon the mayor's commitment to civil rights.[22]

Brooker's articles, like the ones on the Marrow-Horne dispute, were obviously the product of staff "leaks" about dissatisfactions within the agency, but they nevertheless reflected a basic difficulty of the commission structure.[23] Those dissatisfied with the commission's performance not only offered criticisms but also suggested reforms. The Riverside Democratic Club, for example, suggested a reorganization which would eliminate the voluntary commissioners, and an augmentation of the agency's resources. A paid

[22] *Amsterdam News,* May 4, 1963, and April 27, 1963.

[23] Another source of dissatisfaction was the belief among staff members that the commission was not "representative" because a black commissioner (unnamed) was not, in effect, militant enough. Booker cites an incident in which the "aging" commissioner, "who seldom goes out of his house except to attend a Commission on Human Rights meeting," failed to back a staff report when questioned by a white commissioner. This, Booker wrote, led to the "frustration of the dedicated staff workers who had spent long hours to get the facts" (*Amsterdam News,* May 4, 1963).

full-time chairman, paid hearing officers, an adequate staff, field offices open evenings and weekends, an expanded legal staff, and more vigorous use by the commission of the powers that it had, suggested the club, were all needed if the agency was to be made effective.

In fact, Lowell had long been working for some of the changes suggested by the West Side reformers, and for others which would facilitate and shorten the housing complaint procedure. Unlike the Democratic reformers, however, Lowell was functioning in a real political situation of limited resources and resistance to change. The commission eventually was given a counsel and won other minor procedural points, but there was no change in the "two-commissioner requirement." Currently the commission still must function under this rule, one that is illogical if only because it builds into the administrative process the possibility for a split decision. Chairmen have continually pressed for change but have been rebuffed by city councilmen who see this provision as affording "additional protection for the public." The council, in short, is happy with administrative inefficiency in the area of discrimination complaints.

It is interesting that the thrust of the structural changes sought by the chairman and staff, though it may have been unintended, was to diminish the role in the agency of the voluntary commissioners. In an informal manner, the role of the commissioners in the decision-making process of the agency was largely being undermined, and at the same time their role in the administrative process was being challenged. As was the case in the late 1950's, the commission structure seemed to be the source of many of the CCHR's difficulties.

Staff

Just as reorganization failed to reach the roots of the CCHR's problems at the commission level, it failed too to help alleviate agency staff problems. Recruiting and retaining competent staff was a major difficulty for the commission in the early 1960's as it was for other city agencies, but unlike many other agencies, the CCHR had to contend in this area with the added factor of partisan political considerations in the selection of personnel. After staff was obtained, furthermore, commission executives had to face another problem not entirely common in more established city agencies, the problem of intraagency racial tensions.

Staffing the agency was the responsibility of the executive director, Madison Jones, who faced several elemental difficulties. Starting salaries for professional employees were low ($6,000 to $7,000 a year), especially when viewed in the light of the formal civil service job requirements for the basic "human rights specialist" title (a bachelor's degree and four years' work experience, or a satisfactory equivalent). Furthermore, competition from newly created and "more glamorous" city agencies with higher pay scales was increasing, and adding to pressures from the private sector that affected the entire city employment picture.[24]

Like Frank Horne, Jones was faced with continual attempts to staff the commission with politicial appointees. As positions became vacant, prospective employees had to be cleared by Mayor Wagner's patronage dispenser, assistant to the mayor Frank Doyle, before they could be retained by the commission.[25] This, of course, slowed the agency's hiring process and stopped it entirely when the mayor was trying to hold down the city budget.

Fiscal stringencies, besides leading to an informal freeze on hiring, led the city budget office to resist salary increases and personnel upgrading at the CCHR. This led to dissension within the commission, leaks to the *Amsterdam News,* and the loss of key personnel to other agencies. By the end of the 1962–63 fiscal year, the commission had lost two of its chief intergroup relations officers and had made no replacements; half of its ten senior intergroup relations officers had resigned and only two of their spots were filled. Resignations often came from among the agency's most competent and long-tenured staffers. By late in 1962 the situation

[24] See David T. Stanley *et al., Professional Personnel for the City of New York* (Washington: The Brookings Institution, 1963).
[25] Stern, p. 8.

had reached crisis proportions; fully half of the CCHR's professional posts were vacant (eighteen of thirty-six, including supervisory personnel) and few had any immediate prospects of being filled.[26]

In this crisis with the mayor's office the staff enjoyed the support of the commissioners. Early in January 1963 chairman Lowell was able to forestall a mass protest resignation by the entire commission only by promising to bring the matter before the mayor. This he did in a letter in which he pointed out the demoralizing affects of the city's personnel and salary policy for the staff of the commission. The letter got no results, and the administration took no action even after further talks with mayoral assistant Julius C. C. Edelstein.[27]

Finally, disgusted with the delays, seven commissioners joined Lowell in a wire to the mayor and disclaimed any responsibility for the tasks assigned to the CCHR until legitimate staff grievances were dealt with. They wrote: "At a regular monthly meeting of the city Commission on Human Rights today the undersigned agreed to inform you that there has been no resolution of the problems spelled out in our letter to you of March 25 calling attention to the impossible administrative situation in this agency. Since the solution of such administrative problems is outside of our power and control we cannot continue to take responsibility for the tasks assigned to the commission by local laws and the city charter." [28] The pressure of the commissioners, when combined with staff dissatisfactions and some unrest in the agency's constituency groups, was enough finally to win some concessions from the mayor. After several meetings, Wagner got the CCHR

[26] Memo, Bernice McCrory to Wagner, Sept. 28, 1962, files of the mayor, Municipal Archives, box 5578; *Amsterdam News,* April 27, 1963; New York City civil list, 1962–63. All documents cited in this chapter, unless otherwise noted, are in the Municipal Archives.

[27] Memo, Edelstein to McCrory, April 3, 1963, files of the mayor, box 5578; this memo refers to and summarizes the Lowell letter.

[28] Telegram, Lowell, Juan Aviles, Eleanor Clark French, Louise Glover, Murray Gross, Vincent Lacapria, Theophilis Lewis, and David Litter to the mayor, April 25, 1963, files of the mayor, box 5578.

leaders to agree that "the sole problem has been salary grades" and pay increases were promised.[29]

In the agreement, nothing was said about the politicization of the commission hiring process and the low priorities that the administration seemingly placed on the CCHR's activities. Mayoral action was a palliative, not a cure. In 1964 and 1965, the agency continued to complain about personnel shortages and financial stringencies.[30] When Mayor Lindsay came into office in 1965, Mr. Doyle was still in his key spot in the hiring process, a freeze on vacant salary lines remained, and there were twenty-six jobs vacant (sixteen of these professional positions in a staff of eighty). One commission subunit, the community relations division, was down to less than half strength.[31]

Staff difficulties at the commission went beyond questions of political interference with staffing and levels of staff compensation to the basic relationship among different staff members within the agency. Work on the commission seemed to be especially attractive to a certain kind of person, characterized by one interviewee as "the ideologue." The ideologue was interested in working at the commission because often he or she had personally been the object of discriminatory behavior and had very firm convictions on how to deal with it. Though committed to the CCHR's overall goal, the tendency of this type of person, once he came to the agency, was to "go into business for himself." Viewing racial problems from intensely personal perspectives and convinced that theirs were the only solutions, the ideologues on the commission often had a psychological stake in the failure of official agency policies or in approaches to problems suggested by colleagues at odds with them.[32] The "ideologue" as described here is analogous to the "zealot," a general bureaucratic type described by Anthony Downs: "The peculiarities of zealots' behavior spring from two

[29] Press release, office of the mayor, May 14, 1963; press release, CCHR, May 10, 1963, files of the mayor, State Division of Human Rights.

[30] See, for example, CCHR, *Annual Report, 1965* (New York: The Commission, 1966), p. 2.

[31] Stern, p. 11.

[32] Interview with Irving Goldaber, Jan. 13, 1969.

characteristics. The narrowness of their sacred policies and the implacable energies they focus upon promoting those policies. . . . They tend to concentrate their energies and resources on their sacred policies regardless of the breadth of their formal responsibilities, thereby ignoring important bureaucratic functions. Moreover, they antagonize other officials by their refusal to be impartial and their willingness to trample all obstacles." [33]

Furthermore, again perhaps because many of the employees of the commission had been denied other opportunities because of their race, race became a criterion in reverse for internal agency organization and promotion. A careful racial and ethnic balance was maintained at every staff level. When Earl Brown replaced Stanley Lowell as the commission's first paid chairman, he inadvertently upset this balance when he brought with him his two white secretaries (Brown is a black). Brown felt it necessary, when he learned of the consternation he had caused within the agency, to call a special plenary staff meeting to explain that race was not going to be a criterion for hiring or promotion within the agency while he was chairman.[34]

Constituency

As during the late 1950's, the CCHR under Lowell and Jones had a bifurcated constituency. The organizations most interested in it were primarily white and Jewish, but services were provided mainly to middle-class blacks, and, to a lesser extent, Puerto Ricans. In addition, the commission attempted to expand its constituency through community organization and public-relations work and by seeking special relationships with several loosely defined subgroups in the city.

Organized Groups

As is evidenced by the relative stability in the distribution of commission seats, the relationship of the CCHR with its organized

[33] Anthony Downs, *Inside Bureaucracy* (Boston: Little, Brown, 1967), pp. 109–110.
[34] Interview with Earl Brown.

constituency remained constant during Lowell's tenure. In every annual report of the agency issued between 1961 and 1965 the closeness of this relationship was stressed.

In 1961, just after Lowell took office, the commission sponsored a massive conference "to consider intergroup problems and to analyze its program in depth." [35] Representatives of more than thirty city agencies and private civil rights groups participated, and the list of participant groups very much resembled the one that Morris Sass had drawn of sponsor organizations for the COIR eight years before.

In following years commission reports stressed cooperation on various problems with such groups as the Metropolitan Council for Housing, the American Jewish Committee, the NAACP, the Citizens Committee for a Fair Housing Practices Law, and the New York office of the Commonwealth of Puerto Rico. In 1965, the commission noted that contacts with private groups occurred almost daily, and that formal meetings with individual groups, like the National Association for Puerto Rican Civil Rights, were frequent. [36]

The lists of groups consulted for three conferences, one in 1961, one in 1964, and one in 1965, illustrate that the organized constituency relationships of the CCHR begun in the early 1950's were still intact (see Table 3). Generally the lists vary to reflect changes in the scope and subject matter of the conferences (the first was general, the second on discrimination in housing, and the third on strengthening the fair housing law), but the commission continued to consult the core Jewish groups (the American Jewish Congress, the American Jewish Committee, and the Anti-Defamation League) on almost every issue. Some marginal groups dropped from the agency's constituency (including Jewish organizations such as the Jewish War Veterans), and there was increased activity among black and Puerto Rican organizations (the Urban League, the Commonwealth of Puerto Rico, CORE), but for basic, continued support, the commission turned to the Jewish agencies that had originally brought it to life.

---

[35] COIR, *Annual Report, 1961,* p. 8.
[36] CCHR, *Annual Report, 1962,* p. 5; *1963,* p. 22; *1965,* p. 3.

Table 3. Groups consulted for three conferences by the commission, 1961, 1964, 1965

Group	1961	1964	1965
American Civil Liberties Union	x		
American Jewish Committee	x	x	
American Jewish Congress	x	x	x
Anti-Defamation League of B'nai B'rith	x	x	x
Catholic Interracial Council	x		x
Citizens Committee for Children of New York City	x		
Committee on Civil Rights in Metropolitan New York		x	
Commonwealth of Puerto Rico, Migration Division	x	x	x
Community Council of Greater New York			x
Community Service Society of New York			x
Congress of Puerto Rican Hometowns		x	
CORE	x	x	
Holy Rosary Roman Catholic Church	x		
Metropolitan Council for Housing			x
Mobilization for Youth		x	
NAACP		x	
National Community Relations Advisory Council	x		
National Conference of Christians and Jews	x		
National Scholarship Service	x		
New York Civil Liberties Union	x		
New York State Committee on Discrimination in Housing	x	x	
Protestant Council of the City of New York	x		
Puerto Rican Forum, Inc.	x		x
United Neighborhood Houses of New York	x		
United Parents Associations	x		
Urban League of Greater New York	x	x	x

Source: Lists of conference participants in commission annual reports, 1961, 1964, and 1965. The commission did not list every participating group in each conference.

Other more general indicators also reflect the close relationship between the commission and the private civil rights organizations in the city. In 1964, for example, in an effort to generate increased complaints under the fair housing law, the commission began to accept complaints in the offices of private civil rights groups. The groups that participated in this program were predominantly black and Jewish and though the program was not a great success this cooperation does reveal CCHR-constituency ties.[37]

The source of the commission's personnel is a more quantifiable indicator of the closeness of this relationship. Some data on the work experience and community activities of professional staff of the CCHR hired between 1960 and 1964 are available from the newsletter published quarterly by the commission. The information is admittedly fragmentary, but it does suggest that a substantial minority of the staff of the city commission were either trained in the private agencies that comprised the CCHR's organized constituency or participated in the activities of these agencies with some degree of intensity as interested citizens. Of thirty-four professionals hired by the commission during this period for whom background data is available, more than a third had either been employed by one of the related private agencies or had been an active lay person in one of them (see Table 4).

Table 4. Background of professional personnel hired by the CCHR, 1960–1964

Background	No.	%
No experience	1	3
Unrelated experience	2	6
Unrelated government experience	3	9
Related government experience	10	29
Labor union	2	6
Constituency organization	12	35
Private organization, unrelated "liberal cause"	4	12
Total	34	100

Source: COIR Reporter and *CCHR News,* vol. 3, no. 1 (1961) through vol. 6, no. 4 (1964). These newsletters succeeded each other and are numbered consecutively.

Other interesting relationships are also suggested by these figures. Even beyond its ties with the traditional constituency groups, the CCHR seems to have drawn the bulk of its professional em-

[37] *CCHR News,* vol. 6, no. 3 (1964).

ployees from organizations engaged in similar work. These included governmental organizations (human relations officers from federal, state, or city agencies, former employees of city departments with a social service orientation), private nonprofit groups (the Fellowship of Reconciliation, the Civic League for Good Government), and unions with liberal inclinations or a large minority-group membership (ILGWU, Furniture Workers of America).

Few new workers at the commission had totally unrelated job experience. From this it seems that the civil rights arena in New York City in the early 1960's was rather self-contained. Employees of agencies engaged in "the struggle" moved from job to job, from public to private agency and back again, always maintaining and developing their contacts. This movement into the commission of staff people from the agency's constituency could not help but strengthen the CCHR's ties to these organizations.

Community

Efforts to tie the commission more solidly to the New York City community at large and to provide it with a large base of associated neighborhood groups continued under the new chairman in the early 1960's. Within the commission, the divisions of community relations and public relations were the ones primarily concerned with the agency's neighborhood and citywide constituencies.

In the neighborhoods of the city the CCHR, in the 1960's as before, sought to encourage the organization of local community groups to promote integration. This technique, in the hands of the commission, was both preventative and ameliorative. Through organization the commission attempted to anticipate the tensions that would arise from the erection of public housing or the integration of a school in a segregated neighborhood; a local group favoring the change could help prepare the community, provide a common meeting ground for supporters, and help avoid tensions that might arise from a change in the status quo during the critical first few days.[38] Through organization as well the CCHR attempted to pro-

---

[38] In anticipation of the erection of a public housing project in Astoria, Queens, for example, the CCHR suggested the creation of a community council (*COIR Reporter,* vol. 3, no. 1 [1961]).

vide a forum that would bring conflicting groups together after an incident had occurred. This would, hopefully, provide the basis for the avoidance of future incidents.

The commitment of the CCHR to the "community council" idea is summarized in a leaflet entitled "Neighborhood Clinic" issued by the agency early in 1961. The leaflet urged neighborhood people to write to the CCHR, which would then have its staff (1) consult with them, (2) run a "community audit" to analyze and diagnose problems, (3) help formulate an action plan and provide "resource aid," (4) aid the local people in formulating a program, and (5) aid them in dealing with city agencies. In order to help local activists determine if the commission's aid was necessary, a "checklist for appraising conditions in your neighborhood" was included on the back cover of the pamphlet.[39]

Commission efforts to "provide a focus for coordinated activity at the local level for local organizations and city agencies" was not limited to attempts to stimulate neighborhood organization. Throughout the early 1960's the agency held clinics and workshops in intergroup relations techniques and sought cooperation from neighborhood conservation and urban renewal groups.[40]

Despite these efforts, the CCHR was not successful in establishing a network of neighborhood organizations throughout the city, or even in New York's most racially tense neighborhoods. By 1963, the commission had motivated the establishment of only six local groups (in Riverdale, Highbridge, Village-Chelsea, Bushwick, East New York, and Bellrose-Hollis). Most of these were initiated in crisis situations, and even the best of them functioned only sporadically once the crisis for the particular locality had passed. Limited in staff and resources, especially in the community relations division, the commission could not sustain these groups, and without

[39] In a press release on April 13, 1961, Stanley Lowell called this program his "prescription for nervous neighborhoods." Leaflet may be seen in the files of the Municipal Reference library.

[40] *Annual Report, 1964,* p. 5. The entire neighborhood organization approach is summarized in John P. Dean and Alex Rosen, *A Manual of Intergroup Relations* (Chicago: University of Chicago Press, 1955), a book that won a prize in the intergroup relations field in 1955.

crisis, in the words of one former commission staff member, they "simply faded away." The community council technique was successful in occasionally dealing with particular problems in particular neighborhoods and in making the agency somewhat better known in the city, but it failed to provide the commission with a solid and continuing base of local support.

The public relations division of the CCHR addressed itself to the task of giving the agency "a presence" in the larger community. Under Lowell the commission attempted to use all the media in the city to relay its message; radio, television, flyers, posters, films, spot announcements, press releases, speakers, and quarterly newsletters, were some of the techniques used. The fact that either the chairman or the executive director appeared on radio or television almost biweekly during 1962 and that in 1963 the commission prepared two regularly scheduled radio shows illustrates something of the intensity of this effort.

Nevertheless, the CCHR remained relatively unknown in the city at large. Television and radio stations that carried its messages did so at odd hours, or on stations (like WNYC) that had a circumscribed audience. Speaking retrospectively, Stanley Lowell noted that, although his tenure as chairman had occurred during an era when concern for civil rights was growing in the city, the commission under him had rather "low visibility" in city affairs.[41] This suspicion is confirmed by examining the number of times the agency and its leadership was mentioned in the *New York Times* during this period.[42] References in the press were not only infrequent but were usually tucked away in obscure corners of the paper. An examination of the *Amsterdam News* for one test year, 1960, indicates that the CCHR's low visibility extended to the minority press as well, despite special agency efforts to cater to this publicity outlet.

Individuals

During the early 1960's, the characteristics of the individuals served by the CCHR remained the same as they had been in the

[41] Interview with Lowell.   [42] See Table 2.

late 1950's. In an article published in 1961 based upon the first three years of administering the fair housing law, commission staffers Harold Goldblatt and Florence Cromien reported:

> Of all those to whom the Law offers protection, only the Negro came forward in the first three years in sizable numbers to avail himself of its provisions. Eighty-one per cent of all cases were filed by Negroes, and those complainants who filed more than one complaint were almost always Negroes. Puerto Ricans constituted the second largest group of complainants, filing 8 per cent of the total. Complaints by Jews accounted for 3 per cent. The remaining 8 per cent of the complaints were brought by members of various ethnic groups and included persons who filed complaints on behalf of others, usually spouse or friend.
>
> What is more, not all classes of Negroes availed themselves to an equal extent of the protection of the Law. One class came forward in numbers greatly disproportionate to its total numerical strength in the Negro community. This was the young middle class. Thirty-seven per cent of the Negro complainants were college graduates, another 22 per cent had some college education, and an additional 32 per cent were high school graduates. As to occupation, 39 per cent were employed at the professional or managerial levels, and 27 per cent in other white-collar occupations. Thirty-three per cent reported incomes of $100 or more a week.[43]

The vast majority of the agency's individual constituency remained young, middle-class, and black.

A commission report issued late in 1964, though much less thorough, generally confirms that the trend noted in the Goldblatt-Cromien research had continued up until that time. In its quarterly newsletter the commission described its "average complainant" as being a family man, black, between the ages of twenty-five and twenty-nine, earning $75–$100 a week. He was a high school graduate and seeking middle-income housing for his family.[44]

Though the levels of income and education for the "average

---

[43] H. Goldblatt and F. Cromien, "The Effective Reach of the Fair Housing Practices Law of the City of New York," *Social Problems*, 9 (1962), 366–367.

[44] *CCHR News*, vol. 6, no. 5 (1964).

complainant" seem to have slipped between 1961 and 1964, this description still places him in the black middle class of the city.

Nationality Subgroups

During the early 1960's, the commission expanded the number of particular subgroups within the city to which it attempted to give special attention. In addition to its now traditional appeal to Puerto Ricans, the agency attempted to court minority nationalities (Chinese and Italians, for example) with special programs.

In 1961, the COIR continued its special efforts to "plant the seeds of responsiveness" in the Puerto Rican community of the city, and to "orient that community towards the Commission on Intergroup Relations."[45] Workshops and training programs for selected Puerto Rican "neighborhood leaders" were established by the agency in cooperation with the Congress of Puerto Rican Hometowns in order to pursue this goal. During November 1961, twenty-five such leaders completed an eleven-week course; the commission hoped that they would "bring new skills in dealing with living problems in their neighborhoods to their respective organizations" and become "orientation officers" from these areas.

Efforts to reach the Puerto Rican community continued throughout the Lowell-Jones period. Commission literature was printed in Spanish, cooperation was sought from the Spanish-language press in order to bring an awareness of the commission to their readers, and various "crash programs" of forums and workshops were tried. An example of the later was a "community housing workshop" run by the CCHR in 1965. To culminate this effort the agency issued "neighborhood leader certificates" to program graduates.[46]

Though it is thus apparent that the commission sought support from the Puerto Rican community and attempted to serve it, there is little indication that the community either responded to these initiatives or benefited from them. Few Puerto Ricans brought

[45] *COIR Reporter*, vol. 4, no. 2 (1962), and COIR press release no. 44, Nov. 16, 1961.

[46] For description of commission efforts in the Puerto Rican area see: *CCHR News*, vol. 5, no. 3 (1963); vol. 6, no. 3 (1964); vol. 6, no. 7 (1965) and *Annual Report, 1965*, p. 9.

complaints to the commission. Of those who knew of it, many saw no reason to distinguish the CCHR from other agencies in the city's bureaucracy. Critics believed that the Human Rights Commission was too abstract in its approach, interested too much in the "Puerto Rican problem" and too little in the "problems of Puerto Ricans." [47] Even Puerto Rican leaders who worked with the CCHR believed that for it as for other city agencies, Puerto Rican–oriented programs were afterthoughts, undertaken with the resources left over after the needs of the black minority were met.[48]

The commission's appeal to nationality subgroups reflects an attempt to give credence to the oft repeated claim that the agency "served the entire population of the city." The CCHR thus viewed service to nationalities as a "second front" in its community relations work, and early in 1963 a nationalities service bureau was established at the agency. The job of this bureau, as it was described in a letter to the mayor, was to inform the various nationalities in the city of the availability of the commission's services, and to work with them so that they would "refrain from creating problems and tensions." [49]

From time to time, the commission did succeed in providing services for members of minority nationalities. In 1962, for example, it was able to arrange a meeting between leaders of the Chinatown community on the Lower East Side of Manhattan and police officials so that racial tensions in that area could be discussed. A 1964 effort to "lure Italian-Americans from their ethnic isolation," however, met with little success beyond the publication, for a time, of a weekly column in *Il Progresso*.[50] In the minority nationalities area, the commission was clearly the suitor and the minority

[47] Dan Wakefield, *Island in the City* (Boston: Houghton-Mifflin, 1959), p. 231.

[48] Interview with Joseph Monserrat and with Ralph Rosas, director of the New York City office of the Migration Division of the Commonwealth of Puerto Rico, both Feb. 17, 1969.

[49] *CCHR News,* vol. 5, no. 3 (1963); Rae Lesh to Wagner, April 11, 1963, files of the mayor, box 5578.

[50] CCHR, *Annual Report, 1964,* p. 4.

groups the reluctant bride. Most of the latter simply did not view their collective problems as proper matters for commission action.

Intergovernmental Relations

The CCHR's contact with the federal government remained minimal during the early 1960's, and its relations with state agencies were largely confined to jurisdictional squabbles. For a time just after Lowell assumed the chairmanship, the state legislature seemed to be preparing to covertly pre-empt the city agency's jurisdiction in housing through legislation extending the powers of the State Commission Against Discrimination. Previous state legislation had specifically provided for concurrent jurisdiction for the city, but the bill before the governor in February 1961 did not. In light of precedents in other states, the city agency's fear of preemption was not unfounded.[51]

In a letter to the governor written late in February, Stanley Lowell implored Rockefeller to act to preserve the city's jurisdiction in this area. The New York City legislation, he said, had broader coverage than that of the state, the city had valuable experience in this area of administration, and besides, the commission had always been able to work closely with the SCAD. If the state removed the city's enforcement powers, Lowell went on, the educative function of the COIR would be compromised as well, for the two were intertwined.[52]

Apparently the governor's actions left the situation undefined, for in October the city and state agencies signed what amounted to a treaty in the area of the administration of fair housing laws. Taking official notice of the fact that the new state legislation and the augmentation of the city commission's powers left their respective jurisdictions unclear, the two agencies agreed that (1) SCAD would receive all public housing and commercial space complaints, (2) COIR would get all complaints concerning discrimination in one- and two-family housing not in blocks of ten units, (3)

[51] 5 *Race Relations Law Reporter* 269–295 (1959).
[52] Lowell to Rockefeller, Feb. 25, 1961, box 4123.

either agency could process all other complaints, and (4) a daily record of complaints would be exchanged. A final caveat written into the legislation reflects the state of the relationship between the two agencies: "In view of SCAD's conviction that its jurisdiction in this area, to the extent that it has enforcement powers, is exclusive and preemptive, and COIR's conviction that it has concurrent jurisdiction with SCAD, the agreement is recommended pending the resolution of this issue by appropriate legislation or a court determination." [53]

Until the final passage of legislation authorizing local commissions and allowing the city concurrent jurisdiction later in the 1960's, the state agency was willing to live with the city agency, but only reluctantly.[54] This reluctant coexistence led to an undertone of competition between the city and the state agencies during this period. Stanley Lowell, for example, noted that private civil rights groups liked the city agency better than its state counterpart because "we were more likely to take a stand." In fact, as each agency augmented its formal powers it sought to expand its operations, sometimes at the expense of the other, and private advocates of more comprehensive fair housing legislation attempted to use the expansion of the powers of one agency as an argument for the expansion of the powers of the other.[55]

Relations with Other City Agencies

In its relations with other city departments during the period from 1961 to 1965, the City Commission on Human Rights played two basic roles. On the one hand, it attempted to provide the other departments with a service, to make available to them its expertise in intergroup relations. On the other, it attempted to act as an advocate of minority-group positions within the city government,

[53] COIR press release, Oct. 5, 1961.

[54] This legislation is reported in 8 *Race Relations Law Reporter* 250 (1963).

[55] Interview with Lowell; Joseph B. Robison, "Fair Housing in the City and State of New York," in Thomas W. Casstevens and Lynn W. Eley, eds., *The Politics of Fair Housing Legislation* (San Francisco: Chandler, 1968).

either by making demands upon its sister agencies or by seeking information from them about their internal affairs. As was the case in the late 1950's, the CCHR's success in both these roles was ultimately dependent upon the nature of its relationship with the mayor.

In its role as provider of services, the commission gained a modicum of acceptance from other city agencies. Agency annual reports indicated that the CCHR had provided consultants in intergroup relations for the city Youth Board and had developed a "pilot human relations course" for the police academy.[56] They had consulted with the Board of Education on interracial matters and had been brought by the board into negotiations on integrating the school system, and had developed an in-service training program for the Welfare Department. The chairman of the commission, furthermore, served on several interagency boards within the city (the City Housing Policy Board and the Board of Mobilization for Youth, among others) and this provided some liason with other agencies at the topmost level.

When the commission went beyond simply providing services to the other agencies, however, difficulties developed. The agency's powers to investigate complaints of discrimination within the city government disrupted the administrative processes of other agencies, and endeared it to none of them. Some commission activities caused tensions with agencies with which the CCHR, acting in other contexts, had cooperated. The agency's survey of the racial background of city employees ran into a solid refusal of cooperation from the Police Department and several other agencies. When the Board of Education realized that the CCHR was an advocate of minority positions on the integration question, the commission was frozen out of the negotiations. When the commission began to prevail upon the city's housing and planning agencies to change their criteria for renewal and relocation, they became more a problem than a source of aid.

After a time, the commission leadership came to accept this lack of cooperation with other city departments as an inevitable

[56] CCHR, *Annual Report, 1964,* p. 7; *1965,* p. 11.

result of the agency's role in the political process. Speaking retrospectively, Stanley Lowell noted, "The agency's advocacy in different issue areas didn't make it popular with other city agencies. . . . It was not my job to be popular." [57]

The mayor however, could not afford to be as sanguine as his commission about these differences between city departments, for ultimately he had to cope with them. For Wagner, during his third term as during his second, the optimum role that the CCHR could play was the moderation of conflict, not its creation. The commission was most useful to him during election campaigns when he could use it to illustrate his record on civil rights and from time to time during the period between campaigns when, with a minimum expenditure of resources, this record could be bolstered in a similar manner.[58]

As is evident from an examination of the commission's administrative difficulties, the CCHR was not a topmost agency in the mayor's set of political priorities. This observation is confirmed by an examination of Wagner's actions when the commission tangled with other city agencies. There were, in Stanley Lowell's terms, "certain agencies that the mayor just would not take on" in support of the commission.[59] One of these was the Police Department on the matter of the ethnic survey.

Lowell, who had seen city politics from the perspective of the mayor's office and had been a close aide to Wagner, understood the pressures on the mayor and thus could be sympathetic to his failure to support the CCHR in its intragovernmental difficulties with more powerful city departments. High-level commission staff, however, viewing things from a different perspective, were not as charitable. For deputy executive director Irving Goldaber, "politics" was an impediment to the commission's work. Another highly

[57] Interview with Lowell. This was a problem of some magnitude. In 1965, twenty-seven such complaints were received and investigated (*Annual Report, 1965*, p. 7).

[58] During the 1961 campaign against "the bosses," Wagner referred to the COIR by name fifty-two times, more than any other city agency (*Annual Report, 1961*, p. 1).

[59] Interview with Lowell.

placed executive in the agency agreed. Public commissions on human rights, he said, "should get into the gutty issues" but "could only do so much" because of political controls over money and personnel, and because of the administration's sensitivity to controversy.[60]

Because of the mayor's failure to support the commission in its advocate role, and the concomitant distrust within the commission of "political restraints," even basic communications between the CCHR and the mayor's office began to break down. In 1965 the commission was reduced to attempting to communicate with Wagner on the problem of Columbia University expansion into neighboring Harlem by means of a telegram, much to the amusement of the Board of Estimate.[61]

Wagner had begun to despair of the CCHR as an administrative device with which to deal with minority problems, but this despair was rooted as much in his relationships with the commission as in the shortcomings of the agency itself. In turn, the difficulties that Wagner caused the commission were not the result of a lack of personal commitment to the work of the agency (even this mayor's harshest critics did not doubt his personal commitment to civil rights), but were rather the product of the unique perspectives and demands of the office of the mayor. An examination of the commission's efforts in several issue areas illustrates the basic differences between the mayoral perspective and the commission perspective on different civil rights problems, and the conflicting demands that these differing outlooks placed upon the agency.

Housing

During the period from 1961 to 1965 housing discrimination remained the only substantive area in which the City Commission on Human Rights had a legislative mandate to act. It is not surprising, therefore, that the agency's energies in this area were

[60] Interviews with Goldaber and an interviewee who wishes to remain anonymous.

[61] Stern, p. 14.

largely absorbed in the administration of the city's fair housing practices law and in lobbying for amendments that would make the law more effective.

Though the day-to-day administration of the law did not involve the mayor, attempts to alter local legislation did, and the history of this period is a story of lack of administration support for most changes proposed by the commission. Because of the concentration of its efforts on the fair housing law, the attempts by the CCHR to affect the broader housing policies of this city during this period as during the late 1950's were necessarily circumscribed. The resources that remained were devoted to a highly publicized campaign to fight "blockbusting" [62] in the city's outlying boroughs and to urging a "more humane" housing and relocation policy upon city officials and private developers.

Administration of the Fair Housing Law

The number of complaints of housing discrimination filed with the city commission reached a peak in 1960, soon after the law was passed, and then declined in each succeeding year until 1964 (see Table 5). An upsurge in that year can be attributed to the efforts of Jack Wood, who came to the commission from the post of national housing director for the NAACP. Wood's objective was to coordinate the efforts in housing of all the city's civil rights organizations through the commission. Under his guidance ten organizations made available seventeen offices in which complaints could be filed around the city and also agreed to cooperate in education and enforcement programs. Tasks were divided among the agencies. The Urban League, for example, agreed to work to secure black and Puerto Rican applicants for housing, and the Committee on Civil Rights in Metropolitan New York volunteered to recruit white "checkers" whose efforts could help provide proof of discrimination.[63]

[62] A practice of unscrupulous real estate men, whereby panic selling by whites of properties in neighborhoods in transition is promoted, and then these, obtained at depressed prices, are resold to blacks at inflated prices.

[63] *New York Times,* Feb. 19, 1964, p. 30, col. 8; Feb. 1, 1964, p. 21, col. 3. "Checkers" are white persons, usually volunteers, who apply for

Wood's intensive efforts helped reverse the downward trend of complaints coming to the commission, but the cases filed in 1964 did not exceed those completed in 1960, the previous high year, and the number again declined slightly in 1965. Intense activity was able to motivate complaints, but hardly in numbers, according to experts in the city, that approximated the incidence of housing discrimination.[64]

Table 5. Sworn housing complaints filed with the COIR and the CCHR, 1958–1965

Year	Number	% change
1958	175 (April–Sept.)	
1959	194	
1960	269	+38.7
1961	256	−4.8
1962	235	−8.2
1963	207	−11.9
1964	269	+30.0
1965	264	−1.8

Source: CCHR, *Annual Report, 1965,* p. 20.

The commission attributed the reluctance of complainants to come forward to many factors. Certainly, despite all commission efforts, there were still people in New York, estimated commissioner Charles Zimmerman, who did not know of it. Others who did know of the CCHR hesitated to use a government agency to confront the discrimination problem. There was known exclusion of Jews from fashionable East Side cooperatives in Manhattan, for example, but the victims of the discrimination rarely came to the commission. When the help of the commission was enlisted by people of this sort the event was unusual enough to make news,

---

apartments after they have been denied to blacks. They present the same social and economic credentials as did the black applicant, and if the apartment is obtained and the black applicant was told it was rented, a prima facie case of discrimination emerges.

[64] *New York Times,* Feb. 19, 1964, p. 30, col. 8. In an optimistic moment Wood predicted 275 complaints a day.

and the publicity usually caused the wealthy complainants to drop their cases.[65]

Long drawn-out commission procedures also contributed to the dearth of complaints. Even after a potential complainant had come to one of the available offices (often at the sacrifice of a day's pay) and had taken formal action, he had to wait while the commission sought to conciliate the problem with the landlord, as required under the law. If the landlord resisted conciliation, the complainant had to retain his patience until the commission went through the processes of determination of "probable cause," referral to the full commission, and referral to the Corporation Counsel for Court Action. It was estimated in 1961 that this whole process took three or four months.[66]

By this time, of course, the complainant would probably have found another place to live and lost all interest in the case. It is reasonable to assume that some potential complainants, confronted with this administrative apparatus, simply refused to come forward.[67] The commission realized this difficulty and worked for amendments to the law that would speed up the process. Though a few of these were passed and the time necessary to process a complaint was reduced somewhat, the commission was not able during this period to handle complaints with the necessary dispatch, especially when the initial attempt at conciliation failed.

A potential complainant would be discouraged not only by the commission's lengthy procedures but also by its record of achieve-

---

[65] *New York Times,* June 2, 1960, p. 27, col. 4; see, for example, the *Times'* accounts of the case of Mr. and Mrs. Daniel Rose, April 5, 1963, p. 17, col. 1, and April 26, p. 37, col. 8.

[66] *New York Times,* Nov. 19, 1961, section VIII, p. 1, col. 8. In 1961, an amendment to the law removed the Fair Housing Practices Panel, another level of appeal.

[67] A survey done in Newark, New Jersey, on the administration of that state's fair housing law is instructive here. Of a random sample of blacks in Newark, 71 per cent knew of the state civil rights division. Nevertheless, 81 per cent said that when discriminated against they did nothing. Only 2 per cent turned to the division. The reputation of the division, the author concluded, was "mediocre, at best" (L. Zeitz, "Negro Attitudes toward Law, 19 *Rutgers Law Review* 294–311 [1965]).

ment. Of the 1,741 complaints adjusted by the commission between 1958 and 1965, about half, 869, were "satisfactorily adjusted" (see Table 6). Of these, in only 275 cases (31.6 per cent) did the complainant accept the original apartment he sought or an alternative dwelling unit (see Table 7). By the time the administrative process had been completed, 298 complainants (or 34.3 per cent of those whose cases had been "satisfactorily adjusted") no longer wanted the original unit or the alternative offered them. The remaining 296 complainants (34.1 per cent) were not even offered these alternatives but were placed on waiting lists or received offers from rental agents to "process" their requests. In some of these cases, the commission reports that landlords gave the agency policy commitments not to discriminate but fails to indicate what the result was for the complainant. In light of the previous categories, one can only assume that these individuals received little beyond a sense of frustration for their experience with the commission.

Table 6. Types of adjustment of sworn housing complaints, 1958–1965

Year	Satisfactory		Administrative		No probable cause		Total
	No.	%	No.	%	No.	%	
1958	22	35	18	28	23	37	63
1959	132	57	60	26	39	17	231
1960	127	50	40	16	85	34	252
1961	135	48	102	37	42	15	279
1962	102	46	64	29	55	25	221
1963	95	50	43	23	52	27	190
1964	130	49	70	27	64	24	264
1965	126	52	76	32	39	16	241
Total and average %	869	50%	473	27%	399	23%	1,741

Source: CCHR, *Annual Report, 1965,* p. 21.

When we look beyond the "satisfactorily adjusted" category in Table 6 we find that in 399 cases (23 per cent of all those brought to the commission) the complaint of discrimination was not substantiated, and that in 463 (27 per cent) it was dismissed for administrative reasons. Disregarding the first category (for it is a commission function to protect landlords against undue harassment), it is apparent that some of the administrative dismissals occured in cases where discrimination was perhaps present but where the complaint was incorrectly drawn or withdrawn for some reason. Again, a substantial number of complainants, perhaps with legitimate grievances, could find no redress at the commission.

Table 7. Types of satisfactory adjustment of sworn housing complaints, 1958–1965

Action by respondent	Action by complainant ($N = 869$)			
	Total	Accepted	Rejected	Not specified
Apartment offered				
Original dwelling unit	417	234	182	1
Alternative unit	166	41	116	9
Total	583	275	298	10
% of total complaints	67.1	31.6	34.3	1.2
Some commitment offered to complainant				
Waiting list	124	73	26	25
Rental agent to process	54	23	25	6
Total	178	96	51	31
% of total complaints	20.5	11.0	5.9	3.6
No action for complainant				
Landlord signed policy commitment	63			
Landlord gave oral policy commitment	5			
Other	4			
Total	72			
% of total complaints	12.4			

Source: CCHR, *Annual Report, 1965,* p. 23.

When the performance record of the city commission is considered in tandem with the nature of the agency's administrative procedures, it ceases to become surprising that the victims of housing discrimination did not seek legal redress for their ills. The objective, after all, was to find a place to live within a reasonable amount of time, and going to the CCHR was not the way to do this.

Seeking Procedural Change

Commission leaders, convinced that most of the difficulties they faced in the administration of the fair housing law were procedural, sought from the mayor and city council amendments to the legislation that would allow the CCHR to act with more speed and with less solicitude for the interests of the landlords accused of discrimination.

Soon after he came into office, Stanley Lowell called for several amendments to the law which, besides increasing the scope of its applicability, would eliminate several impediments to quick administrative action. The changes Lowell advocated included diminishing the number of commissioners required to sit on a housing hearing from three to one (or alternatively the substitution of hearing officers paid on a per diem basis, whose presence could be guaranteed, for commissioners, whose presence could not), giving subpoena power to any one commissioner or the executive director (rather than three commissioners acting together), removing the cloak of confidentiality that covered the commission's proceedings until the final stage, and eliminating appeals of commission decisions to the Fair Housing Practices Panel.[68]

Other suggestions for change were aimed not so much at commission procedures as at the apparent inability of the agency to get offending landlords to take ameliorative action in cases where discrimination was found. These included proposals that the CCHR be given the power to issue cease and desist orders and that it be allowed to require violators of the law to take "affirmative action" against discrimination. In addition, expanding the coverage of the legislation by including more actors in the "home

[68] COIR press release (quoting Lowell), Dec. 20, 1960; Lowell to Wagner, Jan. 30, 1962; files of the mayor, box 4018.

sale and rental process" (i.e., realtors and lending institutions) and increasing the number of dwelling units to which the existing law applied would have the ancillary effect, the commission pointed out, of augmenting the power of the agency by reducing the number of excuses the discriminatory landlord could make for his actions and by reducing the evasive alternatives available to him.

During the early 1960's, the commission had some success in convincing the mayor and city council of the necessity of some of the reforms it sought. In 1960 the coverage of the fair housing law was extended considerably, and the hearing requirement was, in a compromise, cut down to two commissioners. In 1962, under continuing pressure from Lowell and others, the law was again amended in order to "eliminate glaring weaknesses included in it originally by people who were not really in favor of it." [69]

Under this new amendment, which satisfied the mayor's 1961 campaign pledge to "expand and speed up the administration of the fair housing law," the commission was allowed to seek an injunction to prevent the sale or rental of property about which a complaint was being processed. In addition, the Fair Housing Practices Panel was eliminated, and the CCHR was permitted to publicize cases earlier in its proceedings and to use publicity as a weapon for settlement. These changes, it was hoped, would alleviate the CCHR's major problem, "the failure to obtain a dwelling unit" for the complainant. [70]

A final procedural reform was added in 1963 when the mayor, over the objections of corporation counsel Leo A. Larkin, allowed the commission to hire its own counsel, so that it could appear in its own behalf in the courts without having to wait for cooperation from the corporation counsel's office. Since the commission's counsel was not associated with that office, however, he could not appear in court in the city's name, but only in the name of the commission.

Though some procedural changes were thus instituted at the

' [69] COIR press release, May 15, 1961, files of COIR, box 4123; *New York Times,* July 12, 1961, p. 4, col. 1, and April 5, 1962, p. 33, col. 1.
[70] *New York Times,* May 3, 1961, p. 28, col. 3.

commission during the early 1960's, it is clear that they influenced neither the caseload of the agency nor the proportion of cases in which an apartment was obtained for the complainant. Until Wood's efforts in 1964, the number of cases that came to the commission declined annually, and the proportion of cases that resulted in "satisfactory adjustment" remained relatively constant through this period. Despite tinkering, the complaint procedure remained relatively unchanged. It relied greatly upon the work of volunteer commissioners (and two on each panel may in fact have been worse than the original three since a division would provide no decision), contained several levels of appeals, and was therefore slow and unwieldly.

Furthermore, the heart of the process, the dependence upon the initiative and tenacity of the individual voluntary complainant, was open to question as a method for launching a broad attack on housing discrimination. Concern with the case-by-case approach—"trying to empty the ocean with a spoon" [71]—directed and absorbed the commission's energies and prevented it from trying different approaches that might have had broader effects.

Though the agency reported negotiations with large-scale realtors, brokers, and managers, it did not have the resources either to seek public commitments to integration from them or to follow up these commitments if they were made.[72] When the CCHR did get involved with larger housing questions, as in the case of the confrontation between the NAACP and the Metropolitan Life Insurance Company in 1963, it was often the result of the agency's other responsibilities and not its housing program. Though a commission survey in 1962 of "25,000 controllers of property" in the city revealed "no widespread change" in New York housing practices (that is, discrimination remained the norm), the agency did not take this as a cue that it should change its techniques in the housing area.[73]

One of the reasons for this was, again, procedural. By law, the

[71] Earl Brown, quoted in the *New York Times*, Dec. 16, 1965, p. 40, col. 3.

[72] *Annual Report, 1964*, p. 14.

[73] *COIR Reporter*, vol. 5. no. 1 (1962).

byproduct of the debates of the early 1950's, the commission could not initiate actions or investigations without the approval of the mayor. This was one of the provisions that the commission leadership was unsuccessful in changing in the early 1960's. Beyond this, however, a rationale for the case-by-case approach began to develop. This is evident in the oft expressed opinion of the commission leadership that "the number of complaints doesn't reflect the full impact of the law." [74] The satisfactory adjustment of a complaint, it was argued, assures that another sector of the housing market controlled by a particular landlord will cease to be discriminatory. This may mean, the commission claimed, the integration of thousands of units of housing in some cases.

In fact, the commission offers little evidence for the contention beyond a 98-per-cent favorable response from landlords involved in past commission cases to the question: "How do you feel about the complainants as tenants?" [75] It could equally plausibly be argued that a landlord caught discriminating by the CCHR might have to rent one apartment to a black family (this happened in less than a third of the cases in which discrimination actually occured) but would be "more careful" about being covert in his discriminatory practices in the future. Early research has indicated that the commission, where it did obtain apartments, was simply facilitating the movement of middle-class blacks from one already integrated neighborhood to another.[76] In a more general sense, Taeuber and Taeuber's "index of segregation" shows that in New York, where some form of human rights commission had been in operation since 1943 and a fair housing law since 1958, integration had not advanced substantially beyond the level of that of the rest of the cities in the northeastern United States.[77]

---

[74] Madison Jones, quoted in the *New York Times,* July 27, 1964, p. 27, col. 2.

[75] *CCHR News,* vol. 6, no. 5 (1964). A positive response to this inquiry may have been designed by some landlords to ward off further commission interest.

[76] Goldblatt and Cromein, p. 269.

[77] Karl E. Taeuber and Alma F. Taeuber, *Negroes in Cities* (Chicago: Aldine, 1965), pp. 32, 37.

Blockbusting

Aside from individual complaints, the practice of "blockbusting" was the major concern of the CCHR in the housing area in the early 1960's. A series of hearings held at the commission in 1962 and 1963 revealed that unscrupulous real estate operators were flooding East New York and other neighborhoods in Brooklyn and the Bronx with postcards and phone calls designed to promote "panic selling" of one- and two-family homes. Residents were advised that blacks were moving into their neighborhoods and that this would "lower property values." In some cases, blacks were hired to walk up and down the streets, posing as potential house purchasers.

After mounting the campaign, the realtors bought houses from panicky owners for prices below the market value and sold them at inflated prices to blacks desperate for adequate housing. Of an average of eleven transactions in East New York, the realtor paid $12,000 and resold the property for $20,000, whereas its assessed value was actually $10,000–$14,000 and its market value was $8,125–$13,125. The problem was complicated because black purchasers could not get bank financing and thus had to add to their costs by taking second and third mortgages from the realtors at high rates of interest.[78]

Lacking any statutory power, the commission was forced to employ an amalgam of methods against this practice. Publicity was used to expose the blockbusters, and local property owners organized to resist their appeals. These approaches did tend to curb campaigns in some localities, but the realtors, instead of giving up, simply moved to other neighborhoods. In addition, local legislation aimed at unlicensed real estate operators was suggested to the city council, but no action was taken.

The only effective sanction in this area, license revocation, was in the hands of the secretary of state and was only applicable, of course, to licensed brokers.[79] This power was used sparingly and

[78] *New York Times,* Oct. 3, 1963, p. 21, col. 1.
[79] *New York Times,* Nov. 2, 1962, p. 11, col. 2.

was not the focus of a cooperative effort between the city commission and the state agency.

Housing and the Commission's Role in City Government

In the area of housing during the early 1960's the CCHR had the least difficulty with the contradictions inherent in its dual advocate-apologist role. New York was the first political jurisdiction in the country to have an open housing ordinance that was applicable to privately owned housing, and this measure was one of Mayor Wagner's prime liberal credentials. Thus in enforcing the law (and acting as an advocate) the commission was reinforcing an important segment of the mayor's political image (and acting as an apologist). This was especially important in 1961 when the mayor, with Liberal party and Reform Democratic support, vanquished the city's Democratic machine.

The existence of the fair housing law, furthermore, channeled the commission's advocacy into an area hedged about by great procedural and structural constraints. The commitment of resources in this direction necessarily limited other commission efforts in the area of housing and guaranteed that few individuals in the city would be inconvenienced by the agency's advocacy. In fact, the fair housing law helped during this period to perpetuate the status quo in housing integration in the city by institutionalizing a device that seemingly was working for change but in fact guaranteed that change would proceed very slowly.

In short, the CCHR's efforts in housing during this period offered the mayor a device that embellished his liberal record and at the same time caused him no political difficulties. Aside from the administration of the fair housing law, commission advocacy in the housing area was minimal and rarely occurred outside of city government. The fight against blockbusting, in fact, was an effort by the CCHR to maintain the status quo in many changing neighborhoods, not to change it.

To be sure, the mayor and the city council did pass some of the procedural and substantive changes in the fair housing law that were offered to them during the early 1960's. It is nevertheless true that, though it soon became apparent that no large-scale changes in the pattern of housing discrimination in the city could be effected through the procedures in the law, neither the city government nor the CCHR took any action to ameliorate the basic problems in that legislation. For the mayor and the city council, responsive to different constituencies than the commission, the status quo was functional. The commission, faced with the political difficulties of achieving change, convinced itself that the case-by-case approach was producing desirable social change.

Not until December 1965, when Mayor Wagner knew that he would not have to cope with the problems that would arise from his actions, did he sign into law a bill that sanctioned basic changes in the commission's powers, procedures, and jurisdiction. The commission was given the power to initiate its own investigations, and its jurisdiction was expanded to match that of the state commission (that is, it obtained statutory authority to act in employment, public accommodations, and the like). Violation of commission orders was made a misdemeanor punishable by a fine of up to five hundred dollars or imprisonment for up to one year. The commission was given the power to issue cease and desist orders after a finding of "probable cause" of discrimination, and in the area of housing it was empowered to post a sign on an apartment for ten days while allegations of discrimination in the rental of that apartment proceeded.[80] These far-reaching changes would have their consequences, not only in housing but in other substantive areas, but not until the next administration came to power.

Education

The dichotomy between the commission's two roles is more visible during this period in its activities in the area of education, where the agency had taken an advocate position from the beginning. It endorsed every plan proposed during the early 1960's for integrating the city's schools from "Open Enrollment" in 1960, through "bussing, rezoning, site selection for integration, and the Princeton Plan" in 1963–64, to educational parks in 1965.[81]

---

80 *New York Times,* Dec. 16, 1965, p. 40, col. 3.

81 *COIR Reporter,* vol. 3, no. 2 (1960); CCHR press release no. 35, April 27, 1962; *Annual Report, 1965,* p. 9.

Throughout this period the commission stressed the need to train teachers working in minority communities in human relations and to get the best teachers assigned to the minority areas.

Integration, the commission acknowledged, would not be easy. The groundwork for it would have to be laid in both black and white areas through intensive educational workshops for parents, teachers, and civil rights activists. Neighborhood school-community coordinators for the Board of Education would have to be trained. Tensions would arise in the schools and devices would have to be developed to deal with them. These the commission saw to be its responsibilities, for, despite the difficulties, integration was necessary for the educational advancement of minority children, and possible under the proper conditions.[82]

The commission presented evidence to prove this latter point. A study it sponsored in cooperation with the East Harlem Project illustrated that students who were bussed from East Harlem into Yorkville, a neighboring white area, showed improvement in attendance and in interest in school work.[83] Furthermore, commission efforts in the Glendale-Ridgewood area made clear that, with the cooperation of the Board of Education and other city and private agencies, minority parents, and supportive groups in the recipient neighborhoods, local anti-integration forces could be beaten with a minimum of confrontation.[84]

Though thus clearly an advocate, the CCHR soon found that, perhaps because of the decisions of the Supreme Court in 1954 and the prointegration policy declared by the Board of Education in 1958, advocacy in this area had particular legitimacy in the city. In fact, the commission's clear position on school integration and its official status as a city agency put it in a particularly advantageous position to mediate the then emerging conflicts between civil rights groups and the board.

From its very inception, the commission's ties with the Board of

[82] For an example of the commission position see COIR report on Newton High School Feb. 2, 1962, files of the Municipal Reference Library.

[83] CCHR press release, Sept. 12, 1962.

[84] CCHR pamphlet, *A Tale of Two Boroughs: A School Integration Success Story* (New York: The Commission, 1961).

Education had been closer than with any other official agency of city government, and these ties continued through the early 1960's. During 1961 and 1962, the commission reported continued cooperation with the board's human relations unit on training programs and a joint effort to develop an "interracial community agency" in Queens. Though Madison Jones was not as close to the city's educational establishment as his predecessor (Horne was named as part of Superintendent of Schools John J. Theobold's "black cabinet" in the 1950's), he or representatives from his agency were regularly heard at board hearings on integration. In short, the commission enjoyed a congenial relationship with the board.[85]

This relationship allowed the commission to "play a dual role as both mediator [between the board and civil rights groups] and representative of civil rights interests." [86] In this dual role, the CCHR in 1960 and again in 1963 was able to help the city avoid conflict in its educational institutions. In 1963, for example, the commission was able to forestall a boycott by bringing civil rights groups and the Board of Education together. This time a settlement was made on the basis of a promise by school superintendent Calvin Gross that he would produce a desegregation timetable for the schools by December of that year.

Subsequent events illustrate the basic weakness of the CCHR. Neither the promised timetable nor concrete steps toward integrating the schools was in evidence by December. In two meetings, one with civil-rights-group representatives present and the other without, the commission pleaded with the superintendent to take some steps to head off threatened demonstrations in December and January. They were not, commission representatives stressed, asking for "instant integration" but for a "flexible and moderate plan." [87]

When the educators held firm in their refusal to act, the com-

---

[85] David Rogers, *110 Livingston Street* (New York: Random House, 1968), p. 34. There is no claim intended here that the commission was intimately involved in the board's decision-making process. Its ties to the board were simply closer than to other agencies.

[86] *Ibid.*, p. 438.   [87] *Ibid.*, pp. 233ff.

mission felt constrained, in order to keep faith with the minority-group representatives in the negotiations, to issue a statement critical of the board. The commission urged that "positive integration ideas" be considered by those involved in the struggle, offered its own services to help pursue this end, and said: "Members of the Commission on Human Rights feel strongly that while the task of desegregating and integrating our schools is not one that can be accomplished over night, it is possible and necessary to project some sort of time schedule to measure progress toward the agreed final goal . . . integrated education of the highest possible quality for every child in the system." [88]

This clear, albeit moderate, advocate stand estranged the commission from the Board of Education. In February, the board rejected chairman Lowell's offers to mediate the school boycott because the commission, it said, had "sided with civil rights groups" and therefore could not be an impartial judge or mediator.[89] In short, the educators thought that the CCHR's proper role was to keep civil rights groups in line. When it became apparent that the commission was serious enough about its responsibilities as an advocate for minorities to publicly criticize the workings of a "sister agency," the board acted to exclude it from the decision-making process.

The commission was vulnerable to this type of action by the board because it had no legitimacy in the education area beyond that allowed to it by the larger agency. To be sure, the CCHR could enter certain racially tense situations on the basis of its legislative mandate, but it could not be effective in them without cooperation from the board.

At the same time that the commission was excluded from the negotiations, the board's inaction hampered it in its relationships with civil rights groups. After all, the commission had sponsored a settlement in September that, as it developed, simply provided the Board of Education with more time in which to do nothing. Despite its advocacy, as an official city agency the commission remained suspect. It seemed to be the "Mayor's buffer against the

[88] CCHR press release, Dec. 22, 1963.
[89] *New York Times*, Feb. 7, 1964, p. 29, col. 1.

Negro and Puerto Rican Community," designed to keep racial tensions down while ostensibly pressing for integration but actually doing little.[90]

Thus, because it tried to play two roles, the CCHR found itself unable to play either. As a city agency that had worked with the Board of Education and had "protected" it against two school boycotts, its role as apologist was suspect among the civil rights groups; as an agency with a commitment to these groups, its role as advocate was suspect at 110 Livingston Street. The consequence of this was the effective exclusion of the commission from the political arena of education integration in the city. As one of the foremost students of the integration controversy in New York during that period has concluded, "Since 1964 the commission has had a less influential role in public education controversies; . . . [and has had] little impact on school policy or in encouraging innovation." [91]

Employment

Whereas in housing the conflicting roles of the CCHR are obscured within the structure of the fair housing law, and in education, because of the semiautonomous nature of the Board of Education, they are not defined in relation to the mayor, in employment during this period these roles are quite clearly defined and focused on the relationship between the mayor and the commission. It is in this substantive area that the commission clearly tested the limits of its mayoral support, and in so doing it revealed once again the inherent contradictions in its role in city government.

As we have seen, Stanley Lowell was convinced that employment discrimination lay at the root of all other race relations problems in the city. Because of this sense of priorities, early after he became chairman he urged upon the mayor a two-pronged attack

[90] Rogers, p. 439. In fact, the commission's actions were functional for the mayor because they sought to minimize racial tensions in the city. The commission is viewed here, however, in relation to the board because in this instance the board determined the commission's role.

[91] *Ibid.*, pp. 438–439.

on this seminal problem. First, because Lowell believed that the city government should provide the model for fair employment practices in New York, he sought an examination of the city's pattern of employment to determine if, in fact, this function was being performed. Second, Lowell advocated the use of the city's contracting power as a device through which the government could affect discrimination in the private sector of the economy. Consequently, he sought from the mayor authorization for a "step by step procedure" to guarantee nondiscrimination in the hiring practices of city contractors. This would affect about 4,000 companies that did more than a half billion dollars' worth of work annually for the city.[92]

There had been nondiscrimination clauses included in most city contracts for some time, but, as was evident during the late 1950's, the commission could do little to enforce them without a formal mandate from the mayor. That mandate was finally forthcoming in early 1962, satisfying another of the mayor's campaign pledges: "to use the city's purchasing power against discriminatory employers." [93] On February 7, Wagner, in an executive order, instructed all contracting departments in city government to add an equal employment clause to their contract forms (if such clauses were not already included) and to cooperate with the CCHR in its review of contracts for compliance with this clause.[94] Contractors doing business with the city were required by the order to agree to allow the commission to review their records of compliance, and in addition were instructed to post signs and notices of nondiscriminatory practices at work sites.

Later in 1962, the mayor took steps to implement the other half of Lowell's employment program. He directed the commission to "initiate a review of the ethnic composition of the civil services" so that a basis could be established for "upgrading the skills of minority employees" and in order to "enhance and implement more ef-

---

[92] *New York Times,* Dec. 31, 1961, p. 36, col. 5.

[93] *New York Times,* Aug. 23, 1961, p. 24, col. 3.

[94] Executive Order No. 4, 1962 (endorsed by the city council on June 5, 1962).

fectively . . . [the city's] whole program of equality of opportunity." [95]

Four major commission initiatives grew out of Wagner's actions. These were the commission's contract-compliance program and its concomitant investigation of "bias in the building trades"; Stanley Lowell's advocacy of "preferential treatment" for black and Puerto Rican workers; commission attempts to integrate the skilled work force at the Bronx Terminal Market job site; and the commission's ethnic survey of city personnel. These events, of course, did not occur in a vacuum, but were paralleled and affected by a growing national awareness of employment discrimination.

On the national scene this awareness stemmed from the fight over the passage of federal fair employment practices legislation. Locally, the context was the extensive civil rights activity of the summer of 1963. City and state building projects were being picketed by an *ad hoc* organization, the Joint Committee on Equal Employment Opportunity, that demanded a 25-per-cent black and Puerto Rican work force on all ongoing government construction in the city. Sporadic violence led to the halting of construction at the Harlem Hospital Annex and at the Downstate Medical Center in Brooklyn. Marathon sit-ins outside the mayor's and governor's offices (the former lasted forty-four days), sponsored by CORE, dramatized minority demands, and the confluence of the employment problem with the threatened school boycott accentuated the crisis.

In employment, then, the CCHR was acting in an area that was at the very center of the civil rights struggle in the city in the early 1960's. Its achievements and limitations in this area of policy during this period therefore serve to illustrate clearly the agency's role in the political system of the city at large.

Contract Compliance

Immediately after receiving the mayor's mandate in February 1962, the commission began to take steps to get into the business of policing the compliance of city contractors with the nondiscrimi-

[95] Press release, mayor's office, Dec. 6, 1962.

nation clause. First, additional funds were sought from the city for this new function, and the agency created a business and employment division to reflect this change in focus.

Then, following the mayor's desires that the CCHR's traditional conciliatory procedures be tried first, chairman Lowell publicly warned both employers and unions that they must "take steps to promote and assure equal employment opportunity or face the possibility of losing city contracts." Compliance, Lowell warned, was *required* for all city contractors. In order to help them with these new regulations, he said, commission field consultants would be made available.[96]

In order to provide a sound basis upon which it could proceed beyond the initial stages of conciliation and consultation, the CCHR mailed 2,200 questionnaires to contractors throughout the city. The answers to these, the agency hoped, would provide it with information about the racial composition of their work forces. On the basis of this information, timetables would be established for the elimination of obvious instances of discrimination through conciliation. If consultation failed to remedy the evil, the commission planned to proceed upon the basis of this and other evidence of a "segregated pattern of employment" against the offending contractors.[97]

Construction contractors, upon whom the compliance plan was focused, complained that the unions, not they, were responsible for discriminatory practices. When jobs were available they hired whomever the union sent to them for employment.[98] Lowell realized the complications that union involvement added to the compliance program and attempted to include union apprentice training programs within the scope of the commission's activity, but he was limited in this because the legal basis for city activity in this area remained the contractual relationship.

[96] *New York Times,* Feb. 8, 1962, p. 2, col. 6; Feb. 25, 1962, p. 68, col. 3.

[97] CCHR press release no. 19, Feb. 19, 1963; *CCHR News,* vol. 5, no. 5 (1963).

[98] *New York Times,* Feb. 10, 1962, p. 24, col. 1; May 20, 1962, p. 71, col. 1.

When the crisis was precipitated in June 1963 by the picketing of construction sites by the Joint Committee on Equal Employment Opportunity, the unions provided the focus for the complaints of the civil rights groups, and the commission had to proceed on this basis. The agency had to act to meet the crisis, and could no longer proceed with its more far-reaching plans. After union leaders refused to appear for informal discussions with minority leaders and government officials, public hearings on employment patterns were scheduled by the CCHR and the recalcitrant leaders were subpoenaed.[99]

At the hearings, held in mid-August, the general contractors for the Harlem Hospital and the Downstate Medical Center projects denied allegations that they had engaged in discriminatory activity. Union leaders issued similar denials but were less convincing for they were confronted at the hearings with evidence of "massive" discrimination in apprenticeship programs and journeymen assignments presented by Michael J. Sachs in a study prepared for the New York State Advisory Committee of the United States Commission on Civil Rights.[100] The testimony of union leaders often increased the impact of Sachs' findings. Michael J. Salzarullo, for example, denied that there was any discrimination in Local 2 of the United Association of Plumbers and Steamfitters, citing its twenty-four black members (out of 4,100) to prove his case. Further questioning by hearing commissioners revealed the fact that six of these twenty-four were dead.[101]

The report published by the commission as a result of these hearings placed the blame for discrimination in employment equally upon the contractors and the unions but indicated that city government too was in part culpable. The employers, the commission said, had failed to work against the "pattern of exclusion"

[99] F. Ray Marshall and Vernon M. Briggs, Jr., *The Negro and Apprenticeship* (Baltimore: Johns Hopkins University Press, 1967), p. 53.

[100] Walter Fogel and Archie Kleingartner, "Discrimination in the Building Trades: The New York Case," in *Contemporary Labor Issues* (Belmont: Wadsworth, 1966), p. 288; *New York Times,* Aug. 6, 1963, p. 10, col. 2.

[101] *New York Times,* Aug. 21, 1963, p. 23, col. 1.

induced by union practices, and government had refrained from enforcing laws passed to deal with this situation.

The City Commission on Human Rights finds a pattern of exclusion in a substantial portion of the building and construction industry which effectively bars nonwhites from participating in this area of the city's economic life.

The commission finds the foregoing condition is the result of employer failure to accept responsibility for including minority group workers in staffing their projects, union barriers to Negro admittance, and government failure to enforce regulations barring discrimination.[102]

The report, issued in December, was just a footnote to a crisis that had been effectively quieted during July and August. The interesting fact about this controversy for understanding the commission's role in the city lies in the circumstances of the settlement. Although the CCHR had been mandated by the mayor to vigorously pursue contract compliance as a policy, when the crisis came, Wagner took matters into his own hands.

When the civil rights demonstrations began, the mayor was out of the country. After acting mayor Paul Screvane failed to quiet the escalating situation during the week of June 13, Wagner returned to the city and began intensive negotiations with union leaders Peter Brennan and Harry Van Arsdale. After receiving assurances from them that more jobs would be made available for "technically qualified" minority people, the mayor presided over a series of negotiations among labor, employer, and civil rights groups. At these meetings a recruitment and screening program was hammered out through which minority job applicants could be referred to union locals. Competition with a similar program established by the governor, and the pressure of the commission's hearings, expedited the implementation of this program.[103]

An incipient conflict between labor and civil rights groups was

<hr>

[102] CCHR, *Bias in the Building Trades: An Interim Report to the Mayor,* (New York: The Commission, 1963), p. 10.

[103] Marshall and Briggs, pp. 53–54; *New York Times,* June 22, 1963, p. 1, cols. 2 and 3.

an important political problem for the mayor, for each of these coalitions was an important part of his personal constituency. Because of this, as the situation became more and more sensitive, Wagner felt it necessary to step in and moderate it personally. He had mandated the commission to act, but CCHR advocacy was limited by other, more immediate, priorities. Ultimately, the mayor solved the problem by compromise, by accommodating all groups, rather than by giving the commission its head in enforcing the law. This was the course of least political cost.

During the crisis and afterward, the commission served as a resource for the mayor. It was a place to which individual complaints of discrimination could immediately be referred and through which concern for the issue could be dramatized. Its hearings, and the revelations attendant to them, gave the mayor a degree of leverage in his negotiations with the other actors in the crisis. Its final report offered a convenient way of "closing the case." In the final analysis, however, the mayor could not allow the CCHR, acting in its advocate role, to be the sole voice of the city in the area of contract compliance. The political stakes were too high.

Preferential Treatment

Other commission experiences in the employment area illustrate further the nature of the relationship between it and the mayor. During an interview on WABC radio held soon after the construction hearings, chairman Lowell released a policy statement for the CCHR which advocated "preferential treatment," for a limited time period, for "qualified minority people" so that the "inequities of a hundred years" could be rectified. "Color blindness hasn't worked," said Lowell, "we must move on to color consciousness. The protection of human rights needs the fist of government." [104]

This statement touched off a furor in the city. Black leaders hailed the position but recognized it as nothing new, except that now the advocate was a public official rather than its originator, Whitney Young of the Urban League. Some, like Bernard Katzen

[104] *New York Times,* Oct. 28, 1963, p. 1, col. 2.

of the State Commission Against Discrimination and George Rundquist of the ACLU, denounced Lowell's statement as illegal and advocacy of "discrimination in reverse"; others, like George Fowler, Katzen's colleague on the state commission, endorsed the sentiment but not the wording.[105]

The mayor at first was hesitant. This certainly was not city policy, he said, but he had never required city departments to clear their positions with him. Officials at city hall were reported to be uncertain about the meaning of the phrase "preferential treatment." Lowell for a time stuck to his guns, saying that his only objective was to "get Negroes jobs in lily-white unions, businesses, and industries." [106] Official silence greeted this until, on November 1, on WOR radio, Wagner pointed out that job preference on the basis of race for the civil service was illegal. Although he hadn't read Lowell's statement, the mayor said, he agreed with the sentiment, "to give Negroes a much better break." [107]

Later, at an Anti-Defamation League dinner, Lowell backed away from the words "preferential treatment" because of the "unfortunate interpretation they have been given by others" and substituted "equalization approach" and "affirmative action." In his speech, which was later published by the commission, Lowell said, "We are convinced that the basic definition of equal opportunity must be broadened to include the recognition of the urgent necessity for special effort and action to overcome the inequities resulting from past discrimination." [108]

This added gloss, however, serves only to obscure the basic issue. The mayor would not prevent the CCHR from taking an advocate role, but he would not be bound by it. In this case, the mayor destroyed the agency's advocacy by ignoring it. Since whatever power the commission had was based upon its relationship with the mayor, Wagner's inaction effectively limited the commission's impact.

---

[105] *New York Times,* Oct. 29, 1963, p. 1, col. 7.   [106] *Ibid.*

[107] *New York Times,* Nov. 1, 1963, p. 20, col. 2.

[108] CCHR, *Equality in Our Time: What We Said, What We Did Not Say* (New York: The Commission, 1963).

The Bronx Terminal Market Case

The limitation by the mayor of commission advocacy is again illustrated in the Bronx Terminal Market case. Early in 1964 commission representatives contacted the prime contractors for the Hunts Point Terminal Market in the Bronx, a city project, and informed them of their obligation under the law to take affirmative action to integrate their work force.[109] After several meetings, the contractors agreed to hire minority workers supplied by the commission. On April 30, one black and three Puerto Rican plumbers recruited by the CCHR appeared at the job site to begin work. Forty-one union plumbers walked off the job and began what was to be a twelve-day work stoppage. A confrontation was touched off which drew the attention of President Lyndon Johnson, Secretary of Labor Willard Wirtz, and AFL-CIO president George Meany, not to mention local civil rights activists. The four minority plumbers, put out of work by the strike, filed complaints with the commission against Local 2 of the plumbers union, and the CCHR began proceedings to cancel the construction contract.

Finally, two weeks after the strike had begun, a settlement was reached in negotiations between Meany and Wagner. The four minority plumbers would be allowed by the union to take the journeyman exam, and work on the site would resume. Meany was not happy about the role of the CCHR in recruiting minority workers, and this was to be expected, but neither was Wagner: "Mayor Wagner also sharply rebuked the CCHR for its role in this affair, claiming that the dispute had gotten out of hand and that the CCHR was "never again to act as an employment agency for minority groups." As of that date, in fact, CCHR was removed as a party to the subsequent proceedings by directive from the Mayor." [110]

Once again the mayor was drawn into a politically sensitive area by the commission, and this time he could not avoid acting. Commission advocacy of minority positions had led to crisis; the

[109] This account relies on Marshall and Briggs, pp. 64–65, and *CCHR News,* vol. 6, no. 4 (1964).

[110] Marshall and Briggs, p. 65.

mayor's reaction to this advocacy was to limit it in the case at hand (by entering the situation personally) and to limit the possibilities for such action in the future.

Ethnic Survey

A final example, drawn from the CCHR's experience in gathering the data for the ethnic survey of city employees authorized by Wagner, illustrates further the centrality of mayoral support for commission effectiveness.

Despite the executive order authorizing the survey and an accompanying letter signed by Wagner and circulated to all city departments and agencies, the heads of bureaucratic establishments employing about one quarter of the city's employees refused to cooperate with the CCHR on this matter.[111] Noncooperating departments included the Board of Elections, the Board of Higher Education (professional personnel), the Board of Water Supply, the Department of Investigation, the Law Department, the Police Department, the Probation Department, the Transit Authority, the Youth Council Bureau, the district attorneys of New York, Kings, and Richmond counties, and the civil, criminal, and family courts.

The commission's study was considerably affected by this noncooperation. Only 58 per cent of the city's 19,585 "operators," 49 per cent of its 9,998 "officials," and 63 per cent of its 77,847 service workers were enumerated; the remainder were employed in the resistant departments. Though the findings were encouraging for the city—they showed a high level of minority employment in the upper reaches of the bureaucracy—the procedural problems were discouraging for the commission. When difficulties arose, the necessary backing from the mayor to give commission projects respectability in the eyes of the rest of the city's bureaucracy was simply not forthcoming.

Moderating Disputes

The cases set out above are largely chronicles of commission failures, failures marked by a lack of support from the mayor or

[111] *Annual Report, 1963,* p. 14.

intervention by the mayor to limit the scope of commission activity. The commission did have some successes in the area of employment during this period, and these, as much as its failures, help illuminate the agency's dual role in city government.

Most of these successes came, not in cases in which the commission took the initiative, but rather in situations in which the agency responded to the initiatives of others, usually civil rights groups. In reacting, the commission served a valuable political function by defusing potentially explosive situations. At the same time, the CCHR was often able to secure jobs for minority-group members by working closely with civil rights groups. Thus, the agency was able simultaneously to fulfill its employment and tension-reduction functions and to meet the needs of its constituency.

The commission's activities in 1963 provide several good examples of this activity. In that year, complaints against the employment practices of Chock Full o'Nuts, White Castle, Ebinger's Bakeries, the Waldorf Astoria, the Stork Club, Safeway-Trails bus company, and several city departments were satisfactorily resolved. The commission reports:

In most of these cases, CCHR, through delicate negotiations, succeeded in bringing about a better relationship between the business concern and the minority community and won from the employer not only the promise to discontinue discriminatory hiring and promotion practices, which in some instances had provided picketing and the threat of violence, but also to adopt a policy of active recruitment of qualified minority personnel. After a satisfactory agreement had been negotiated, CCHR kept in close touch with the progress of integration in each company or establishment, seeing to it that qualified minority group applicants were referred to them, that a reasonable number actually won jobs, and that these have continued to receive treatment comparable in every way to that received by fellow employees.[112]

In 1965 similar work was done with other companies; an especially notable industry-wide agreement involved five brewers, the International Brotherhood of Teamsters, and the Negro American Labor Council. Thirty-one jobs were opened immediately,

[112] *Ibid.*, pp. 20, 21.

and mediation machinery was set up to handle future complaints of racial bias.[113]

Generally, in the area of employment during the period from 1961 to 1965, the commission was most successful when it acted as apologist, reacting to the initiatives of others, keeping the visibility of the issues low, and avoiding the involvement of the city's major political actors. When the agency assumed an advocate stance or took positions that involved the mayor rather than protecting him from involvement, it was likely to find itself a victim of his differing political priorities.

Tension Control

As was the case during the late 1950's, during this period the CCHR's tension-control function permeated all of the agency's other work. When the commission sought to establish neighborhood councils, moderate controversies over the integration of education, or seek solutions to racially based employment controversies, it was engaged in tension control. In fact, in these other substantive areas, tension control corresponded with the commission's apologist role and was the primary justification for the agency's existence.

Occasionally, following the precedents of the 1950's, the CCHR took specific steps to treat tension control as a separate area of concern. In 1962, for example, a twenty-four-hour phone service was established for reporting incidents of racial tension, so that violence could be avoided.[114] Indeed, when violence finally came to the city, the commission was hardly consulted on how to deal with it. As is evident from the racial violence in New York during the summer of 1964, agency efforts to anticipate and deal with tensions were largely ineffectual.[115] As with other racial problems, as the issues became more immediate and more important they became the concern of the mayor and other major political actors and were removed from the aegis of the CCHR.

[113] *Annual Report, 1965,* p. 11.
[114] *New York Times,* Aug. 2, 1962, p. 11, col. 8.
[115] Fred C. Shapiro and James W. Sullivan, *Race Riot* (New York: Crowell, 1964).

Transition at the Commission

By early 1965, Stanley Lowell had decided to give up his post as chairman of the CCHR. As the demands placed upon his time by his law practice increased, Lowell found himself less and less able to give commission business the attention he had given it earlier. Consequently, he was increasingly required to take responsibility for commission actions initiated by the executive director, actions about which he was informed only after they had been put into effect. Though Lowell was aware that these difficulties were due to his absence from the commission offices, they nevertheless contributed to increased tensions between him and Jones, and to his conviction that "you cannot have a split of authority between the commission and the executive director." [116] These difficulties, in turn, reinforced Lowell's belief that the only possible course for him was to resign.

Thus, on April 13, Lowell wrote to the mayor of his intentions. In order to smooth the transition, the chairman proposed that he, with the cooperation of city administrator John Connorton, would draft a set of administrative recommendations to Wagner advising changes in the commission's structure. The key recommendation would be the long-contemplated change in the chairmanship of the CCHR to a full-time paid post. This, Lowell thought, would solve the "split of authority" problem. The commission would be retained "as a policy advisory board to the paid chairman . . . to serve as representative of the overall community on the vital problems facing the commission." [117] In fact, Lowell's suggestion offered the mayor a political opportunity. Wagner owed Earl Brown, then the deputy borough president of Manhattan, a political favor for stepping aside so that Constance Baker Motley could receive the unopposed Democratic party endorsement for the borough presidency. Some influential Manhattan Democrats were prepared to make a fight for Brown, who had become acting borough president when Edward Dudley accepted a judgeship and was considered to be "in line" for the job. Brown's gracious with-

[116] *New York Times,* April 24, 1965, p. 16, col. 4; interview with Lowell.
[117] *New York Times, ibid.*

drawal avoided an intraparty battle and, Wagner thought, deserved a reward. The proposed commission chairmanship, made attractive with an annual salary of $25,000, seemed to be the answer.

An exposé of the personnel and budgetary problems of the commission and charges that the mayor "only gave lip service to the commission's task," made first by president William Booth of the state NAACP and then by anonymous commissioners and staff members, for a time threatened Lowell's resignation scenario, but finally, on April 24, the chairman announced his decision.[118] He would, Lowell promised, stay on until the law could be altered to provide for the administrative changes he had suggested and until a paid successor could be found.

The changes in the structure and powers of the CCHR that Lowell recommended had important implications for some of the difficulties that the commission had faced during its first ten years, but they nevertheless failed to reach the roots of the agency's problems. The elevation of the chairmanship to a full-time paid post did eliminate the problem of bifurcated direction for the agency, but it also had some less obvious implications.[119] The chairman, now in a position to dominate the executive director, was also strengthened in his relationship with the other commissioners. This change, coming on top of structural changes that diminished the role of the commissioners within the agency, could contribute to the transformation of the commissioners into a group functioning formally, but without any real power in CCHR decision making.

With the appointment of a powerful chairman this potential emasculation of the commission would become a reality. The commission had never functioned well as a policy-making body; with

---

[118] Booth to Wagner, March 22, 1965, files of the mayor; *New York Times,* April 18, 1965, p. 1, col. 1; April 24, 1965, p. 16, col. 4; March 22, 1965, p. 26, col. 8.

[119] It will be recalled that the commission's powers were greatly augmented at the end of the Wagner administration. These structural changes, then, were put into effect at the same time that the agency's jurisdiction was expanded to parallel that of the state commission and at the time that it was given the power to initiate its own investigations.

this final change it would become a *de jure* body masking what was in fact a departmental agency structure. Despite the realities of this situation, however, observers of the agency would perceive it as a representative commission, and this would shape their expectations of it. Because Lowell's changes were not directly or even indirectly aimed at their roles in the agency, even the commissioners themselves would retain these perceptions and expectations. An old source of tension had been eliminated, but a new one was potentially created.

Similarly, though Lowell's proposed changes were not aimed at the basic source of the commission's difficulties (that is, the agency's role conflict), the strengthening of the chairman gave the CCHR the potential for the strongest executive leadership in its history. If the difficulties the agency had encountered over its ten-year history were not ameliorated after this basic structural change was made, the hypothesis would be confirmed that the problems were not with the structure of the commission but were to be found in the contradictory tasks assigned the agency and in its roles in the political process of the city.

6

The Commission on Human Rights, 1966-1969: The Enforcement Years

The fortunes of city politics made the Brown chairmanship a short one. With the victory of the Lindsay reform forces in 1965, the commission came under close scrutiny—as did all city departments during the transition—and was the subject of a critical report which, after considering and rejecting suggestions that the agency be abolished, recommended retrenchment and the appointment of "a strong and effective fighter" as chairman.[1] The job went to William Booth, state chairman of the NAACP. Acting in the context of the escalating national and citywide concern for racial problems that stemmed largely from the violence of the mid-1960's, Booth attempted once again to restate the commission's philosophy, redefine its goals, and reorder its priorities. For a time the new chairman had some success in this endeavor, but eventually the agency under his direction foundered on the same shoals as it had under his predecessors: the conflicting roles demanded of it by the city's political system, the contradictory desires of its different constituency groups, and the ever changing political priorities of the city's major political actors.

The Commission under Earl Brown

Earl Brown, the transitional chairman of the City Human Rights Commission, was by experience and temperament a moderate man. Born in the South, he had worked his way through

---

[1] Henry J. Stern, "Freedom When?: A Report on the City Commission on Human Rights Prepared for the Task Force on Economic Development of New York City," typescript, 1965, p. 22; prepared during the Lindsay campaign and on file at the mayor's office.

Harvard College as a porter and, after a long career in journalism, had risen to an editorship with *Life* magazine. Entering New York politics in the late 1940's, Brown reached the city council by defeating the lone elected communist official in the United States, Benjamin J. Davis of Harlem. Throughout the 1950's, therefore, he was a part of the Democratic majority that controlled the council. Though he worked for measures that promoted integration (he co-sponsored the Sharkey-Brown-Isaacs Act), councilman Brown was not a "race man." He was used to the give and take of city politics and became accustomed to settling matters of policy by compromise, far from the public view. Publicity, Brown believed, should be used only if all else failed. He was interested, he said, in results, not notoriety.[2]

Brown brought this approach to the commission. His role, he thought, was not to take the black or white side in any dispute, but rather, as a city official, to seek a compromise solution. Thus, when faced with renewed charges of discrimination in the building trades Brown attempted to arrange a solution without publicity by bringing together involved city officials, contractors, and union leaders. Similarly, in housing, Brown rejected the case-by-case approach as unproductive of anything but tension and instead advocated private meetings with large-scale builders and landlords to obtain nondiscrimination pledges.

Two major factors, however, acted to prevent Brown's approach from becoming the approach of the commission. First, since he was appointed late in the Wagner administration and then retained on a temporary basis by Mayor Lindsay after the November election, he never felt that he had the freedom or legitimacy to alter the agency's structure or processes. Second, and certainly more fundamentally, Brown was skeptical about the value of the agency he was appointed to head. As a member of the city legislature he had thought it inefficient and ineffective. His new vantage point gave Brown no reason to change his mind.

For his ten-month tenure at the CCHR, then, Brown largely

[2] Interview with Brown, summer 1968. The next several paragraphs are based upon this interview.

maintained the policies of the Lowell commission. Noting that a number of civil rights advocates considered the agency "practically impotent," the new chairman did seek an "impartial" report from the office of the city administrator on strengthening the commission's structure. In anticipation of this report, no changes were made, and in the rush of the last days of the Wagner administration, the report was not forthcoming. Brown's major structural innovation at the agency was therefore his refusal to appoint an executive director, a step he took to compensate, in part, for his $25,000-per-year salary.

In short, though the establishment of the new paid chairmanship created possibilities for redefining the basic relationships among the topmost actors in the CCHR, the first man who held this post did not realize its new power or choose to use it. His personality, his experience, and the circumstances of his appointment to and service at the agency disqualified him for this role. Brown held a new job, but chose to perceive himself as being in the job's old framework. It remained for a different sort of man to accept the redefinition of the position and to use it effectively.

Leadership, Philosophy, and Goals

Change at the City Commission on Human Rights was hardly a top-priority concern of the Lindsay administration during its preparations for the transfer of power in the city. When Wagner, early in December 1965, reappointed all the commissioners (fourteen of whom had been serving beyond the expiration of their terms of office) including Brown for another three years, Bethuel Webster, a Lindsay advisor, attributed the outgoing administration's failure to consult with him to "inadvertence" and was only slightly annoyed. In fact, as we have seen, later that month the mayor-designate found it expedient to ask the incumbent chairman, Earl Brown, to remain at the commission on an interim basis.[3]

The Stern report, released on December 29, 1965, recommended strongly that Brown be replaced, but it was not until February that Lindsay found his new man. William Booth, chair-

[3] *New York Times,* Dec. 3, 1965, p. 1, col. 8; Dec. 4, 1965, p. 28, col. 6.

man of the state conference of NAACP branches and an outstanding criminal lawyer from Queens, had campaigned hard for the new mayor. A longtime critic of the commission from his vantage point at the NAACP, Booth nevertheless was convinced by Lindsay to take the newly reinforced chairman's job and turned down a position as chief trial assistant in the office of Queens district attorney Nat Hentel to take the post.[4]

The appointment of Booth was significant for the course that the CCHR would take, for he was fundamentally different in several ways from his predecessors (see Table 11). Whereas all of them (with the exception of Earl Brown) had been white, he was black. Whereas most of them had had previous experience in government, Booth's experience had been with criminal law—a profession that by definition demands a high degree of advocate behavior—and with a pressure group. The new chairman was used to acting upon government from the outside, rather than to working within the constraints of office. His role in the governmental process had been to demand action of others. From the perspective of this role, strong advocacy was highly valued, and compromise was viewed negatively, as an occasional bleak necessity.

The framework of this experience suggested to Booth a new philosophy for the CCHR, a philosophy that was implicitly endorsed by Mayor Lindsay's "broad mandate" to him.[5] The commission, Booth thought, was not a "human relations" agency but a "human rights" agency. Too often, he believed, people who violated the law were permitted to have their past actions remain unpunished if they promised future reforms. Under his administration, the law, strengthened in December 1965, would be enforced. "Immediate enforcement" would be combined with conciliation, the agency's traditional approach to problems of discrimination.[6]

Booth furthermore stressed that the CCHR was a "city commission," not a "mayor's commission." Its job was to enforce

[4] *New York Times,* Jan. 31, 1966, p. 18, col. 2.

[5] *Ibid.,* Feb. 2, 1966, p. 1, col. 2.

[6] CCHR, *Annual Report, 1966* (New York: The Commission, 1967) p. 29; interview with Booth, Jan. 27, 1969.

human rights legislation in various substantive areas and to generally carry out its legislative mandate, but not to run political errands for the mayor. It had a base independent of City Hall.

Despite this new militancy, the goals of the commission under Booth remained substantially the same as they had been under Lowell. Like his predecessor, Booth stressed the primary importance of fighting employment discrimination. On the occasion of his appointment by the mayor in February he singled out for special attention city agencies (specifically the Board of Education and the Department of Highways), major corporations with home offices in New York, and the building-trades unions. The new chairman outlined his priorities about a month later in an interview reported in the *New York Times:* "I won't be satisfied until I get substantive change in discrimination . . . ; jobs, large numbers of jobs; really open occupancy in housing; complete elimination of prejudicial treatment at fine hotels and restaurants and in clubs, some of which are not really open." [7]

Unlike previous chairmen, commissioner Booth did not have to share the leadership of the agency with his executive director. Marrow had inherited an executive director who was senior to him in the agency and who had, in effect, put the commission together. Lowell had helped choose his executive director, but found it necessary to delegate many commission responsibilities to him because of his own unpaid status. Brown had left the executive directorship vacant. Booth, the first full-time chairman appointed at the beginning of a mayoral administration, was also the first who could appoint an executive director responsible to himself alone.

He chose Ramon Rivera, a coordinator of minority programs for the Urban League, who had been trained in industrial management and labor relations at the University of Illinois. Rivera became the "chief operating executive" of the agency and in this capacity functioned as Booth's deputy; the chairman retained veto power over any policy or procedural matters within the agency.

[7] *New York Times,* March 27, 1966, p. 79, col. 3.

The creation of the paid chairmanship had resolved the problem of bifurcated executive direction for the CCHR.

Though Rivera was clearly Booth's subordinate, his efforts were important for the new chairman, for they freed him from the every-day responsibilities of administration and allowed him to be the agency's "public man." Whereas the visibility of the agency in the *New York Times* remained relatively low, and that of the executive director declined further, the index for the chairman soared during Booth's tenure.[8]

Booth viewed publicity not as a burden but as an opportunity. He saw to it that all official statements of the agency were released through him, and that the agency's efforts in the media were focused upon him. During Booth's chairmanship, the commission produced at least four radio shows and one television show weekly, and all were moderated by Booth. For newspapermen, the chairman was a good source: a man of "overwhelming velocity," "forceful, direct, and articulate," and always ready to make a statement.[9] In addition, since he was black, reporters no longer had to go to the executive director for a "minority opinion" as they did when a white man was chairman. After a time, some of them began to see him as something of a publicity seeker. One wrote, "Publicity, in fact, was something else that Mr. Booth took seriously. He had a statement ready for almost every occasion and was always available when a television camera was plugged in." [10] Sympathetic onlookers attributed Booth's constant availability to the nature of his job; the more cynical hypothesized that he "wanted to run for Congress or a judgeship." [11] In either case, this availability made his tendency to advocate the position of the black minority in the city apparent even to the casual observer of the eleven o'clock news. In turn, the coverage that Booth obtained contributed to his advocate tendencies, for unlike Earl Brown, he was a "race man" and he knew that some of those watching comprised his black constituency.

[8] See Table 2.   [9] *New York Times,* March 27, 1966.
[10] *Ibid.,* Feb. 9, 1969, section IV, p. 7, col. 1.   [11] *Ibid.*

Organizational Structure

The advent of the Lindsay administration marked the first time that the City Human Rights Commission had experienced a change in partisan control of city government. This change, however, did not alter the basic directions of administrative evolution within the agency. The tendency to isolate the commissioners at the top of the structure and to devitalize their role in the agency continued and in part reflected changes in the CCHR's constituency, which are discussed below. And, despite still another reorganization, the commission's propensity to act in too many issue areas and thus to fail to concentrate its resources remained.

The Commissioners

During the period of Booth's chairmanship the tendency to remove the human rights commissioners from the center of decision making in the agency, begun under Lowell, was continued. This effort manifested itself in several ways. Through administrative action of the executive director contacts between the staff and the commissioners were minimized. As time passed, commission subcommittees met less and less frequently, and most became moribund.[12] Proposals to transfer the commissioner's hearing function to paid hearing officers, and thus to remove their last link with the ongoing daily work of the agency, were pushed in the city council.[13]

The greatest manifestation of the decline of the role of the commissioners was the transfer of the decision-making power in the agency from the commission to the chairman. When he appointed Booth to the chairmanship, Mayor Lindsay offered him the opportunity to suggest structural changes in the agency, but the new chairman decided to "try it for a while to see how it works." Later, a change to a departmental type of organization, which the chairman came to prefer, became impossible, but nevertheless Booth

[12] Interview with Murray Gross, Jan. 28, 1969; interview with Simeon Golar, Aug. 29, 1969. When Golar became chairman in 1969, he saw as one of the tasks before him the "revitalization" of these subcommittees.

[13] Interview with Booth, Aug. 8, 1968.

took *de facto* power in the agency into his own hands. "The commission," he said, "should be a consultative body. . . . The commission structure is clumsy. I've acted as if this were a department. It is hard to consult with everyone in a fast-breaking situation. . . . This is policy making, but I did it." [14]

The executive director, Rivera, favored Booth's taking control for two reasons. First, he found that commissioners were an administrative nuisance. Second, he felt that the commissioners were a conservative influence in the agency, and that they opposed its new enforcement ethos. The chairman's aggressive public stance, however, discouraged the commissioners from suggesting policy directions to him that they might have pressed upon another in his position.[15]

Commissioners realized the attitude of the major administrators at the CCHR toward their role in the agency. Gilbert Colgate, for example, thought that Booth "saw the commission as an anchor that keeps him from doing what he wants to do." [16] When asked what changes they would like to see instituted at the commission, several commissioners either suggested "more policy making at the commission level" or noted that "the commission, not the chairman, is supposed to decide policy." By the end of 1968, just before the black anti-Semitism crisis engulfed the agency and postponed further debate, several commissioners were seeking to organize a special meeting in order to discuss "at what level policy decisions should be made." [17]

In fact, though the commissioners were justifiably sensitive about being estranged from the policy-making process of the agency, they had brought much of the criticism of the operating officers upon themselves. Though some gave between 20 and 25 per cent of their time to the commission each week, too often

[14] *Ibid.*

[15] Interviewees, staff members at the commission, wish to remain anonymous.

[16] Interview with Colgate, Jan. 30, 1969.

[17] Several interviewees who made these statements have expressed the wish to remain anonymous. One who did not was Murray Gross, Jan. 28, 1969.

there were no commissioners available for the housing discrimination hearings. During the first six months of 1968 six hearings had to be adjourned because of inability to obtain a commissioner to preside. "Thirty-one of the sixty-eight hearings held during this period were held before a single commissioner because it was not possible to persuade a second commissioner to appear on the hearing date. Hearings before one commissioner alone are legally questionable since they are not in conformance with the law and require a waiver from the respondent." [18] During the second half of that year, only six commissioners (40 per cent) had sat on at least seven hearings, or about one a month. This inactivity of some placed a disproportionate burden upon others and slowed the commission's performance of its legally mandated functions.[19]

Commissioners were equally delinquent in other areas of participation in the work of the agency. For the eleven commission meetings in 1968, for example, attendance (excluding the chairman) averaged eight commissioners, or 57 per cent. Attendance records for commission meetings divide the fourteen commissioners into roughly three groups; active, moderately active, and inactive. At one extreme, no commissioners attended all meetings, but two attended ten of eleven; at the other, one commissioner missed all but two.[20]

Inactivity resulted from many factors. Commissioners were unpaid, and their career responsibilities necessarily took precedence over commission work when demands upon their time conflicted. The most active commissioners tended to be women with no other job responsibilities or retirees who made the CCHR an avocation. Some had sought a commission appointment for political or status reasons but did not care for undramatic service on "piddling little hearings." Others viewed their service as a favor to the mayor, who, they thought, had had a difficult time filling the job. The reasons aside, commissioner inactivity made the job of adminis-

[18] Sigmund Ginsburg *et al.,* "Management Review of the New York City Commission on Human Rights," Office of the Mayor, Office of Administration, April 2, 1969, p. 8.

[19] Interview with Booth, Jan. 27, 1969.   [20] Ginsburg, p. 7.

tering the CCHR more difficult and convinced the agency's top officials of the unworkable nature of the commission structure.[21]

While the leadership of the CCHR was becoming increasingly disaffected from the commission as an administrative and decision-making tool, the new city administration was beginning to challenge its "representative" nature. Although Mayor Lindsay was not able to replace many of the city's human rights commissioners because of Wagner's last-minute actions, the five appointments that he did make challenged the philosophy that underlay the representative character of the fifteen-man group.

Wagner, in all of his appointments to the commission, had carefully sought to maintain a racial, ethnic, geographic, and class (i.e., labor, management) balance, but Lindsay seemingly ignored these factors in seeking the "best men" when vacancies arose. Thus Gilbert Colgate, a WASP, was appointed to replace Juan Aviles, a Puerto Rican, and the seat of Morris Ploscowe, a Jewish judge, was given to Kenneth Drew, a black newspaper editor from Queens. Chairman Booth, in an interview, noted this change: "The commission . . . used to be organized along group lines, with each organization having its spot, but not since Lindsay came in. He appoints people who he thinks have a commitment to this type of work." [22]

Though only minimally important in power terms within the agency (for, as we have seen, the commissioners' role in decision making was being minimized), this change in the representative character of the commission had symbolic importance. The commission was the creature of the city's established civil rights groups; it was established, in part, so that their voice could be heard in the agency. Now at the same time that they were being excluded from the constituency base of the CCHR by the chairman, and the role of the commissioners in agency policy making was being minimized, the long understood balance within the commission itself was being

---

[21] Besides the hearings, executive director Rivera estimated that a special commission investigation required about eighty commissioner man-hours. The frequency of these, too, was limited by commissioner availability.

[22] Aug. 8, 1968.

altered. Each of these events reinforced the other and presented a picture of developments in the commission that seemed antithetical to the interests of these established groups.

The Staff

With the chairman acting as the "public member" of the commission, much of the day-to-day administration of the organization was left to the executive director, Ramon Rivera. Rivera, trained in administration (not social work or law as were the rest of the commission's professional staff), was convinced that organization affected the policy directions of an agency and that therefore the ills of the CCHR could be solved by reorganization.

Rivera envisioned a scheme in which the commission was divided into four major functional subdivisions; legal and enforcement; affirmative action; administrative services; and public relations and information. These were three fewer than the number of subdivisions in the agency under Lowell and Jones. The heads of these subdivisions would report through Rivera to the chairman, with the chairman and the executive director regulating all contact of the staff with the commissioners.

Though seemingly cutting down the number of operating units, Rivera's reorganization failed to solve the problem of unwise allocation of commission resources. Below the first level subunits proliferated. Five units, for example, were included in the affirmative action program under deputy executive director Thomas H. Allen. This meant that the CCHR's entire business and employment program was essentially a "two-man operation." The community action subunit under Allen was a bit larger (nine people) but, as indicated in Chart 2, was fragmented to an even greater degree. A glance at the chart reveals that a similar fragmented situation existed under the other major operating officer of the agency, the general counsel.

Rivera's reorganization did effect changes at the commission, some rhetorical and others more substantive. Reflecting the enforcement philosophy, the research division was eliminated and the name of the community relations division changed to "community action." Reflecting efforts to expand the agency's constituency, the nationalities division was reincarnated, and the Puerto Rican–Hispanic division established. Later in 1968, research reappeared under the heading "special projects" when the CCHR received a federal grant to follow up an earlier study by the Equal Employment Opportunities Commission on employment discrimination in the retail trades in New York City.

Chart 2. Organization of the CCHR, March 1, 1968

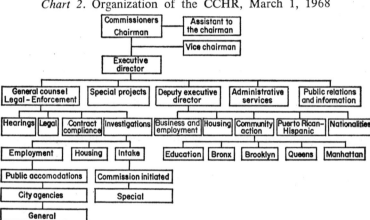

Source: Files of executive director Ramon Rivera.

Generally, however, the structural changes in the agency simply were attempts to do the same number of things (or, in the processing of complaints, even more things) in a slightly different way. In one small agency, subdivisions were organized along functional, service, and constituency lines. People involved with the general problem of employment discrimination, for example, could be found in any one of four subunits: the hearings, investigations, or contract-compliance sections of the general counsel's office, or the business and employment division responsible to the deputy executive director. The nature of the CCHR's organization, in short, contributed to fragmentation and inefficient use of agency resources.

These difficulties with the commission's structure were quite apparent to professional staff who had to function within it. In a letter to chairman Booth written late in 1968 four young staff members urged a reorganization of the agency that would "streamline" it and concentrate its efforts in the areas in which it had "unique authority and capacity to act," notably employment and housing discrimination. Decrying the "lack of communication among divisions," the "lack of willing cooperation among divisions," and the "general lack of effort and morale amongst employees," the staff members noted: "At the present time CCHR is involved in many areas over which it has no real power and in which there is little that it can in fact accomplish with the limited resources at its disposal. This dissipation of endeavours not only diminishes the commission's public image but also tends to demoralize the staff, which gradually becomes convinced that it cannot accomplish anything even if the maximum effort is made." [23]

The structural problems of the commission were reflected both in the confusion of intra-agency procedures and in tensions among professional personnel. Though Rivera was trained in administration and thought administratively, he apparently was not a good practitioner of his art. Simple administrative matters like filing, record keeping, and mail routing were mishandled or not done at all. Consequently, staff members had difficulty in determining precedents, and in coordinating their efforts with colleagues in other divisions. In his study of the agency in 1969, the deputy city administrator wrote: "The Affirmative Action staff is unaware of the activities of the General Counsel's office and vice versa—thus staff members involved in persuading companies to hire more minority group members do not know which companies have poor performance records in the field of discrimination. Investigators handling employment complaints do not know what has been told to the Affirmative Action staff concerning the hiring and promotion policies of the company in question." [24] Standard operating

[23] Memo, Lisa Blitman, Wendell H. Goddard, Lincoln E. McDonald, and Mitchell I. Wald to Booth, Oct. 1, 1968, files of the Commission.
[24] Ginsburg, pp. 10, 13.

procedures did not exist, a condition that slowed agency action and caused it to seem arbitrary. New employees received no in-service training and lacked an overall conception of what the commission did and how their jobs contributed to this effort.[25]

Internal policies that did exist contributed to the intra-agency malaise and to a problem that had been endemic to the commission from its beginnings: racial tensions within the staff. Promotion policies were unknown to the staff. Monthly staff meetings were devoted to discussions of charged general questions (i.e., "integration or separation") that tended to divide the staff. In an interview, Simeon Golar, Booth's successor as chairman, commented that the intergroup relations within the agency were perhaps the worst of any agency in the city. Division heads were subject to the same administrative controls as beginning clerks. The executive director refused to deal with an organization formed by employees to present him with staff grievances.[26]

In suggesting the necessity for reorganization, the dissident young leaders at the commission explicitly rejected the solutions that both Booth and Rivera continually offered for all administrative difficulties: more money and more personnel. Almost immediately upon coming into office, Booth sought from the mayor funds for seven regional offices (two in Brooklyn and Manhattan and one for each of the other boroughs) and for a reinforced team of seventy "human rights inspectors." In 1967, on the anniversary of his first year, the chairman sought money from the administration for two new divisions, one to concentrate on education and the other on youth services.[27] In 1968, under attack by the commission appointed to investigate racial tensions in the city, Booth again indicated that by doubling the budget the commission could handle the problem.[28] Most other commissioners agreed with the chairman about the nature of the problem, if not about the extent of the need; when interviewed they indicated that money and personnel were the CCHR's two major problems.

[25] *Ibid.*, pp. 9, 15.   [26] *Ibid.*, p. 12; interview with Golar.
[27] CCHR press release, Feb. 6, 1967.
[28] *New York Times*, Jan. 18, 1969, p. 19, col. 4.

In fact, though it hardly met Booth's demands, the Lindsay administration did not treat the commission less well than it did other agencies. During Booth's three years, the commission budget did grow at approximately the same rate as the budget of the city at large, something it did not do during the Wagner years, and a few new professional positions were added at the agency. The commission did have difficulties in retaining clerical staff, but this was a problem endemic to the city at large. Turnover among professional personnel was high during the changeover of administrations, but thereafter settled down to a level below that for professionals in other branches of city government, and the agency was able to retain most of its committed longtime employees. A study done in April 1969 showed only seven of forty-five professional positions at the CCHR vacant. This contrasts with the situation during previous administrations and can be explained by a general salary increase for professionals at the commission in 1966 and the concomitant higher salaries paid at each level in the agency in subsequent years.[29]

Despite these facts, however, the leadership of the commission continued to view themselves as "deprived" and to blame personnel and money problems for agency shortcomings. Though these complaints may have been partially justified (the total allocation of city resources in particular policy areas would have to be examined to determine this), it is clear that the agency was not organized to use effectively the resources that it did have. It tried to do too much with too little, failed to concentrate its efforts where success may have been possible, and then claimed that the lack of money and personnel caused the ineffectiveness.

Constituency

There had been, almost from the date of the establishment of the CCHR, the potential for a split in the constituency of the com-

[29] New York City civil list (annual); David T. Stanley *et al.*, *Professional Personnel for the City of New York* (Washington: The Brookings Institution, 1963), p. 31; CCHR press release, Nov. 10, 1966. In 1967–68 salaries for human rights specialists averaged $8,000/year and for supervisory personnel $14,000/year.

mission, for the social, economic, and racial characteristics of the people the agency served were very different from those of the people who afforded it organizational support. With a few notable exceptions, such as the events surrounding the Marrow "resignation," the commission was generally able to minimize the tensions within its constituency during its first ten years. During the late 1960's, however, the increased polarization of groups in the city over the issues of school decentralization and black anti-Semitism resulted in splitting the commission's constituency.

Organized Groups

At the end of Stanley Lowell's tenure as chairman, the organized constituency of the commission looked much as it had in 1953 when the agency was established. With the beginning of chairman Booth's tenure, this emphasis began to change. Early in 1966 monthly meetings were initiated by Booth with about forty private civil rights groups in the city so that public and private efforts in the area of human rights could be coordinated. Representatives of the established groups were invited to these sessions, but in addition, the chairman prided himself on including little-known organizations (such as the Harlem Parents' Association) based in minority neighborhoods.[30]

These meetings soon became a source of tension between the new chairman and the civil rights organizations, and attendance at them serves as a rough index of the relations between the CCHR and its organized constituency. At first attendance was high (Booth estimates seventy or eighty people), but it dwindled until lack of participation forced the commission to discontinue the program.[31] The chairman attributed this decline to lack of interest among the private groups. Agency leaders, on the other hand, contended that Booth simply called the meetings to aggrandize the commission and was not really interested in cooperating with them. One commented, "Booth attended the first [meeting], was late to the second

[30] Interview with Booth, Aug. 8, 1968.
[31] Interviews with Booth and a spokesman for the American Jewish Committee, summer 1968.

and after that didn't come at all. It ended up with just staff talking back and forth to each other . . . and he wanted us to bring our lay leaders as well." [32]

Developments outside the agency also contributed to the change in the CCHR's organized constituency. Federal antipoverty legislation encouraged the creation of community corporations through its "maximum feasible participation" dictum, and these provided alternatives to the more established groups for the commission just as the increased militancy of the civil rights movement seemed to have left the old organizations outside the mainstream. In reaching out to what he considered to be the commission's natural constituency, "grass roots organizations and unorganized individuals," Booth simply moved away from the older groups. "It was not conscious or intentional," he said, "and civil rights groups are another advisory source, but that is the way it worked out." [33]

The commission's report on the New York City Conference on Community Action held under its sponsorship late in 1967 serves as an indicator of the transitional stage in the change of the agency's constituency. Representatives of the traditional organizations that had been associated with the CCHR in the past (the American Jewish Congress, the American Jewish Committee, the NAACP, and the Catholic Interracial Council) helped plan and participated in the conference, but so did people from such groups as the Harlem Commonwealth Council, the Lower West Side Community Corporation, and the Fort Greene Progress Center.[34]

This was not simply evidence of the expansion of the CCHR's organized constituency, for a key bloc in the established organizations, the Jewish groups, were beginning to feel increasingly divorced from the commission's work. As tensions between Jews and blacks in the city grew in late 1967 and early 1968, these groups became progressively less comfortable with chairman Booth's conception of himself as an advocate of black positions within the city government.[35]

[32] Interview with American Jewish Committee spokesman.
[33] Interview with Booth.
[34] CCHR, *New York Conference on Community Action* (New York: The Commission, 1967).
[35] Interviews with Morris Sass, Will Maslow.

The first manifestation of this discontent came early in 1967 when Rabbi Julius Neumann resigned his post on the commission and charged that Booth was "whipping up animosity among people and ignoring discrimination against Jews." The rabbi charged that the chairman had failed to accept complaints from Sabbath observers who had lost their jobs, had been silent about anti-Semitic remarks directed at Intermediate School 201 principal Stanley R. Lisser during the controversy at that school, and had failed to hold hearings on discrimination against Jews in the city's banking industry.[36] Booth professed to be "shocked" by Neumann's statement and offered a defense in which he was backed by the mayor and the whole commission.[37] In a few weeks, the matter seemed to have blown over.

It had not. Although leaders of Jewish groups, like Booth, questioned Neumann's motives and use of publicity, they nevertheless believed that there was a kernel of truth to his charges. By the summer of 1968 they had reached the point of total disaffection from the commission. Upon being interviewed they offered these observations:

The commission must be 80 or 90 per cent black by now, and it is only concerned with Negro and to some extent Puerto Rican problems. It is only responsive to pressure from these groups.

Last time I was there I did not see a white face.

I judge an agency by outputs and the CCHR hasn't done much lately. I can only think of one or two one-shot things that the CCHR have recently cooperated on.

They have been seeking out the militants lately. We are predictable, they are not.

Booth is using the agency for his own personal advancement and shoots from the hip.

The commission has become a black agency and the staff is incompetent. It has defined its constituency as the black militants. All the Jewish groups have given up on it.

[36] *New York Times,* Feb. 15, 1967, p. 1, col. 7.
[37] CCHR press release, Feb. 27, 1967.

Booth made a conscious decision to limit his constituency to blacks. He had political ambitions.[38]

Beyond the chairman's advocacy of black causes, two things bothered Jewish leaders about the commission. First, at the staff level at the agency, there did not seem to be anyone with whom they could talk. Extensive personnel data are not available for this period as they were for 1962–1965, but it is evident from the city civil list that though top commission staff continued to be recruited from establishmentarian black organizations (i.e., the NAACP and the Urban League), Jewish groups had ceased to be a training ground for these positions. Furthermore, the highest placed individual at the commission with connections in the private Jewish agencies, Irving Goldaber, left when he failed to be appointed by the new chairman to the executive directorship.[39] Other Jews joined the commission (it was not as "black" an agency as the Jewish leaders perceived it to be) but they were neither recruited from the established private groups nor known to them.

Second, and more important, Jewish leaders were especially upset by the failure of the chairman to speak up or to use the commission as a vehicle with which to condemn black anti-Semitism. Other black leaders disappointed them as well, but Booth's official capacity, they believed, *required* him to act.[40] When Booth did speak out, as he did to condemn "group libel" in the controversial book prepared from the Metropolitan Museum exhibition "Harlem on My Mind," it was not nearly with the rhetorical flourishes that he used in his black-advocate role. From Booth's point of view, the criticism and concern of the Jewish leaders in the city was "ill advised." After all, he believed, "I've

[38] Interviews with staff and lay leaders of American Jewish Congress, American Jewish Committee, Anti-Defamation League, Jewish Labor Committee.

[39] Interview with Goldaber. Individual contacts take on added importance in light of the report of the Ginsburg investigation team: "There is no central file of agency activities, reports or contacts. Each individual staff member has his own contacts with various groups and agencies, and when he leaves this information is lost to the agency" (Ginsburg, p. 10).

[40] Interview with Morris Sass, fall 1968.

spoken up in these cases and 85 per cent of my constituency is Negro. They want me to go further. The commission is not an antidefamation league." [41]

Though the Jewish groups were thus estranged from the commission, the CCHR did not make concomitant gains among black and Puerto Rican organizations. Puerto Rican groups focused their efforts upon organizing the Puerto Rican community and upon getting more political attention (and patronage) from the mayor; little energy was left over for commission-related activities. Besides, Puerto Rican leaders believed it natural that commissioner Booth should favor his own group. His "treatment of the Puerto Ricans as an afterthought," said Joseph Monserrat of the Migration Division of the Puerto Rican government, was simply typical of the approach of most city agencies to this minority group.[42]

Among the predominantly black organizations, the commission received strong support in its projects from the NAACP (Booth's original organization) and cooperated with CORE in occasional press conferences and programs. Ties were perhaps closest with the Urban League's Operation Open City housing program which was revitalized in the late 1960's with a grant from the city Anti-Poverty Board. One commission staff member commented that ties with the Urban League were so close that communications from them "sounded like interoffice memos."

Consistent support for the CCHR was not forthcoming from more recently organized antipoverty groups and black protest organizations. Representatives of these groups would participate

[41] Interview with Booth.

[42] Interview with Monserrat, Feb. 17, 1969. For a demarcation of Puerto Rican priorities in the city at this time see "A Design for Change: Puerto Ricans Confront Problems of the Complex Urban Society," Community Conference Proceedings, Columbia University, April 15 and 16, 1967. Morris Engle has suggested that Puerto Ricans as a group do not get excited about discrimination because "on the whole . . . [they] do not feel that they have received discriminatory treatment." Only 6 per cent, for example, said when interviewed that they knew someone who had been denied housing because he was a Puerto Rican ("The Puerto Ricans in New York City," in Nathan Glazer and Davis McEntire, eds., *Studies in Housing and Minority Groups* [Berkeley: University of California Press, 1960], pp. 65–66).

in occasional commission conferences, consult with Booth, and cooperate with him from time to time in tension situations, but essentially they were engaged in another arena. The commission, an agency with its roots in the 1950's, was suspect both because it had not emerged from the new militancy of the mid-1960's and because, as a city agency, it was part of "the establishment."

An indicator of the lack of engagement of the commission with the "new" civil rights groups is the absence of large-scale protest by these organizations on the occasion of chairman Booth's removal under fire from the commission in February 1969. Despite Booth's efforts "at the grassroots," protests appeared in the *New York Times* from only four organizations: the NAACP, Harlem CORE, HARYOU Act, and the Queens Interfaith Council. Booth's adoption of the advocate's role had cost the CCHR a large part of its organized constituency, and these groups had not been replaced with an equally stable base.[43]

Individuals

No cumulative data are available on the racial and socioeconomic characteristics of formal complainants to the commission for the period 1965–1968. Because of revisions in commission policies and other factors, many more complaints were registered than in previous years, and chairman Booth estimated that 85 per cent of them were registered by blacks. This is consistent with figures for early periods, and other commissioners noted in interviews that the CCHR served largely the black middle class. These impressions are fortified by the fact that the Urban League's Operation Open City, which was the source for many of the commission's housing complaints, sought apartments predominantly for middle-class black families.[44] It thus seems safe to conclude that the CCHR's individual constituency did not change substan-

[43] *New York Times*, Feb. 5, 1969, p. 1, col. 1. In a letter to the author (June 6, 1973) Mr. Booth claimed that he personally dissuaded protests by dozens of organizations and hundreds of individuals to prevent the dispute from mushrooming.

[44] Planners for Equal Opportunity, New York Chapter, *Planning for Open City* (New York: New York Urban League, 1967).

tially from previous periods; it remained predominantly black and predominantly middle-class.

Communities

As under the previous chairman, the CCHR under Booth attempted to expand its constituency into minority neighborhoods. Learning from the mistakes of the previous administration, the commission ceased trying to organize neighborhoods and instead sought to associate with already established neighborhood groups in order to bring its services directly to individuals in the local communities.

Upon coming to the commission, chairman Booth discerned as one of its primary difficulties that, "the commission and the human rights law that it is mandated to enforce was not nearly well enough known by the community it was established to serve." [45] He attempted to remedy this difficulty by "taking the commission to the communities" through a series of Human Rights Nights. Beginning early in 1967, once a week in each borough, commissioners and staff serving on a rotating basis would hold meetings in neighborhood centers. Gatherings were advertised through handouts and other media, representatives of other city agencies were invited, and local residents were given an opportunity to present their grievances.

Citizens were advised and complaints recorded at the meeting, and subsequently referrals were made if the problem was in the bailiwick of another city agency. Booth believed that the program was successful in "making it easier for people to register complaints with us." [46] The number of complaints processed by the commission did increase fourfold during the first year of the Human Rights Nights program, but other variables (changes in the law, activities of the Urban League in motivating complaints) were at work and thus it is impossible to isolate a causal relationship. The reception by the commission of all kinds of complaints

45 *CCHR 50/50 Reporter*, vol. 1, no. 1 (April 1967), p. 1. This was a successor newsletter to previously cited COIR and CCHR publications.
46 *Ibid.*

and not just those mandated by law involved a question of the commission's proper function. This ombudsman-type practice, with the commission taking the part of the "little man," was attractive to Booth but led to comments like: "the small professional staff spent much of its time investigating complaints about which it could do nothing . . . while valid complaints of discrimination had to wait their turn." [47]

Furthermore, after the first few meetings the CCHR's Human Rights Nights received little media coverage and thus their ability to expand the commission's constituency was limited. Neighborhood people, in order to avail themselves of commission services through this program, still had to be rather highly motivated. They had to come to evening meetings (and thus travel at night, possibly after a hard day's work) that were hardly well-publicized, and once there, they had to feel able to present their grievances to commission officials.

The commission employed both conventional and unconventional means in attempting to make the CCHR known to the city at large. Chairman Booth led walking tours through ghetto areas in four boroughs. The usual publicity devices—press releases, mailings, and television and radio appearances—were used, but they still rarely commanded prime-time or prime-station coverage. Booth made several television and radio appearances weekly, and his chosen advocate role constantly involved him in political battles beyond the formal limits of his office. A member of the public relations staff of the commission commented in an interview that Booth's chairmanship had made his job easier, but that in addition, since Booth had arrived upon the scene, "we've had to wipe up a lot of blood around here." Though Booth was news, he did not, as we have seen, share his visibility with the commission. As one mayoral advisor noted: "He was important because he was Bill Booth, not because he was chairman of the Human Rights Commission."

A better indicator than Booth's visibility in the media of the attentive public for commission activities, then, is the agency's mail-

[47] Ginsburg, p. 15.

ing list. Commission materials were sent to a total of 3,433 individuals and groups in the period from 1966 to 1968. Few of these (19.6 per cent) were individuals (see Table 8).

Table 8. Recipients of the literature of the CCHR, 1966–1968

Recipient	No.	%
City officials and departments	607	17.8
Other governments and commissions	190	5.6
Educational groups, high schools, and libraries	301	8.8
Commissioners and staff	78	2.2
Citywide media	321	9.4
Private agencies	124	3.6
Community newspapers	38	1.1
Individuals	674	19.6
Catholic churches	220	6.5
Jewish groups and media (and clergy)	158	4.5
Negro groups and media (and clergy)	414	11.2
Spanish groups and media (and clergy)	304	8.8
Foreign-language presses	15	0.4
Total	3,433	99.5

Source: CCHR mailing list, revised April 1966.

The majority were agencies in the CCHR's organized constituency or media contacts through which the agency hoped to reach individuals. When these contacts chose to pay little attention to the commission, the reach of the agency's information program was circumscribed indeed.

Nationality Subgroups

As under previous leadership, the CCHR under Booth attempted to expand its constituency by providing services to special subgroups in the city. Special appeals, for example, were made to Puerto Ricans and other national minorities.

The nature of commission services to Puerto Rican New Yorkers changed little with the ascendance of Booth to the chairmanship. Primary activities still included leadership workshops and the participation by the commission in symbolic celebrations like the Puerto Rican Day Parade on Fifth Avenue and the Puerto Rican Folk Festival in Central Park. Commission literature was printed in Spanish in order to facilitate communication with the Puerto Rican community, but this step was hardly an innovation. From time to time the chairman served on special mayoral committees on Puerto Rican civil rights, attempted to moderate differences between Puerto Ricans and blacks, or sought to alleviate tensions between Puerto Ricans and city agencies, but these were steps to meet particular problems and were not part of a continuing program. With respect to most commission programs Puerto Ricans were served incidentally; they rarely availed themselves of agency services.

The circumstances surrounding the creation of the Puerto Rican–Hispanic division of the CCHR illustrate well the nature of the involvement of the agency with the city's Puerto Rican community during the late 1960's. After a number of protests by the National Association for Puerto Rican Civil Rights against the "commission's and Mayor Lindsay's neglect of the city's 700,000 Puerto Ricans," the president of that organization, Gilberto Gerena-Valentin, was appointed to the CCHR's business and employment division. This, both Booth and Gerena agreed, "illustrated that the Commission was on the right track for the first time . . . in its relations with the Puerto Rican Community." [48] Subsequently, Gerena, in a commission reorganization, was given his own division for Puerto Rican—Hispanic affairs. He organized an extensive ten-point program for Puerto Ricans in the city, but little of it was implemented.[49]

For the CCHR, the cooptation of Gerena served to prove the agency's concern for the Puerto Rican community and, because of the Puerto Rican leader's radical background, its willingness to work with "militants." In fact, the employment of Gerena identified the commission with one political faction within the Puerto Rican

[48] *New York Times,* May 2, 1966, p. 15, col. 1; CCHR press release, May 2, 1966.
[49] *New York Times,* July 10, 1969, p. 23, col. 2; July 11, p. 42, col. 6, July 12, p. 14, col. 7, July 16, p. 50, col. 2, and Aug. 4, p. 72, col. 1.

community and thus strained the relationship of the agency with other influential Puerto Rican leaders in the city. Later, when Booth's successor, Simeon Golar, attempted to replace Gerena, the Puerto Rican leader led demonstrations in front of the CCHR offices and went on a hunger strike. His cataclysmic style in a mayoral election year caused observers to wonder whether he was concerned more about anti-Puerto Rican bias or losing his own power base.

Sensitive to criticisms that it had been concerned with black and Puerto Rican problems to the exclusion of other groups, the CCHR in May 1968 re-established a nationalities division. This paralleled steps taken under Lowell and was done over the objections of the chairman, who "did not want to seem to be playing to the several ethnic blocs." [50] In order to inform the leaders of the city's minority nationalities of the services that the CCHR could provide them, the agency called a meeting of the consuls general of the various nations whose ex-nationals were to be served by the new division. The foreign officials were rather unreceptive to commission suggestions because they seemed to believe that there was no discrimination and no need for the commission's efforts; nevertheless, a committee structure was set up, and the CCHR encouraged each nationality to initiate meetings in its own neighborhood, which the staff of the agency would then visit.

In the end, as the consuls general had predicted, nationality groups were unresponsive to commission overtures. The only successful community meeting to come out of the nationalities program was a Human Rights Night on the "lower" Lower East Side of Manhattan, a neighborhood that sheltered an amalgam of Chinese, Italians, Jews, Puerto Ricans, and blacks. A large turnout convinced the CCHR leadership that this meeting was a success, and they planned to return. This, however, was the exception that proved the rule. The nationalities idea had born little fruit for the commission; there was no constituency for the agency here.

In the period from 1966 to 1968, the constituency of the CCHR underwent a fundamental change. The confluence of several events

[50] Interview with Booth.

—the intensification of the racial crisis in the city, the translation of this crisis into a Jewish-black confrontation, and the assumption of the chairmanship of the agency by a dynamic black lawyer who found the advocate role cogenial for both himself and the commission—destroyed the coalition that had supported the agency in the past. Though the commission continued to serve the same individuals it had always served (and even intensified its efforts among them with new types of community-oriented programs), it lost the organizational support formerly afforded it by private Jewish civil rights agencies and failed to replace this with a stable organizational base. To be sure, the narrow base of the established black organizations remained, but it was not augmented by solid continuing relationships with the burgeoning, activist, locally based civil rights groups in the city. In addition, as the commission came under increased criticism for being concerned only with black problems, it found it more and more difficult to expand its individual constituency to include the members of other minorities.[51] Its Puerto Rican program failed to focus the attention of that group upon the commission, and its efforts among white minority nationalities in the city failed completely.

Relations with the Mayor and Other City Agencies

During the first months of the Lindsay administration the relationship between the chairman of the commission and the mayor was closer than at any previous time in the agency's history. For Lindsay, interested in solidifying relationships with the city's minorities after the election, Booth was an important asset. For his part, Booth was convinced of Lindsay's sincerity during the interview in which he was offered the chairmanship, and his conviction was reinforced by the fact of his ongoing high-level access to city hall. The chairman was included in the mayor's weekly cabinet meetings and was frequently consulted by the administration on matters of policy. As he noted in March 1966, "City hall is willing and al-

[51] See Ginsburg, p. 16, for a criticism of the commission's public-relations program for being too heavily oriented toward the black community.

ways available for me to discuss problems. Two or three times a week city hall asks for my opinions on some matter." [52]

At the commission, the chairman's ties to the administration were taken as signs of a new real commitment on the part of city government to the work of the agency; longtime staff members interviewed volunteered a contrast between the support offered the CCHR by the Wagner administration in its last years and "the real commitment of the Lindsay administration." Even critics of the new chairman among the commissioners acknowledged that, "at first, Booth got more support from Lindsay than Lowell did from Wagner." [53]

Beyond the mere fact of access to upper-echelon officials at city hall, Booth was impressed by the mayor's willingness to allow him to differ from the administration publicly on matters of policy: "Lindsay and I have differed, and I could lose my job tomorrow, but the mayor is man enough publicly to allow this and give me full cooperation." [54] This willingness upon the part of the mayor to allow the chairman to play an advocate role in the city is important, for it stemmed from a basically different understanding of the role of the CCHR at city hall from that of previous administrations. As one of the mayor's chief aides in the area of minority affairs noted, "During the Lindsay administration the chairman has been an advocate rather than a moderator. There has been some liberation from the office of the mayor, and this is a good thing. It would not be his role to keep things quiet." [55]

This basic redefinition of the commission's role did not come only from the change in administrations; it was also the result of the increased intensity of the racial problems of the city, the new chairman's perception of his proper constituency, and the political needs of the mayor. When racial tensions were a relatively minor problem in the city (as they were for most of Wagner's tenure), the type of agency that was most functional for the mayor was one that would make the problems that did arise disappear with the fewest

[52] *New York Times,* March 27, 1966, p. 79, col. 8.
[53] Interview with Murray Gross.   [54] Interview with Booth.
[55] Interviewee wishes to remain anonymous.

possible costs. When they became the city's primary problem, a degree of advocacy at the commission became increasingly functional, for the mayor needed all the assistance he could get from aides with "credibility" in minority communities. For Booth, in turn, being "the first black man ever employed by the city who was able to speak his mind" was important both because of his personal conception of his role and because it was upon this image that his usefulness to the administration depended.[56]

Nevertheless, the administration's permissiveness toward Booth's advocacy had its limits. In the 1966 building-trades dispute, for example, Lindsay, at the urging of Liberal party leader Alex Rose, arranged a secret meeting in his office between Booth and labor leaders Peter Brennan and Harry Van Arsdale. Booth, who had been highly and publicly critical of the unions prior to the meeting, emerged from it "satisfied that substantial progress had been made towards getting more Negroes and Puerto Ricans into the building trades unions." [57]

As the political climate in the city changed, further limits on advocacy were defined. The role of the chairman that was acceptable to and even functional for the mayor in 1966 had become, by 1968, a source of difficulty. In 1966 and 1967, the demands of the Lindsay administration upon the CCHR and its chairman corresponded with those of the agency's changed constituency. Booth's predisposition to adopt the advocate role pleased both of these, and the role conflict that we have identified in the agency emerged only infrequently. As outside pressures (from the very Jewish constituency that the commission had lost) caused the city administration to restructure its political priorities in anticipation of a difficult election, however, this conflict problem emerged again in virulent form, to be solved, as in 1960, on the basis of citywide political considerations.

The CCHR during the late 1960's was able to cooperate with its sister agencies in the visible public arena but maintained few

---

[56] Quotation is from an interview with Barry Gottehrer, July 30, 1969.
[57] *New York Times,* June 20, 1966, p. 35, col. 1; see below, p. 223, for further discussion.

working contacts at the staff level. This was probably the result of the chairman's announced intention to "publicly either support or decry conditions or administrative actions within the jurisdiction of other governmental agencies, and even proposals of the Mayor's office, that it believed might help, or harm, the human rights of any group of citizens." [58] It is true, however, that Booth acted not only as a critic of city departments but also as a moderator between them and aroused minority groups. The relationship between the CCHR under Booth's chairmanship and the Police Department perhaps best illustrates the agency's roles as both critic and moderator.

At times, the CCHR was very critical of the department and its policies. When police involved in an incident in Harlem were transferred to another district, for example, Booth publicly objected to this administrative solution and demanded that they be suspended from the force.[59] Similarly, the chairman objected on radio to the department's policy of using Harlem as "a dumping ground for demoted policemen." [60]

When the city considered setting up a civilian police review board, the chairman's outspoken advocacy and his involvement of the commission in the fight for the board earned him the enmity of many rank-and-file police officers. In fact, during this controversy Booth used the commission to run voter-registration drives and sponsor panels explaining the civilian review board in minority neighborhoods. He was publicly critical of police officials who opposed the change, and engaged in a running battle with Police Benevolent Association president John Cassese for his "intemperate remarks" about minorities.[61]

At the same time that he criticized the department, however, Booth's position in this battle placed him on the side of the mayor and the police commissioner, and he used these contacts to help moderate the differences between the police and ghetto residents.

[58] CCHR, *Annual Report, 1966,* p. 2.
[59] *New York Times,* March 2, 1966, p. 29, col. 7.
[60] *Ibid.,* March 7, 1966, p. 17, col. 1.
[61] *Ibid.,* Feb. 18, 1966, p. 18, col. 4; March 12, 1966, p. 8., col. 8; May 19, 1966, p. 40, col. 3; May 29, 1966, p. 42, col. 3.

Under commissioner Howard R. Leary and chief inspector San-
ford D. Garelick, the chairman said, "there had been a total
change in the attitude of the department toward the commission."
Working with Leary, Booth arranged a series of "meetings in a
living room" so that the police administrator could become ac-
quainted with minority community leaders. During the riots in
East New York in 1966 and at Columbia University in 1968,
Booth again served as a moderator between the police and
minority-group participants.[62]

The visible relations between the commission and other major
city departments were much the same as they were with the police
department. Booth was critical of many Welfare Department
practices and programs but nevertheless attempted to arrange
meetings to moderate relations between welfare workers and their
clients.[63] When Fire Department personnel were being attacked
in ghetto areas, the chairman released criticisms of the department
to the press but helped arrange meetings between fire officials and
community groups in order to alleviate tensions. Finally, commission Human Rights Nights provided an ongoing forum in which
representatives of city agencies could meet with community people and deal with their grievances. Criticism of these agencies was
implicit in this program, but the commission hoped in this way to
reduce tensions before they reached the stage of overt hostility
toward city employees and programs.

Though the commission thus had some success in maintaining
constructive relationships with other city agencies on a public
level, this was not the case on a day-to-day operating level. Some
agencies, like the Board of Education, publicly refused to cooperate with CCHR programs.[64] It simply never occurred to administrators of other departments to bring problems to the commission. One black official commented, "As a city administrator, I
never think of going to the commission with a problem. In fact, I

[62] *Ibid.,* March 20, 1966, p. 84, col. 3; March 27, 1966, p. 79, col. 3;
July 22, 1966, p. 1, col. 7.
[63] CCHR, *Annual Report, 1966,* p. 3.
[64] *New York Times,* March 27, 1966, p. 19, col. 3.

think each department should have a unit within its own shop to deal with problems like this, and mine does. I know this is the case in the Manpower department as well." [65] A study done by the city administrator's office confirmed that the commission maintained few formal links with other city departments on the staff level: "The Human Rights Commission is not fully aware of the activities of the human relations and/or equal opportunities staffs of such city agencies as: the Board of Education, Economic Development Administration, Housing and Development Administration, and Human Resources Administration. Consequently, the commission is unable to coordinate its work with these other agencies." [66]

Commission staff members sometimes articulated a feeling that other city agencies saw the Commission on Human Rights as a troublemaker. This feeling is confirmed by the negative attitude toward the commission as a place to work displayed by city hall officials. One assistant to the mayor, for example, remarked in an offhand way that the Commission on Human Rights was the wrong place for a young lawyer to start out in city government. This negative attitude was sometimes reflected in policy decisions. When the administration wanted to give priority to programs in which the commission had been involved (tension control or contract compliance, for example) it did not augment the CCHR budget and staff but instead created a new agency to do the job or transferred the function. Though Booth was important to the administration and though he was able to cooperate on a high level with other top administrative officials, he was not able to transform the confidence in him into confidence in the agency he headed.

Relations with State Agencies

As in previous periods, during the mid-1960's there was no great cooperative effort among city, state, and federal agencies in the human relations area in New York City. Again, in the words

[65] Interview with Eugene Callender, deputy commissioner of housing and development, July 29, 1969.
[66] Ginsburg, pp. 10–11.

of the city administrator's report, "The Commission had no regular liaison with other city, state, federal or private agencies working in the human rights field in New York City." [67] The jurisdictional problem between the city and the state was solved in 1965 when state legislation assured the CCHR concurrent jurisdiction with the state commission, and local legislation then extended the city agency's powers to match those of the state group.[68]

From 1965 to 1968, the tendency of the two agencies to leave each other alone was augmented by differences between the state chairman, George Fowler, and Booth. When Robert Mangum became state chairman some tentative steps toward cooperation were taken. The closest contact at the staff level was between the housing divisions of the two agencies, which established a cross file of respondents' names to aid in investigations. The city and the state commissions met together early in 1968 and divided the responsibility for pursuing an investigation of the communications industry, and later in that year monthly coordinating meetings were begun.[69] The extensive reorganization of the state agency in 1968 (a reorganization which eliminated the jobs of most of the state commissioners) seemed to preclude any great cooperation during that period.

Action in Substantive Policy Areas

The activities of the CCHR in the major policy areas of education, employment, and housing during the period from 1966 to 1968 serve to illustrate further the agency's attempt to solve its advocate-apologist role dilemma by substantially abandoning the apologist role. The confluence of several factors allowed the commission, at least for a time, to do this. These included the new enforcement philosophy and augmented legal powers of the commission, the attractiveness of the advocate role for the chairman and the willingness of the mayor to allow him to perform in this role within broad limits, the changed constituency of the agency, and, finally, the altered structure of the CCHR and the changed power

[67] *Ibid.*   [68] *Race Relations Law Reporter* 467 (1966).
[69] *CCHR 50/50 Reporter*, vol. 1, no. 3 (April 1968), p. 3.

relationships within it. All of these changes, of course, were partly due to a new constant in the city, the constant fear of racial violence, cyclically renewed with the appearance of each summer season.

In a fourth major substantive area, tension control, the acceptance by the city of the CCHR as advocate led to an abandonment of the agency as apologist, and the function was taken from it and given to a new group especially created for the purpose, the Mayor's Urban Action Task Force. Similarly, in the area of employment, the administration reduced the commission's responsibilities by removing from it the job of administering the contract-compliance program, thus illustrating a propensity to remove from the aegis of the CCHR matters of heightened political priority.

Education

During Booth's tenure, the CCHR never reassumed the central role in education that it had had during the school integration controversies of 1961 and 1962. Rather than attempting to achieve a special moderator position, the commission during this period acted as one advocate among many involved in the recurrent crises of 1966, 1967, and 1968.

Chairman Booth's advocacy on school matters earned him several adversaries, most notably the Board of Education and the United Federation of Teachers. On the day of his swearing in, the new chairman revealed what was to be the tone of his administration on educational matters when he protested the mayor's concurrent announcement of the completion of plans for the Flatlands Industrial Park in Brooklyn and argued that the site should be used for an educational park.[70] This early attack was only a harbinger of things to come. In September 1966, Booth denounced the Board of Education for not doing enough to head off the fall school demonstrations. As the crisis developed, the chairman commiserated with "the parents in their attempt to secure action from the board." To be sure, Booth denounced CORE and SNCC for

[70] *New York Times,* Feb. 2, 1966, p. 38, col. 5; Feb. 18, 1966, p. 18, col. 1.

some of their tactics during the dispute, but it was clear that he placed the burden of blame on the board.[71]

During the 1967 strike, Booth's main target became the United Federation of Teachers. He questioned the motives of the striking teachers and offered the opinion that, as professionals, they should not join unions. The union in this case, the chairman alleged, was using the children as pawns and "was not supporting the Negro community in its goal of better education." For this statement Booth earned the enmity of Albert Shanker, leader of the UFT, and was denounced by black union leaders Bayard Rustin and A. Philip Randolph.[72] Needless to say, the mayor quickly disassociated himself from his commissioner's remarks.

While attacking the union, the commission sought a détente with the Board of Education. A subcommittee was established to meet with the board's committee on integration and community relations. In these meetings, however, the CCHR's posture remained mainly that of advocate; it urged upon the board decentralization and active parent participation in school decision making.[73]

During the fall of 1968, during the decentralization–community control controversy, the chairman took on both the union and the board. Early in October he visited the schools of the embattled Ocean Hill–Brownsville district in the company of several principals ousted by the Board of Education and issued a statement "in an official capacity." "I hope," Booth said, "that the courts will undo what was wrongfully done by the Board of Education." Besides antagonizing the board, this action enraged Mr. Shanker, who felt that Booth was "trying to force the schools in the district to accept his presence and the presence of several principals who have been relieved of their duties for defying the Board of Education. [He] . . . has improperly given the city sanction to the school principal's [sic] defiance of the central Board."[74]

[71] *Ibid.,* Sept. 22, 1966, p. 50, col. 3; Dec. 22, 1966, p. 1, col. 1.

[72] *Ibid.,* Oct. 1, 1966, p. 52, col. 1; Oct. 6, 1966, p. 48, col. 3.

[73] CCHR, *Annual Report, 1967* (New York: The Commission, 1968), p. 18.

[74] *New York Times,* Oct. 11, 1968, p. 50, col. 1.

The chairman's actions in this incident are not surprising, for a commission study released earlier in 1968 had clearly identified the agency as a proponent of school decentralization and as an antagonist of the board and the union. Though hardly polemical, the "Report on Three Demonstration Projects in the City Schools" accepted the premises of the proponents of decentralization and implicitly placed much of the blame for the school crisis on the Board of Education and, to a lesser degree, on the UFT. The school system was viewed as "unresponsive," "lacking in flexibility," and the locus of "a massive, almost impenetrable bureaucracy." Its "insensitivity to the views of the parties at interest," said the report, were largely responsible for "parents and students attacking school officials . . . [and for] conflicts within schools among students and faculties."

As for the union, its strike in 1967 was viewed as having "heightened racial feelings in the community," and its boycotting as a result of local governing board policy positions and lukewarm attitudes after initial cooperation in decentralization plans contributed to the difficulties of the projects. In short, said the report: "Despite early support of the plan drafted by two University professors and assertions of support for decentralization in theory, in practice the UFT has opposed the three projects. Leaders of the three demonstration projects repeatedly charged that the UFT has done everything in its power to retard the experiments, and even teachers who support decentralization admitted that the UFT's opposition created great difficulties for them and the projects.[75]

The commission did not totally endorse all that had happened in the demonstration districts. It found it "an unfortunate circumstance," for example, that in the Intermediate School 201 and Two Bridges districts "control was acquired by a group, the source of whose members antagonized many parents and teachers." Nevertheless, the CCHR investigating committee believed that "effective decentralization is an answer to the worsening relations

[75] CCHR, *Report on Three Demonstration Projects in the City Schools* (New York: The Commission, 1968), p. 17. All quotes in these three paragraphs are from this report.

between school and community, and to the rising tensions engendered within the schools by the present system in disadvantaged areas." Failures were due to "hasty and inadequate planning, lack of professional guidance to lay people who organized the projects, lack of cooperation and support from many teachers, supervisors, and the Board of Education, and the many limitations of state law," but not to the inadequacies of the idea itself.

Aside from its relationships with the Board of Education and the UFT, commission advocacy in education during this period was marked by a special awareness of the agency's constituency. In August 1967 an investigation of anti-Semitic outbursts by CORE members in school-community controversies in Brooklyn and Queens was begun by the CCHR, but at the same time the public was assured that complaints filed by black parents and teachers on discrimination in the public schools would also be investigated. Complaints about "racist and antiwhite" statements in the memorial service for Malcom X at Intermediate School 201 would be investigated, said the chairman, but he was sure that this impression came from "parts taken out of context." [76] "There are indications of some racism in the public school system," reported the commission, but "these are reflections of the racism in the society at large among both blacks and whites." [77]

It is clear that in the area of education during the late 1960's the commission and the chairman were identified with one side in a very divisive controversy. Besides contributing to the fragmentation of the agency's constituency, this advocacy left the CCHR outside the education decision-making process in the city and hampered its ability to moderate group conflicts.

Employment

The provision of equal employment opportunities within the city was the policy objective given top priority by chairman Booth during his tenure at the CCHR. With recalcitrant labor unions, the

[76] *New York Times,* Aug. 7, 1967, p. 23, col. 4; March 11, 1968, p. 35, col. 1.

[77] *Report on Three Demonstration Projects,* p. 25.

commission's new advocacy was marked by the more extensive use of public hearings and by the willingness to use the ultimate sanction, the cancellation of city construction contracts. In dealing with the city's large private employers, a new adversary, the CCHR lacked any real sanction beyond the threat of the dissemination of unfavorable publicity, but this, when combined with strong *prima facie* cases of past discrimination, was often enough to convince companies to cooperate with the commission in hiring and training programs. Though commission advocacy had some success with corporate executives newly educated in their social responsibilities by the crisis atmosphere in the city in the late 1960's (and at the same time increasingly pressed for low-priced, semiskilled labor), aggressive techniques made fewer inroads among union leaders, who had been the subject of attack by civil rights groups for some time. Eventually, when the city administration decided to re-emphasize its contract-compliance program, a concurrent decision was made to remove the responsibility for the program from the CCHR.

The Building Trades

William Booth's first official act upon being sworn in as the chairman of the City Commission on Human Rights was to promise to hit the building-trades unions in "their economic breadbaskets . . . not with brickbats, but with the law." The new chairman's initial effort in this campaign was to be a revival of the Lowell investigations of the conditions of employment in the building-trades industries in the city. In this he had the blessing of the mayor, who urged Booth to "make a determined effort to eliminate bias in labor unions . . . [and to] survey everyone doing business with the city with the view of seeking out and eliminating discriminatory practices." [78]

As it proceeded, the commission developed two major focuses for its investigation: contractor hiring practices, and union aprenticeship and membership requirements. Early in March 1966 the representatives of fifteen corporations doing business with the

---

[78] Both quotes from *New York Times,* Feb. 2, 1966, p. 1, col. 2.

tional high schools would be integrated with union hiring practices. Finally, a separate division of the CCHR would be established to enforce these new regulations, to advise job seekers, and to cooperate with governments at all levels in these programs.

The revealing thing about these hearings and the subsequent report with regard to the CCHR's role in city government is that much of the data incorporated in the report was not produced at the hearings. In fact, it had been released to the press in June 1966, three months before the hearings were held and nine months before the final report was published.[86] The hearings were simply a "spur to compliance," a device through which the commission could perform its advocate function.

The commission estimated that its 1966 hearings produced 858 jobs for minority-group members. Other research has shown that more concrete progress was made by cooperative Workers Defense League efforts with unions than through commission attacks on them, though the CCHR dramatized the issue and thus made the "cooperative alternative" a more viable one for the unions.[87] One indication of the commission's lack of effectiveness is that when the report was published in 1967, Peter Brennan said that there would be no conciliation meetings between union and CCHR representatives because "no charges of discrimination had been proved." [88] In the face of this resistance, and without mayoral backing for their plan, the commission could do little.

To be sure, the mayor retained his commitment to challenge discrimination in union practices, but he had become convinced that the commission was not the proper vehicle for the job. In his 1967 annual report, Lindsay articulated a "growing concern over the slow progress of integration in the building trades unions and the persistence of discriminatory hiring practices in the industry." [89] A study produced by the Potomac Institute for the city, however, indicated that the CCHR had been ineffective for too

[86] *New York Times,* June 6, 1966, p. 37, col. 1.
[87] F. Ray Marshall and Vernon M. Briggs, Jr., *The Negro and Apprenticeship* (Baltimore: Johns Hopkins University Press, 1967), p. 80.
[88] *New York Times,* June 12, 1967, p. 44, col. 2.
[89] *Ibid.,* June 25, 1967, p. 1, col. 1.

long to be entrusted with this new initiative: "The inadequately staffed City Commission on Human Rights has been occupied largely in dealing with individual complaints and holding general hearings. While notices of contract awards go from many city agencies to the CCHR, together with employment statistics reports by contractors, these reports have merely been filed away because of lack of staff to review them. Compliance inspections are very rare." [90] The Potomac Institute analysts recommended that a role—the acceptance of complaints of discrimination—be reserved for the commission, but the larger affirmative action program should be administered from the city administrator's office. This plan won the mayor's approval, and in an executive order he chose to implement it rather than the commission's suggestions.[91]

Ironically, the executive order came just at a time when the commission had begun to carry out its threats against noncomplying contractors and unions. On March 5, 1968, it had initiated a complaint against the Manshul construction company and eight unions engaged in building a school annex in Bedford-Stuyvesant, on the grounds that the company and unions had failed to recruit, accept, and refer black and Puerto Rican journeymen and apprentices on the same basis as whites.[92] This was the first general complaint initiated by the commission and aimed at a project rather than at a specific union or employer and the first to ask prior compliance before the project could proceed.

Though the attitudes of mayors Wagner and Lindsay differed on the CCHR's confrontation of union discrimination, in the final analysis they both took steps that limited commission involvement in this area. Wagner expected the commission to play an apologist role and found it necessary to curb the agency when its advocacy threatened his network of political alliances; Lindsay accepted commission advocacy but found that it ultimately prevented the agency from running an effective contract-compliance program.

[90] The Potomac Institute, Inc., "A Fair Employment Contract Compliance Program for New York City" (Washington: The Institute, 1967), p. 34.

[91] Executive Order No. 71, April 2, 1968.

[92] CCHR press release, March 7, 1968.

Private Employers

With the passage in 1965 of legislation granting the city commission concurrent jurisdiction with the state agency within the limits of the city, the CCHR was mandated for the first time to enter unhampered the area of discrimination by private employers in the city. The agency had done some work in this area in a limited way through voluntary conciliation agreements in the past, but now for the first time it was legitimately authorized to act with all the powers at its command.

The CCHR's treatment of private industries followed the general pattern that had been developed in previous dealings with city contractors. First, through informal investigation, detailed research, or even conversations with company personnel officials, data was gathered about industry employment patterns. The data were then measured against commission standards based upon the minority percentage of the total work force in the city and upon knowledge of minority professional employment in other sectors of the economy. Then, if a *prima facie* case of discrimination emerged, companies were confronted with the evidence and asked to take affirmative action—that is, to hire more minority-group members in certain job categories and to allow the commission to check their progress periodically. Often the companies agreed and were then subjected to continued scrutiny by the commission. If they hesitated or refused to cooperate, the commission then turned to press releases and public hearings to bring pressure to bear.

In practice the pattern was not this ordered and simple. Some companies, like Consolidated Edison, New York Telephone, Chase Manhattan, and the Manufacturers Hanover Trust Company were relatively responsive to commission initiatives. They cooperated in establishing training programs for minority workers, in making job specifications more realistic (for example, removing the requirement of a high school diploma for jobs for which this credential was not necessary), and in recruiting workers from community centers and from community agencies.[93] All this

93 *CCHR 50/50 Reporter,* vol. 3, no. 1 (Jan. 1969), p. 2. and vol. 1, no. 1 (April 1967), p. 2.

cooperation was not entirely altruistic, as commissioner Booth pointed out at the federal Equal Employment Opportunities Commission hearings on the banking industry: "I don't want them to take credit for having done so much. They haven't done it except when prodded, except when it's been shown to them that it's in their own interest to make the progress they have made." [94] Nevertheless, a minimum of commission energy was needed to get employers to comply with the law, and the agency was therefore free to act in these cases as a conduit between prospective employers and community groups that could locate job seekers.

In other cases, there seemed little effort to establish a cooperative working relationship between the commission and the industry involved. The commission sponsored a study of retail employment patterns in Manhattan, for example, which documented a tendency to keep blacks in the lowest-paying job categories, but this was a pure research effort.[95] Not until the commission received a further grant did it act to meliorate the conditions revealed in the report. Likewise, the chief purpose of the agency investigation of the advertising industry and communications media (done in cooperation with the state commission) seemed to be to publicize these industries' sins rather than to work for substantive change. Again, as with the unions, the public hearings served as a tool with which to expose a practice that the commission already felt was unsatisfactory. Post-hearing followup was minimal.[96] Only in 1968 did the commission produce a study to determine the impact of one of its hearings, and then suspicions were confirmed. The advertising firms studied had weathered the bad publicity with few

[94] U.S. Equal Employment Opportunities Commission, *Hearings on Discrimination in White-Collar Employment* (Washington: GPO, 1968), p. 502.

[95] Don O. Watkins and David M. McKinney, *A Study of Employment Patterns in the General Merchandising Group Retail Stores in New York City*, 2 vols. (New York: The Commission, 1968).

[96] CCHR press releases, March 23, 1967, and Jan. 15, 1968; CCHR, "Report of the Public Hearings on the Employment Practices of the Broadcasting and Advertising Industries and the Image Projection of Members of Minority Groups on Television and Radio (New York: The Commission, 1968).

changes in their employment patterns. Another study, done two years later, however, did show some progress toward integration in the twelve largest ad agencies.[97]

The experience of the CCHR with private corporate employers during the period 1966–1968 reveals that the weaknesses of the agency were still grave handicaps even when it was able to take an aggressive advocate stance. Though able occasionally to exert pressure on industry for short periods through the use of publicity, the commission was incapable of sustained efforts for long periods over a broad employment spectrum. Its resources were too few and too inadequately marshaled. Though its practices had departed from those that Herbert Hill had claimed constituted "administrative nullification" of antidiscrimination legislation, the city commission could not hope to affect more than marginally industry's "minimum strategic accommodation" to the law.[98]

Housing

Though the integration of housing in the city ceased to be the priority function of the agency for commission leaders during the 1966–1968 period, it remained one of the important substantive areas in which the agency operated. As in other areas, the activities of the commission in housing changed to reflect its new enforcement philosophy. Two symbolic examples make this clear. In 1966 the commission concentrated, as before, on processing individual complaints of housing discrimination; by 1968 it had begun to initiate its own complaints against major realtors in the city. In 1966 housing director Lou Zimmerman asked major apartment owners in the city to list vacancies voluntarily with the CCHR; by 1968 the new housing director, Mitchell I. Wald, was suggesting for commission presentation to the city council legislation that would require that all vacancies and rental transactions in the city be recorded with the commission.[99]

During 1966, the first year of the Booth administration, 821

[97] CCHR, "Affirmative Action Followup on the Advertising and Broadcasting Hearing" (New York: The Commission, 1968); *New York Times,* May 18, 1970, p. 49, col. 3.

[98] EEOC, *Hearings,* pp. 491–492.

[99] CCHR, *Annual Report, 1966,* p. 56; *1968,* p. 8.

complaints of discrimination were filed with the CCHR (see Table 9). There were several reasons for the phenomenal increase over 1965, when 264 complaints were filed. The commission's Human Rights Nights program motivated some complaints, many of which were accepted under the new heading "general information and inquiry." [100] In addition, the Urban League's Operation Open City, funded with antipoverty money, recruited black families, gave them logistical backing to seek housing in white neighborhoods, provided white "checkers" to develop cases against discriminatory landlords, and then brought these cases to the commission. The expansion of the commission's jurisdiction through the 1965 legislation also was a factor, for this made the CCHR eligible to receive complaints that formerly would have gone by default to the state agency (at least the 163 complaints in employment and 52 in public accommodations were added in this way).

Table 9. Complaints filed with the CCHR, 1966 and 1968

Type	1966		1968	
	No.	% *	No.	% *
Housing	405	49	274	50
Employment	163	20	158	30
City agencies	98	12	22	4
Public accommodations	82	10	4	1
Education	11	1	46	9
Other	72	9	27	5
Total	821	101%	541	99%

Source: CCHR annual reports for 1966 and 1968.
* Percentages do not add to 100 because of rounding.

Even when complaint figures are deflated, however, the total in the housing area alone shows about a 50 per cent increase over the highest previous annual total, and this was especially significant in light of the declining trend of the Lowell years. In fact, the CCHR received so many complaints during 1966 that at times it had to remove most of its personnel from other duties on an emergency

[100] That is, the number of complaints went up because the criteria for what constituted a complaint were made less rigorous.

basis so that the volume of work could be accommodated. By 1968, with the commission emphasizing other matters, complaints had declined by about one-third. Except for employment, which dropped slightly, and education, which, reflecting the central race-related issue in the city in 1968, expanded to more than four times the 1966 figure, all areas of complaint dropped substantially.

The commission was not simply handling an increased workload. With its new enforcement orientation and new powers, significant legal breakthroughs in the handling of housing complaints were made and new "firsts" achieved in a number of individual cases. In a series of decisions, the New York Supreme Court approved the commission's use of its "posting power" (this is the power of the commission to post a notice on the door of an apartment to prevent it from being rented to a new tenant while a complaint of discrimination is before the agency), allowed it to continue its practice of awarding compensatory damages to victims of housing discrimination, and allowed to stand monetary penalties imposed by the agency upon landlords who had acted to obstruct the administration of the fair housing law.

Nevertheless, little was done by Booth to deal with the basic deficiencies of the case-by-case approach. Of all the complaints lodged during 1966, fewer than half (49 per cent) were adjusted at all. Only 19 per cent (154) were adjusted to the satisfaction of the commission (see Table 10). In 1968 the record was substantially better, with almost all the cases resulting in some action and about half adjusted to the commission's satisfaction. Most satisfactorily adjusted cases came in the housing area, the locus of most complaints. In 1966 the number in the area was 130, the same as for 1964. By 1968 it had risen by about one-third, to 196. As we have seen from our analysis of the 1961–1965 period, however, satisfactory adjustment hardly meant that some solution (such as an apartment or a job) for the problem of the individual complainant had been found.[101]

101 The failure of the commission to indicate its criteria in listing the adjustment of a case as "satisfactory," "administrative," or "no probable cause" makes analysis in this area difficult.

Despite the commission's more aggressive philosophy and new powers, proceeding through the administrative process was still an arduous task for a complainant. Only if the landlord could be broken down by the initial shock of confrontation with his crime at a quick conciliation meeting in the CCHR offices could the process work. If the landlord resisted, the process could take three months and leave the justified complainant with a small financial reward but without a place to live.[102] For intransigent realtors with large holdings and a lawyer on retainer, individual complaints were an inadequate regulatory device. Such operators, if inured to public opinion, might accept the small fines that the commission was empowered to impose (up to $500) as an operating expense, or even welcome them as the price of "good advertising" in the white community.

Table 10. Complaints adjusted by the CCHR, 1966 and 1968 (in numbers and per cent of all complaints filed)

Type of adjustment	1966		1968	
	No.	%	No.	%
Satisfactory	154	19	265	49
No probable cause	174	21	198	37
Administrative	79	9	74	13
Total complaints adjusted	407	49	537	99
Total complaints filed	821	100	541	100

Source: CCHR annual reports for 1966 and 1968.

Mitchell Wald, a young lawyer who succeeded Zimmerman as commission housing chief, came to the agency convinced of the inadequacies of the case method. He urged the chairman to have the commission initiate legal action against landlords who violated fair housing ordinances. Data would be developed for such cases by requiring by local law that racial and economic data on every rental transaction in the city be filed with the commission. Booth, though convinced of the necessity of the case approach (he thought

[102] *New York Times,* Feb. 9, 1969, section IV, p. 7, col. 1; "A Reporter at Large," *The New Yorker,* Sept. 24, 1966, pp. 188–220.

it "gave the small man a place to go and a feeling he had redress") was attracted by his aide's impulse to confront large realtors. This impulse was put into operation late in May 1968, when, for the first time in its history, the commission initiated a housing complaint on the ground of *de facto* discrimination.

In its brief the commission charged that the Metropolitan Life Insurance Company had engaged in "deliberate, intentional, and systematic" exclusion of blacks and Puerto Ricans from its Stuyvesant Town, Peter Cooper Village, and Parkchester housing developments. Minority applicants, the CCHR charged, were channeled by the company to its "black property," the Riverton Houses in Harlem. Consequently, few of them applied at the "white developments" because they believed that it would be "futile and embarrassing." [103]

The commission had chosen its first target well. Though the company denied the allegations, the publicity had its effect and Metropolitan Life entered into negotiations with the CCHR. Subsequently, an agreement was reached. The company agreed to end the practice of showing preference for incumbent tenants' relatives, to seek applicants for its other developments at Riverton, to consider black and Puerto Rican applicants concurrently with those already on waiting lists, to issue instructions on nondiscrimination to its project staffs, and to open its records for CCHR inspection. In the five months after this agreement was signed, 19 of 106 apartments in Parkchester, 19 of 106 in Stuyvesant Town, and 5 of 81 in Peter Cooper Village were rented to nonwhites. Furthermore, the same approach was used by the commission to open up the Glen Oaks, Fresh Meadows, and Phipps Gardens developments in Queens.[104] These agreements seemed to be a great victory for the CCHR, but they were the object of a considerable amount of criticism both from within and from outside the agency. In conversation, commission personnel pointed to them as examples of the "limits of what you can accomplish within government" rather

[103] *New York Times*, May 28, 1968, p. 7, col. 4, quoting Booth.
[104] CCHR and Metropolitan Life Insurance Company, concurrent press releases, July 18, 1968; CCHR, *Annual Report, 1968* (New York: The Commission, 1969), p. 7.

than as indications of the extent of what could be accomplished. External critics of the agency were less circumspect. Eileen Lee of the Urban League's Operation Open City called the Metropolitan Life agreement a "sellout" of the open housing program; two hundred apartments at Parkchester, she said, should have been reserved for immediate occupancy by black and Puerto Rican families.

Commission activities in the area of housing during the late 1960's illustrate the agency's increased advocate stance during this period, and in doing this further highlight its basic dilemma. As commission techniques changed, the context changed with them. What would have been viewed as extreme aggressiveness and a great settlement in 1963 (the Metropolitan Life agreement) was, by 1968, termed an amoral compromise by pressure-group leaders. Regardless of the degree of its advocacy, the CCHR remained a city agency. Though the limits of advocacy expanded as the political context changed, there remained limits. The fact of the agency's conflicting roles within city government could be ignored or, for a time, forgotten, but it remained an underlying reality.

Tension Control

As riots by blacks in ghetto areas became a continuing threat in New York, riot prevention was transformed from the relatively minor task of dealing with infrequent incidents as they arose to a full-time, top-priority job that often commanded the attention of the mayor himself. When circumstances caused this change in focus, it apparently never occurred to the administration to leave tension control in the hands of the CCHR. After all, the role of the agency was to advocate minority positions, and thus it could hardly be expected to act to control the actions of minorities. Besides, the commission had previously been ineffective in this area, and the problem was now too important to leave to the CCHR.[105]

The commission's Human Rights Nights program, conceived by chairman Booth, was a forerunner to the city's ultimate solution to

[105] Interview with an assistant to the mayor, who wished to remain anonymous.

the tension-control problem, but the program was administered through a new agency, the Mayor's Urban Action Task Force, headed by Barry Gottehrer, an assistant to the mayor. Commissioner Booth was included as one of the fifty-five high-level city leaders on the task force, but there was no institutional participation by the CCHR.

As an institution, the task force was able to achieve, in a short period, what the CCHR in ten years of tension control had been unable to accomplish. It managed to establish a close working relationship with the Police Department and an information network that let it know quickly and accurately of potentially explosive situations. Neighborhood offices, staffed by paid neighborhood personnel, provided the local touch points for this network; to these, and to Gottehrer, information flowed from everyone from police captains to neighborhood leaders. The commission had been talking about this kind of network for several years but had never been able to put it into operation.[106] Again, as in the case of contract compliance, the growing importance of an issue for the city administration led to the removal of the responsibility for that substantive area from the CCHR.

Booth Loses His Job

By the end of 1968, chairman Booth's three-year term had expired and the matter of his reappointment became a focus for the enmity of the CCHR's estranged Jewish constituency. The chairman had been under scattered attack by Jewish leaders and union officials during the fall of that year, and these attacks had even occasionally necessitated the mayor's public expressions of support, but on the whole these did not cause Booth much concern. The problem reached a new degree of seriousness, however, when he was condemned by the New York Board of Rabbis for "a singular insensitivity to anti-Semitic incidents." [107]

Though not universally supported by Jewish leaders, this condemnation was reinforced by findings, at about the same time, of "appalling signs of racial bigotry" by the special commission ap-

106 Nicholas Pileggi, "Barry Gottehrer's Job Is to Cool It," *New York Times Magazine*, Sept. 22, 1968, p. 28.
107 *New York Times*, Jan. 30, 1969, p. 41, col. 2.

The Commission on Human Rights, 1966–1969   237

pointed by the mayor to investigate racial tensions in the city.[108] By
recommending that a long-term inquiry into racial, religious, and
ethnic conflicts be made by a permanent conference of representatives that was to be drawn from private religious, human rights,
and civil rights agencies, and by calling for a permanent committee
to continue its work, the Botein commission was implying a criticism of the CCHR. Though the mayor had taken the tension-
control function from the commission, parts of its constituency still
expected the agency to perform it. In the opinion of the *New York
Times:* "The Mayor's special study group, headed by former justice
Bernard Botein, stopped just short of a flat accusation that the
Human Rights Commission has not been functioning properly—
not maintaining communication among various New York groups,
not investigating vigorously enough the circulation of hate literature
and the sharp upsweep in incidents of racial vandalism. By suggesting strongly the need for a separate committee to perform
these functions, the Botein group indicted the rights commission.[109]

Finally the mayor, under increased pressure to repair his political
position with the Jewish community in anticipation of an election
year, decided, in the words of one of his aides, "that [Booth] could
no longer function effectively in the job. . . . He . . . had to
spend all his time defending himself against charges of racism, and
we had to spend all of our time defending him." [110] With "mixed
pleasure and considerable reluctance" Lindsay offered Booth a
judgeship.

Protest from black organizations was relatively minimal, perhaps because the mayor and the chairman treated the convergence
of pressure from Jewish groups and the judgeship appointment as
coincidental; the judgeships, they said, had been in the works for
several months. In fact, the job had been offered to Booth several
months before, but he had turned it down. His feelings came out
to some extent at the press conference called to introduce Simeon

108 *Ibid.,* Jan. 17, 1969, p. 1, col. 3.

109 *Ibid.,* Feb. 5, 1969, p. 44, col. 2 (editorial).

110 Interview with Barry Gottehrer. Mr. Gottehrer stressed that, though
he personally did not believe the allegations made by union leaders, many
people did and this made Booth's position tenuous.

Golar, his successor as chairman. "The ambition of any lawyer is to become a judge," Booth said, but upon being questioned further he noted that "a person is never happy to leave the job he loves." [111] The chairman's last official act was the circulation of a press release in which he attempted to demonstrate the continuous CCHR concern for its Jewish constituency during his term of office.[112]

Thus, just as chairman Alfred Marrow was largely the victim of black displeasure with his performance on the CCHR, William Booth was the victim of Jewish displeasure. Booth had succeeded in altering the agency's operating philosophy and its conception of its role in city government (if not the role itself), and in doing this had altered the CCHR's constituency relationships, but Jewish expectations of the commission were not changed by his actions. Rather, Jewish groups chose to look at this term as an aberration and hoped that under a new leader the commission would be, once again, responsive to their needs.

During the late 1960's, the City Commission on Human Rights adopted a more aggressive advocate stance, in its rhetoric and its actions, than ever before in its history. This type of behavior was most useful, during this period, for the protection of the interests of the city administration. Nevertheless, though "advocacy" was freer than ever before, it remained limited by the political priorities of the mayor and by the needs of the commission's diverse constituency.

Substantively, the CCHR's new militancy changed only marginally its effectiveness in major policy areas. Success was still limited by the agency's lack of resources, by its attempts to act in too many areas, and by inadequate organization for the proper use of the resources that were available. The aura of inadequacy at the commission, fostered by this lack of success and lack of recognition by other city departments, led to the removal from its aegis of policy areas that it had traditionally handled as these became important to major political actors in the city.

[111] *New York Times,* Feb. 5, 1969, p. 28, col. 1, and interview with Gottehrer.
[112] CCHR press release, Feb. 4, 1969.

7

An Appraisal

The foregoing analysis illustrates that the New York City Commission on Human Rights is an anachronism. It is an agency established in the 1940's and reaffirmed in the 1950's to deal with minority problems through discussion and the promotion of good will, and it cannot cope with the heightened racial tensions that are endemic to contemporary New York. Though its leadership and philosophy have changed since its early days, it remains structurally ill suited to deal with its divided constituency and to administer the substantive programs that have been superimposed over the responsibilities originally given it. This inability feeds upon itself and gives the commission a reputation for incompetence throughout the political and administrative structure of the city. In turn, this reputation further hampers the agency's effectiveness.

From the mayor's perspective, though the CCHR was once a useful tool for building a reputation in the area of civil rights, it has recently been more of a liability than an asset. In every administration examined in this study since the statutory establishment of the agency, a major embarrassment to the mayor either has emerged from the commission or has been avoided only through emergency mayoral action. Under these circumstances, it is not the agency's substantive achievements that have kept it alive (these have been shown to be minimal), but rather the conviction of successive administrations that a redistribution of the commission's functions, however justifiable in management terms, would be misinterpreted as an "illiberal act" and carry with it high political costs. The commission, in short, has been retained because it is believed to be a symbol of the city's commitment to equal rights for all its citizens.

239

The question that remains, however, is: "Is the CCHR in fact such a symbol to New York's minority populations?" It may well be that to the groups the commission has sought to serve it has become a symbol of failure, the failure of the administrative process to work for them in the areas of housing, employment, and educational equality.

The usefulness of a human rights commission for furthering the interests of minorities in the city is inversely related to the centrality of racial issues and the emphasis given them by major political actors. Cities may be viewed as passing through stages of development in their responsiveness to these issues. In early stages commissions are useful for giving such issues legitimacy and providing minorities with some access to the political process. In later stages, however, when the question of race becomes central to almost every decision in the city, such agencies are eclipsed. It may well be that New York has now reached this point in its political development.

Philosophy and Goals

Between the official founding of the Unity Committee in 1943 and the early 1960's, the philosophy and goals of official human rights agencies operating within the city government remained relatively constant. There was a basic belief that the prejudices against racial, religious, and ethnic minorities could be overcome through conciliation, compromise, and an educative approach. This outlook was partly the product of the hesitancy of the mayor and the city council to give the human rights agency powers beyond those that made this approach a practical necessity; but it was more than that, as is evidenced by the fact that the conciliatory philosophy survived even as the formal powers of the agency were augmented. In fact, this philosophy had great staying power because it was the one, during this period, that was most compatible with the role of the human rights agency within the city's political system: the protection of the mayor.

The conciliatory approach was eventually undermined by changes in the national civil rights struggle, changes that were reflected in black political demands within the city. The early 1960's were a period of transition. Stanley Lowell began his chairmanship as an advocate of conciliatory techniques but three years later found himself calling for changes in the city's fair housing law to allow more rigorous enforcement, asking for "preferential treatment" for minority-group job applicants, and taking on the city's politically powerful labor unions on questions of employment discrimination.

During the late 1960's the agency's role as advocate of minority interests in the city was emphasized, and there was a conscious effort away from conciliation and toward a policy of law enforcement. Discriminators were viewed, not as innocents who had wandered from the path of righteousness and could easily be convinced to return, but as violators of the law who would be made to pay to the full extent for their actions. This more militant stand by the agency reflected the growing militance of minorities in the society at large and was facilitated by the continual strengthening of the laws that the commission was mandated to enforce.

Throughout the period of this study the constant goal of the commission was the creation of an integrated society in the city. Only during the late 1960's in some policy areas, notably in education, did the CCHR begin to question this goal.

Leadership

The nature of the leadership of New York's official human rights agencies over the period of this study offers some insights into those agencies as entrée points for minority-group members into the administrative structure of the city. At the same time, changes in leadership characteristics serve as indicators of changes in the civil rights movement in the city, and thus of the milieu in which each agency functioned (Table 11).

During the very early years of the Unity Committee, neither the chairmanship nor the executive director's post was held by a minority-group member. When Edith Alexander finally captured the chief administrative post in that organization she seemingly

Table 11. Trends in commission leadership

Period	Years	Organization	Chairman		Executive director	
			Name	Racial or ethnic group	Name	Racial or ethnic group
Conciliatory 1943–1960	1943–1947	Unity Committee	Hughes	WASP	Dodson	WASP
	1948–1949	Unity Committee	Roosevelt	WASP	Stewart	Jewish
	1949	Unity Committee	Lazansky (acting)	Jewish	Alexander	Black
	1949–1955	Unity Committee	Wallander	WASP	Alexander	Black
	1956–1956	COIR	Swope	WASP	Horne	Black
	1956–1960	COIR	Marrow	Jewish	Horne	Black
Transitional 1961–1966	1961–1965	CCHR	Lowell	Jewish	Jones	Black
	1965–1966	CCHR	Brown	Black	None	
Enforcement 1966–1973	1966–1969	CCHR	Booth	Black	Rivera	Black
	1969–1970	CCHR	Golar	Black	David	?
	1970–1973	CCHR	Norton	Black	David	?

defined it as a "black job," for all subsequent executive directors of successor agencies were black.

Until the Wagner administration, the chairmanship of the city's minority-oriented commissions remained in the hands of "ethnic neutrals," and Wagner's first appointment continued this trend. The next two chairmen (spanning nine years of the commission's history) appointed by Wagner, however, were Jewish, reflecting the dominance of the organized constituency of the CCHR by Jewish organizations and Jewish leadership in the civil rights movement in the city during this period. No black was appointed to the chairmanship until the last days of 1965, when this became a full-time, salaried post. Since then, all chairmen have been black. It might be said that the city human rights agency was led by "non-minority" chairmen during the period when conciliation was the dominant philosophy, by Jewish chairmen during the transitional period, and by black chairmen during the "enforcement period." Though hardly proof of any causal relationship, this progression is a rough indicator of the changing nature of the civil rights struggle in New York. Furthermore, as we have seen in previous chapters, leadership predilections have had a considerable impact upon the approach (if not the goals) of the official human rights agency in the city.

Organization

The two predominant trends that emerge from a comparative analysis of decision making in the human rights agency over time are the progressive minimization of the role of the voluntary commissioners, and the inability of the leadership of the commission to find a viable organizational structure for itself.

The Commissioners

On the Unity Committee the voluntary commission was the locus of agency decision making. Though the executive director participated in Unity Committee meetings, policy decisions were made by the committee, as we saw with the statement on segregation. With the creation of the COIR, policy-making responsibilities were again vested in the commission, but because the commissioners were willing to devote different amounts of time, resources and interest to their work, control eventually tended to devolve to the chairman. The chairman depended upon the commission to legitimize his actions, but not to guide them. In the early 1960's the trend to minimize the policy-making role of the voluntary commissioners was paralleled by an attempt to remove them from involvement in the day-to-day functioning of the agency.

This process reached its culmination with the events following the creation of the paid chairmanship in 1965. The chairman's prime organizational reference point became the staff rather than the commissioners. Attempts to minimize contacts between commissioners and staff increased. The chairman made the effective decisions for the agency and presented the commission with *faits accomplis;* the involvement of commissioners in the work of the agency (such as on subcommittees) diminished and may have atrophied entirely if agency attempts to amend the requirement that they preside over hearings had succeeded in the city council.

The committee structure was chosen by Mayor La Guardia for the Unity Committee at a time when it was believed that many of the tensions that existed between different groups in the city could be dispelled simply by creating a forum in which the problems could be discussed by the leadership of those groups. In addition, of course, La Guardia's committee was a device for political recognition and was envisioned as an organization that would engage, on the staff level, almost entirely in research. This type of structure was perpetuated in the Commission on Intergroup Relations because of the desires of the civil rights groups in the city that championed the creation of the agency, and because Mayor Wagner, like La Guardia, realized that such an agency must provide the means for recognition of the many racial and ethnic groups in New York. Wagner made the commission a representative body and maintained it as such. Only with the advent of the Lindsay administration was the concept of representativeness challenged, and because of Wagner's last-minute appointments, the new mayor could do little to effect any change of this type during his first term.

The voluntary representative commission was not originally designed for administrative decision making. It was designed as a research organization, perpetuated for political reasons and involved in the process of administering laws through a sequential series of *ad hoc* steps over time. In fact, other research suggests that representative committees are not effective devices for decision making [1] and that many preconditions must exist before committee decision making can be effective. Two of these seem to be the agreement of committee members to some overriding goal and the development within the committee of strong behavioral norms with which members can identify. [2]

Given these factors, it is not surprising that the preponderance of decision-making power passed into the hands of the chairman. This may well have been the case if the chairman had not been strengthened by being made the chief administrative officer of the agency. Nevertheless, the continued existence of the voluntary commissioners tends to obscure the real locus of power at the agency, to make the allocation of responsibility for its actions more difficult, and to help create a series of false expectations of it.

Agency Structure

Between 1955 and 1970 the commission was completely reorganized three times and other major overhauls were planned or recommended but never carried out. Much energy was spent in puzzling over the deficiencies of operating structures or in designing alternatives that the agency hoped would finally do the job.

This constancy of structural change offers a clue to one of the agency's major difficulties. Though there are some constants on the commission's discarded organization charts (legislatively mandated functions must be caried out), the generally vague mandate

[1] Richard Fenno, *The President's Cabinet* (Cambridge: Harvard University Press, 1959). See also Governor's Committee to Review New York Laws and Procedures in the Area of Human Rights, *Report to the Governor* (Albany: The Committee, 1968), p. 13.

[2] See James D. Barber, *Power in Committees* (Chicago: Rand-McNally, 1966), and Robert L. Peabody and Nelson W. Polsby, *New Perspectives on the House of Representatives* (Chicago: Rand-McNally, 1963).

of the agency leaves it in the position of "always looking for something to do." This lack of a firm function makes the commission the dilettante of government, investigating employment discrimination here, getting involved in education there, and finding *causes célèbres* everywhere. Dilettantism in turn results in constant reorganization to meet the imperatives of the moment (the creation of the division for Puerto Rican and Hispanic affairs is a case in point).

Continuous organizational change is also symptomatic of the CCHR's tendency to attempt to do too much. Lacking one firm goal, the agency tries to solve all the minority problems of the city at once. The result is the proliferation of administrative subunits and the concomitant dissipation of limited resources ineffectually in many different directions.

Constituency

Until 1965, the constituency of the CCHR and its antecedent organizations remained divided but relatively stable. At the organized level, most consistent support was gained from citywide Jewish civil rights groups. These groups had provided manpower for the early Unity Committee, had fought for the creation of the commission, and were closely cemented to it through commissioner appointments. At the individual level, the commission mainly served middle-class blacks in the city. Such people constituted most of the complainants in cases of housing discrimination, and in the areas of education and employment the agency, when not restrained by other considerations, championed positions that served their needs.

Tensions between these two elements of the CCHR's constituency occasionally came to the surface, but before 1966, with the exception of the Marrow-Horne case, they were manageable by the agency's leadership. After that year, however, the convergence of several factors served to upset this delicate balance.

First, issues emerged in the city at large, especially in the school system, which pitted the Jewish middle class against the increasingly militant black minority. The Jewish agencies, the members of which had generally supported activities in the area of civil rights in the city, now found their individual constituents increasingly at odds with the individuals served by the commission. Second, at the same time that this polarization was occurring, the leadership of the commission came into the hands of William Booth, the first effective black chairman, who envisioned a more forceful advocate's role for the agency. Third, within the CCHR the new chairman felt himself constrained by the commission structure and acted to minimize its importance. But by now this structure was the traditional locus of activity in the agency for the Jewish groups, and they believed that actions to minimize its role were indirectly aimed at them. One final factor further complicates the picture. As time passed, chairman Booth increasingly came to symbolize in his own person the black position in the city. As this happened, leaders of Jewish groups, besides perceiving Booth as "ambitious" and "opportunistic," became convinced that his agency was "all black" and that they could not work with it.

The developments of 1966 and 1967 did not totally remove Jewish groups from the constituency of the agency, however, but simply made them a latent factor. Late in 1968, with an election in the offing, these groups were able to help effect a change in its leadership, just as had black groups in 1960. In each case, the groups involved were not the sole cause of the change, but they did help to convince the mayor that some action was politically necessary.

To replace Booth, Lindsay appointed Simeon Golar, a black with strong ties to Jewish leadership in the city through his Liberal party affiliation. Golar's was a year-long caretaker administration, and after the 1969 election he returned to the chairmanship of the city Housing Authority. As chairman of the commission, Golar tried to re-establish its ties to its Jewish constituency. He gave visibility to alleged cases of discrimination against Jews, said he was "personally saddened" by black-Jewish differences, and generally muted the agency's advocate role in most policy areas. Golar's successor, Eleanor Holmes Norton, has also been sensitive to her agency's bifurcated constituency. She has been more ready than was Golar to have the CCHR adopt positions of advocacy in major policy areas (especially education and employment) but has often channeled advocacy into support for the newly emergent cause of women's rights, one that has not divided the agency's constituency along racal lines. Though recent chairmen have thus been sensitive to the CCHR's constituency problems, the underlying cause for these problems remains, and events in the city to which the commission might be required to react can bring differences to the surface at any time. The situation is a highly unstable one.[3]

Intragovernmental Relations

Within the city government, the CCHR and its antecedent organizations were unable to establish close and lasting relationships with the major operating agencies. The Unity Committee, in the late 1940's and early 1950's functioned not as a peer of these agencies but as a subordinate device, sometimes called upon for minor services.

Later, when the COIR was established, commitments from other agencies were more rhetorical than real. Occasionally, as in the case of the Board of Education in the early 1960's, the commission was able to act as a mediator between city departments and the black minority, but more often these departments were reluctant to cooperate with the CCHR or even to supply it with information when directed to do so by the mayor. During the late 1960's, as minority problems increased in intensity and as the commission assumed an active role as minority advocate within the city government, the public contacts between its leadership and that of other agencies increased in frequency and cordiality, but cooperation at the staff level remained minimal.

The difficulties that the commission faced in gaining cooperation from the operating agencies of the city government can be traced to the nature of its relationship with the mayor. One available indicator of the strength of this relationship is the amount of city

[3] *New York Times,* Feb. 12, 1970, p. 29, col. 5; April 25, p. 40, col. 5; Sept. 24, p. 93, col. 4.

resources that the mayor was willing to allocate to the commission and the rate at which he was willing to increase these resources as the problems with which the agency was supposed to deal became more important. A comparison of the rate of change of the commission budget and the rate of change of the city expense budget (Table 12) makes it apparent that, though concern for race relations problems grew tremendously in the city between 1960 and 1973, few of the resources that the city committed to deal with these problems went to the commission. In fact, the rate of increase of the commission budget exceeded that of the city budget only twice during this period, and in three years there was an absolute decline in the money available to the agency.

Table 12. Rate of growth of the commission budget compared to rate of growth of the city expense budget, 1955–1974

Year	City exp. budget (in millions of dollars)	% change	Commission budget (in thousands of dollars)	% change
1955–56	1,736			
1956–57	1,854	+6.6	120	
1957–58	1,934	+4.3	153	+25.6
1958–59	1,992	+3.0	200	+30.8
1959–60	2,175	+9.2	371	+85.5
1960–61	2,345	+7.9	483	+30.2
1961–62	2,542	+8.4	476	−1.4
1962–63	2,785	+9.5	514	+8.0
1963–64	3,093	+11.0	578	+12.3
1964–65	3,351	+7.7	566	−2.1
1965–66	3,876	+15.7	629	+11.1
1966–67	4,615	+15.0	716	+13.8
1967–68	5,178	+12.2	814	+13.7
1968–69	6,003	+15.9	935	+14.9
1969–70	6,723	+12.0	971	+3.9
1970–71	7,800	+16.0	1,094	+12.7
1971–72	8,659	+11.0	1,192	+9.0
1972–73	9,561	+10.4	1,132	−5.0
1973–74 (est.)	10,160	+6.3	1,250	+10.4

Source: New York City Expense Budgets, 1955–1974.

Within the city government the CCHR and its predecessor agencies functioned as apologists for the mayor, protecting him from the adverse effects of racial issues. Under La Guardia, O'Dwyer, and Impellitteri, this role meant that the racial nature of issues would be minimized whenever possible, and that problems, when they arose, would be settled quietly, behind the scenes. During the Wagner administration, the mayor found it useful to allow the commission some advocacy of minority positions within the government and, in the early 1960's, outside the government as well. Under Mayor Lindsay, the commission as advocate was given still broader freedom.

Although in each succeeding administration the city human rights agency was able more easily to adopt an advocate stance on public issues, the crucial point is that in all cases this advocacy was limited by the mayor's perception of what was functional for him. The power of ultimate solution of the agency's advocate-apologist dilemma was not in its hands.

Peabody and Rourke point out that some bureaucracies have been able to liberate themselves from executive dominance by cultivating independent ties with the legislature. A relatively minor agency in size, and not one that provided direct services to the white middle class (the effective constituents of most city councilmen), the CCHR was never able to do this. Here again the commission's divided and changing constituency was a liability: "[A] necessary part of any agency's strategy in securing legislative support is the task of winning a sufficient degree of public esteem to impress the legislature with the political risk involved in refusing the agency's requests for financial and other resources. In short, it has been held that administrators, like politicians, have to nurse their constituency to more than survive." [4]

For the mayor, commission needs were rarely matters of the first priority. Its demands for funds had to be balanced against the

[4] Robert L. Peabody and Francis E. Rourke, "Public Bureaucracy," in James G. March, ed., *Handbook of Organizations* (Chicago: Rand-McNally, 1965), p. 824.

needs of other agencies and its requests for support weighed against the effects of this support upon mayoral relationships with other city departments. In this constant process of balancing costs and gains the commission was at a disadvantage, for it only came to the mayor's attention when it was causing a problem (by upsetting the status quo), failing to do its job (when a racial incident occurred), or having internal difficulties.

In its daily operations the agency produced little basis for a close relationship with the mayor, or little reason for him, if he did happen to inquire into its operations, to trust its competence. Thus, in 1965 under Wagner, communication between the mayor and the human rights commission was minimal. Under Lindsay, the commission did receive relatively equitable financial treatment, and its chairmen were major administration figures. Mrs. Norton, the most recent chairman, has in addition been a highly-placed mayoral aide. Though Lindsay's relationship with Booth and later with Norton may have helped the CCHR on budgetary matters, the mayor's ties to the commission chairmen did not indicate a commitment to the agency but rather to the individuals involved. During the Lindsay years the commission was a platform for prominent black leaders within the administration, but as an institution it actually lost responsibility for major functions such as contract compliance and tension control.

Intergovernmental Relations

The relationship between the CCHR and organizations doing similar work at other levels of government has never been more than minimal. With federal agencies contacts have been limited to the administration of a few research grants and agreements to exchange information if such an exchange is ever necessary. With the state, agreements have been reached on jurisdictional questions, but real cooperative efforts have not been made in any policy areas. Interagency rivalry rather than cooperation between the state and the city has been the norm.

The result of this has been the development in New York City of two parallel bureaucracies acting in the same areas. In 1968 the state agency processed more complaints and probably spent more money in the city than did the CCHR. It maintained a main office and five branch offices within the city limits, two of the later in Manhattan and three in the outlying boroughs.[5] Between 1963 and 1968 the state commission received more complaints than did the city agency in all but one year, though, as is evident from Tables 13 and 14, its complaints were concentrated in a different issue area than were those received by the CCHR.

Table 13. Number of complaints received in New York City by city and state human rights agencies, 1963–1968

Year	NYC	State (in NYC only)
1963	207	605
1964	269	579
1965	264	n.d.
1966	821	603
1967	n.d.	707
1968	541	782

Source: Annual reports of the CCHR and the State Division of Human Rights, 1963–1968.

Though these parallel efforts may have been justified at one time because of the different degrees of power that each of these agencies had to act in alternative policy areas, by late in the 1960's these jurisdictional and procedural differences had largely been eliminated. Both agencies were doing the same things in the city, and statistical indices indicate that the state commission was doing a more extensive job, if only because its resources were greater (see Table 15). In serving the middle-class black and Puerto Rican communities, the CCHR was only duplicating the efforts of the state agency.

[5] State Division of Human Rights, *Annual Report, 1968* (Albany: The Division, 1969), p. 2.

Table 14. Comparison of types of complaints received
in New York City by city and state human rights
agencies, 1966

	City	State
Housing	405	172
Employment	163	404
Public accommodations	82	19
City agencies	98	—
Education	11	8
Other	42	—
Total	821	603

Source: 1966 annual reports of the CCHR and the State
Division of Human Rights. This is the last year for which
complete comparative data are available. It is not, however,
a typical year because it overemphasizes the extent of the
city effort. This was a peak year for the city agency and the
only one during the period of this study for which its total
exceeded that of the state.

Table 15. Comparison of resources and complaints received by the
New York City and New York State human rights agencies, 1968

	City	State
Nonwhite population	1,374,903	1,834,026
Budget	$935,000.00	$2,980,000.00
Expenditure per nonwhite resident	$0.68	$1.62
Complaints		
Total	541	2,019
In New York City	541	782
Expenditure per complaint	$1,055.00	$1,480.00

Sources: Population: New York State Office of the Budget, *Statistical
Yearbook, 1968–1969* (New York: Office of the Budget, 1969), p. 16. The
reported statistics are estimates of the State Division of Human Rights for
1967. Budget: New York City Expense Budget for fiscal year 1968–69,
Budget of the State of New York for fiscal year 1968–69. Complaints:
CCHR, *Annual Report, 1968,* p. 20; State Division of Human Rights, *Annual Report,* 1968, p. 2.

Has the CCHR a Future?

The establishment and strengthening of local human rights commissions has been encouraged by the federal government, the state government, influential private law-making groups, and legal experts in the field of civil rights. Both the 1964 and 1968 national civil rights laws include a clause which requires that the federal agencies in charge of administering this legislation defer to state and local agencies, where they exist, in processing individual complaints of discrimination in employment and housing.[6] This perforce encourages the creation of commissions on the local level, if only to keep the national government from entering the scene and upsetting the local status quo between the races.

In New York, furthermore, the state government encourages the creation of local human rights commissions through its Division of Human Rights. State legislation authorizing the establishment of the commissions was passed in 1965, and the division distributes a model statute outlining the powers and duties of these organizations for localities that wish to act upon this authorization. As a result, sixty-two commissions have been established, some with rather extensive powers, budget, and staff, and others without the wherewithal to answer their mail.[7]

New York's practice has been in accord with the recommendations of the National Conference of Commissioners on Uniform State Laws, and especially its committee on the Model AntiDiscrimination Act chaired by Norman Dorsen, professor of law at New York University. The model statute recommended by the committee encourages the establishment of local commissions that would "exercise some but not all the powers of the state commission." [8]

The rationale for encouraging the establishment of local commissions finds its roots in the presumed familiarity of local officials with local conditions and in the need to develop indigenous civil

[6] 42 *U.S. Code* §2000C-5(b) and 3609(c)(d).

[7] Correspondence by the author with all the agencies in the state produced a return of less than 50 per cent.

[8] Norman Dorsen, "The Model Anti-Discrimination Act," 4 *Harvard Journal of Legislation* 275–278 (1966).

rights leadership in local areas. The case is summed up by Joseph Witherspoon:

> Continued proliferation of the effects of discrimination must be halted by the enactment of laws prohibiting discrimination and by the effective enforcement of these laws by an official government agency equipped to receive and fairly dispose of complaints of racial discrimination. The most important functions of this agency are to allow the tensions that build up within the minority group to be vented and to force the majority group to confront the civil rights problem it has produced. . . . The above functions can best be performed by local rather than state or federal agencies. Local agencies are likely to be conversant with local problems and to be more influential with the leadership of the majority group.[9]

According to Professor Witherspoon, local commissions would serve nine basic functions in the area in which they are established. They would resolve intergroup conflict; control activities which unreasonably obstruct members of minority groups; process complaints against the police; cooperate with the police, the board of education, and other city departments; study local human rights problems and recommend resolution of them; provide services to minority groups and coordinate the efforts of private groups (in cooperation with public and private agencies); develop local leadership and training programs; enlist the services of talented leaders throughout the community; and direct attention toward civil rights problems.[10]

Though little has been written about local human rights commissions, these recommendations were not devised in a vacuum, for the legal fraternity had for years debated the merits of state fair employment practices commissions.[11] The consensus among these

[9] Joseph P. Witherspoon, "Civil Rights Policy in the Federal System: Proposals for a Better Use of the Administrative Process," 74 *Yale Law Journal* 1176–77 (1965).

[10] *Ibid.*, p. 1204.

[11] See, for example: Anon., "California FEPC: A Stepchild," 18 *Stanford Law Review* 187 (1965); R. B. Dyson and E. B. Dyson. "Commission Enforcement of State Laws against Discrimination: A Comparative Analysis of the Kansas Act," 14 *Kansas Law Review* 29 (1965); A. E. Bonfield, "Institutional Analysis of Agencies Administering Fair Employment Prac-

observers was that, though these organizations had not been very successful in eliminating discrimination, with augmented powers and more adequate funding and staffing they could do the job. The problem was not with the organizations themselves, but with the scope of their powers and resources.[12]

The conclusions of this study differ from those of the law reviews. Their analysis focused upon the formal powers of human rights agencies and holds out hope for future achievement; the present analysis focuses upon the political role and substantive achievement of one such agency over time, and reveals inherent limitations.

The New York City Commission on Human Rights is the most powerful local agency of this kind in the nation. It is one of the two urban human rights agencies with a paid chairman, has the largest staff, may initiate investigations, and has subpoena power. In 1968 its budget ranked fourth in size among all state and local human rights agencies in the United States (exceeded only by three state agencies).[13] Yet during the past twenty-five years it has performed well few of the functions outlined for such an agency by Professor Witherspoon. It has not been able to resolve intergroup conflict. It has not been able to work closely with other city agencies or with private groups in a sustained fashion. It has not substantially affected the patterns of discriminatory conduct in the city at large. In fact, the chief function of the agency has been to act as apologist for the mayor and occasionally for other major political actors in the city, and not as advocate of minority positions. Permission to play the latter role has been contingent upon the effectiveness of the former.

Acting within the constraints of this political reality, the CCHR has achieved relatively little in substantive policy areas. Individual housing complaints are processed, but the overriding pattern of

tices Laws," Parts I and II, 42 *New York University Law Review* 823, 1035 (1967); Anon., "Discrimination in Employment and Housing," 82 *Harvard Law Review* 834 (1969).

[12] More recently critics have attacked the administrative agencies for not using the powers they do have effectively.

[13] "Note: Municipal Fair Employment Practices Ordinances: A Legal Survey and Model Ordinance," 45 *Notre Dame Lawyer* 258 (1969).

discrimination in housing in the city remains. Employment discrimination is attacked, and progress is made, but discrimination remains the norm, not the exception. Certainly, the commission did not help the city avoid the racial discord arising out of the 1968 school disputes, nor did it enable New York to fare better than cities without commissions in coping with the rioting that swept the nation in the mid-1960's. Preliminary research on cities in the United States with 10,000 or more blacks shows a statistically significant correlation between those that had human rights commissions and those that suffered at least one major racial incident. The existence of a commission in a city in the early 1960's was thus a good indicator that the city was ripe for a riot, and New York was no exception.

What the CCHR does do can probably be done better by other city agencies or, alternatively, by the State Division of Human Rights. Housing complaints could be handled just as efficiently by an augmented staff of the human relations section of the city Housing and Development Administration or by the Mayor's Complaint Bureau, and are now being concurrently dealt with by the state human rights agency. Other complaints can similarly be received by the proper subunit of the city agency involved (i.e., employment complaints by a division of the Human Resources Administration) if city officials do not wish to leave sole responsibility to the state. Broad investigations could be undertaken by a civil rights division of the corporation counsel's office, an agency which commands considerably more respect, within and outside the government, than does the CCHR.

If the city commission's substantive activities could better be performed elsewhere, it is also true that the agency is no longer needed as an advocate of minority positions within city government, or as a conduit for blacks into the administration. Unlike the situation in 1943 or even 1955, presently questions of minority policy are central in the New York City political process and daily command the attention of the mayor himself. Blacks and Puerto Ricans hold high administrative posts in almost every city department and in the mayor's office, and through them minority views on substantive policy matters are made known and advocacy occurs much closer to the seat of power than it could through the CCHR. In addition, minority-group leaders within the city have sharpened their skills in pressure-group politics, and, unrestrained by political ties to the administration, can be more vociferous in their advocacy than can the commission.

Thus the CCHR performs few substantive chores that cannot be done elsewhere and is no longer needed for an advocate role in the city's political process. But the problems with the commission go further, for it continues to exist as a vestigial organ in the city's body politic, serving no purpose but remaining always a potential source of trouble.

As we have seen, the commission has a constant impulse to advocacy; though this impulse can be controlled by the mayor, it is always a potential source of trouble and embarrassment for him. Beyond this, the existence of something called a "Human Rights Agency" creates a latent series of expectations within the Jewish population in the city, a group that the agency does not normally serve in its everyday work. In this work the agency tends to identify itself with the interests of the black and, to a lesser degree, the Puerto Rican minorities in the city, and this identification makes it unwilling (or unable) to cope with the needs of its latent constituency when they come to the fore. This may be especially true when the needs or positions of the several constituencies conflict.

Certainly it is more politic for the mayor to create an occasional *ad hoc* group to deal with the manifestations of prejudice that emerge from the racial and ethnic political clashes in the city than to have to deal intermittently with these problems through a permanent agency that perforce identifies with certain minorities because, for the overwhelming majority of the time, it serves them. Certainly it is politic for black, Puerto Rican, and other groups in the city that have lost confidence in the commission to acquiesce in the elimination of an agency that has promised so much and achieved so little, especially if an ancillary result is the strengthening of the administration of civil rights legislation that has already been enacted.

In short, the New York City Commission on Human Rights continues to exist because it has existed, and because of the notion that to abolish it would be "bad politics." Abolition, it is said, is a good idea but would appear to be a step backward. In fact, a consensus has been growing since the mid-1960's among minority-group leaders and former commissioners and staff members that the CCHR was an "agency of the 1950's," has "outlived its usefulness," and "ought to be abolished." [14] If done properly, political protest against abolition could be minimized, especially if replacing the commission with other administrative devices is stressed.

At one time, the City Commission on Human Rights performed some positive functions for New York. It helped blacks gain access to the political process, helped define minority affairs as a legitimate area for government concern, and initiated action against discrimination in housing and employment when these were not central issues in city affairs. Now that blacks have reached the uppermost posts in many city departments and the minority-group variable has become central to almost every mayoral decision, the commission has been eclipsed. Moreover, there is nothing that the CCHR does that cannot be done elsewhere in the city or state government, and perhaps better elsewhere, since the commission acting in the present suffers from its past history of lack of achievement.

Politically, the agency is more of a liability than an asset for the mayor and the major political actors in the civil rights arena that has been described during the course of this study. It is the major conclusion of this study that the agency ought to be abolished and its remaining functions redistributed, and that this can be done.

[14] Interviews with Stanley Lowell, Earl Brown, Eugene Callender, and others. See also the opinion of interviewees in Henry J. Stern, "Freedom When?: A Report on the City Commission on Human Rights Prepared for the Task Force on Economic Development of New York City," typescript, 1965 (on file in the mayor's office).

Bibliography

Unpublished Materials

American Jewish Committee, Jacob and Hilda Blaustein Memorial Library, New York City.

American Jewish Congress, Files, New York City.

Anti-Defamation League of B'nai B'rith, Files of Morris Sass, New York City.

Municipal Archives, New York City.

Municipal Reference Library, New York City.

New York State Division of Human Rights, Library, New York City.

Published Materials

Abrams, Charles. *Forbidden Neighbors.* New York: Harper, 1955.

——. "Segregation, Housing, and the Horne Case." *The Reporter,* 13 (Oct. 6, 1955), 30–33.

Allen, James E. *The Negro in New York.* New York: Exposition Press, 1964.

Allport, Gordon. *The Nature of Prejudice.* Garden City: Doubleday, 1958.

American Jewish Congress. *Report on Eighteen State Anti-Discrimination Agencies and the Laws They Administer.* New York: The Congress, 1957.

Anti-Defamation League. *Comparative Analysis of State Fair Employment Practices Laws.* New York: The League, 1959.

Bamberger, Michael, and Nathan Lewin. "The Right to Equal Treatment," 74 *Harvard Law Review* 526–589 (January 1961).

Banfield, Edward C., and James Q. Wilson. *City Politics.* New York: Vintage, 1963.

Barber, James D. *Power in Committees.* Chicago: Rand-McNally, 1966.

Berger, Morroe. *Equality by Statute.* Rev. ed. Garden City: Doubleday, 1967.

Binder, Betty. "Administrative Action against Residential Discrimination in New York City." M.A. essay, Columba University, 1962.

Blalock, Hubert M. *Toward a Theory of Minority Group Relations.* New York: John Wiley, 1967.

Blau, Peter. *The Dynamics of Bureaucracy.* Rev. ed. Chicago: University of Chicago Press, 1963.

Blumrosen, A. W. "Anti-Discrimination Law in Action in New Jersey: A Law-Sociology Study," 19 *Rutgers University Law Review* 189–287 (1965).

Bonfield, A. E. "An Institutional Analysis of the Agencies Administering Fair Employment Practices Laws," Parts I and II, 42 *New York University Law Review* 823–879, and 1034–1086 (1967).

——. "Origin and Development of American Fair Employment Practices Legislation," 52 *Iowa Law Review* 1043–1092 (1967).

——. "Substance of American Fair Employment Practices Legislation," Parts I and II, 61 *Northwestern University Law Review* 907–975 (1967) and 62 *Northwestern University Law Review* 19–44 (1967).

Brink, William, and Louis Harris. *The Negro Revolution in America.* New York: Simon and Schuster, 1964.

Brown, Earl. *Why Race Riots? Lessons from Detroit.* New York: Public Affairs Committee, 1944.

Caraley, Demetrios. *New York City's Deputy Mayor–City Administrator.* New York: Citizens Budget Commission, 1966.

Clark, Kenneth. *Dark Ghetto!* New York: Harper & Row, 1965.

——. "Group Violence: A Preliminary Study of the Attitudinal Pattern of Its Acceptance and Rejection—A Study of the 1943 Harlem Riots," *Journal of Social Psychology,* 19 (May 1944), 319–337.

Connorton, John V. "Unfinished Business: A Report by the Deputy Mayor–City Administrator to Mayor Robert F. Wagner on the Work of the Office of Administration." New York: Office of Administration, 1965.

Davies, Clarence J. *Neighborhood Groups and Urban Renewal.* New York: Columbia University Press, 1966.

Dean, John P., and Alex Rosen. *A Manual of Intergroup Relations.* Chicago: University of Chicago Press, 1955.

Dodson, Dan W. "Balance Sheet for One City," *Common Ground,* 6 (1946), 88–91.

Dorsen, Norman. "The Model Anti-Discrimination Act," 4 *Harvard Journal of Legislation* 212–278, (1966).

Downs, Anthony. *Inside Bureaucracy*. Boston: Little-Brown, 1967.

Dyson, Richard B., and Elizabeth D. Dyson. "Commission Enforcement of State Laws against Discrimination: A Comparative Analysis of the Kansas Act," 14 *University of Kansas Law Review* 29–58, (1965).

Eiberson, Harold. *Sources for the Study of the New York Area*. New York: City College Press, 1960.

"Employment Discrimination," 5 *Race Relations Law Reporter* 569–598, (1959).

Fogel, Walter, and Archie Kleingartner. *Contemporary Labor Issues*. Belmont: Wadsworth, 1966.

Frakt, A. N. "Administrative Enforcement of Equal Opportunity Legislation in New Jersey," 21 *Rutgers Law Review* 442–477 (1967).

Franklin, John Hope. *From Slavery to Freedom*. [1st ed.] New York: Knopf, 1947.

Ginsburg, Sigmund, *et al.* "Management Review of the New York City Commission on Human Rights." New York: Office of the Mayor, Office of Administration, April 2, 1969.

Glazer, Nathan, and Davis McEntire, eds. *Studies in Housing and Minority Groups*. Berkeley: University of California Press, 1960.

Goldblatt, H., and F. Cromien. "The Effective Reach of the Fair Housing Practices Law of the City of New York," *Social Problems,* 9 (1962), 365–370.

Governor's Committee to Review New York Laws and Procedures in the Area of Human Rights. *Report to the Governor*. Albany: The Committee, 1968.

Greenberg, Jack. *Race Relations and American Law*. New York: Columbia University Press, 1959.

Grimshaw, Allen D. "Lawlessness and Violence in America and Their Special Manifestations in Changing Negro-White Relationships," *Journal of Negro History,* 44 (January 1959), 52–72.

———. "Negro-White Relations in the Urban North: Two Areas of High Conflict Potential," *Journal of Intergroup Relations* 3 (Spring 1962), 146–158.

———. "Three Major Causes of Colour Violence in the United States," *Race,* 5 (July 1963), 76–87.

Grodzins, Morton. *The Metropolitan Area as a Racial Problem*. Pittsburgh: University of Pittsburgh Press, 1958.

Gross, Bertram. *The Managing of Organizations*. 2 vols. New York: The Free Press, 1964.

Handlin, Oscar. *The Newcomers.* Cambridge: Harvard University Press, 1959.

Harlem Youth Opportunities Unlimited. *Youth in the Ghetto.* 3d ed. New York, 1964.

Hentoff, Nat, et al., *Black Anti-Semitism and Jewish Racism.* New York: Shocken, 1970.

Higbee, Jay A. *Development and Administration of the New York State Law Against Discrimination.* University, Ala.: University of Alabama Press, 1966.

Horne, Frank. "Interracial Housing in the United States," *Phylon,* 19 (April 1958), 13–20.

——. "Open City—Threshold to American Maturity," *Phylon,* 18 (July 1957), 133–139.

——. "The Past Decade in Fair Housing Legislation," *Journal of Intergroup Relations,* 1 (Winter 1959), 52–56.

Kesselman, Louis C. *The Social Politics of FEPC.* Chapel Hill: University of North Carolina Press, 1948.

Lee, Alfred M., and Norman D. Humphrey. *Race Riots.* New York: Octagon, 1968.

Lloyd, Kent. "Urban Race Riots vs. Affective Anti-Discrimination Agencies: An End or a Beginning," *Public Administration,* 45 (1967), 43–53.

Lockard, Duane. *Toward Equal Opportunity.* New York: Macmillan, 1968

Lowi, Theodore. *At the Pleasure of the Mayor.* Glencoe: The Free Press, 1964.

McEntire, Davis. *Residence and Race.* Berkeley: University of California Press, 1960.

McKay, Claude. *Harlem: Negro Metropolis.* New York: Dutton, 1940.

Mann, Arthur. *La Guardia—A Fighter against His Times.* Philadelphia: Lippincott, 1959.

Marrow, Alfred J. *Changing Patterns of Prejudice.* Philadelphia: Chilton, 1962.

Marshall, F. Ray. *The Negro and Organized Labor.* New York: John Wiley, 1965.

—— and Vernon M. Briggs, Jr. *The Negro and Apprenticeship.* Baltimore: Johns Hopkins University Press, 1967.

Marx, Gary T. *Protest and Prejudice.* New York: Harper & Row, 1967.

Mayhew, Leon H. *Law and Equal Opportunity.* Cambridge: Harvard University Press, 1968.

The Mayor's Commission on the Conditions in Harlem. *The Negro in Harlem.* New York: The Mayor's Commission, 1935.

Miller, Elizabeth W. *The Negro in America: A Bibliography.* Cambridge: Harvard University Press, 1966.

Miyamoto, S. Frank. "The Process of Intergroup Tension and Conflict," in E. W. Burgess and D. J. Bogue, eds., *Contributions to Urban Sociology.* Chicago: University of Chicago Press, 1964.

Morsell, John. "The Political Behavior of Negroes in New York City," Ph.D. diss., Columbia University, 1950.

Moynihan, Daniel P., and Nathan Glazer. *Beyond the Melting Pot.* Cambridge: MIT Press, 1963.

"Municipal Interracial Councils," *American City,* 59 (August 1944), 74.

Myrdal, Gunnar. *An American Dilemma.* New York: Harpers, 1944.

New York City Commission on Human Rights. *Annual Report, 1961–1969.* New York: The Commission, 1961–1970.

New York City Commission on Intergroup Relations. *Annual Report, 1956–1959.* New York: The Commission, 1957–1960.

New York City Police Department. "Report to the Mayor on the Disturbances in Harlem." New York: The Department, 1943.

New York Council on Civil Liberties and Civil Rights. "Report Concerning a New York City Mayor's Committee on Intergroup Relations." Mimeographed, n.d.

"New York's Anti-bias Statute," 18 *New York University Intramural Law Review* 269 (May 1963).

New York State Division of Human Rights. *Annual Report, 1968.* Albany: The Division, 1969.

Norgren, Paul, and Samuel Hill. *Toward Fair Employment.* New York: Columbia University Press, 1964.

"Note: Discrimination in Employment and in Housing: Private Enforcement Provisions of the Civil Rights Act of 1964 and 1968," 82 *Harvard Law Review* 834–863 (1969).

"Note: Municipal Fair Employment Practices Ordinances: A Legal Survey and Model Ordinance," 45 *Notre Dame Lawyer* 258–313 (1969).

"Note: The Operation of State Fair Employment Practices Commissions," 68 *Harvard Law Review* 685–697 (1955).

"Official Interracial Committees Established by Thirty-one U.S. Cities," *Public Management,* 26 (July 1944), 211–212.

Ottley, Roi. *New World A'Coming.* Boston: Houghton-Mifflin, 1943.

Padilla, Elena. *Up from Puerto Rico.* New York: Columbia University Press, 1958.

Parsons, Talcott, and Kenneth Clark. *The Negro American.* Boston: Houghton, Mifflin, 1966.

Pearl, Laurence, and Benjamin Terner. "Survey: Fair Housing Laws— Design For Equal Opportunity," 16 *Stanford Law Review* 849–899 (1964).

Planners for Equal Opportunity, New York Chapter. *Planning for Open City.* New York: New York Urban League, 1967.

The Potomac Institute, Inc. "A Fair Employment Contract Compliance Program for New York City." Washington: The Institute, 1967.

Rabkin, Sol. "Progress in Civil Rights in State Legislatures," *Journal of Intergroup Relations,* 2 (Summer 1961), 273–279.

Reitzes, D. C. "Institutional Structure and Race Relations," *Phylon,* 20 (March 1959), 48–66.

Robbins, Richard. "Local Strategies in Race Relations: The Illinois Experience with Community Human Relations Commissions and Councils," *Journal of Intergroup Relations,* 2 (Autumn 1961) 311– 324.

Robinson, Joseph B. "Fair Housing in the City and State of New York," in Thomas W. Casstevens and Lynn W. Eley, eds., *The Politics of Fair Housing Legislation.* San Francisco: Chandler, 1968.

——, and B. Flicker. "Summary of 1964–65 State Anti-Discrimination Laws," 3 *Law in Transition Quarterly* 94 (Spring 1966).

Rogers, David. *110 Livingston Street.* New York: Random House, 1968.

Rose, Arnold, M. ed. *Race, Prejudice, and Discrimination.* New York: Knopf, 1951.

Ross, Arthur M., and Herbert Hill, eds. *Employment, Race, and Poverty.* New York: Harcourt, Brace, and World, 1967.

Ruchames, Louis. *Race, Jobs, and Politics.* New York: Columbia University Press, 1953.

Sayre, Wallace, and Herbert Kaufman. *Governing New York City.* New York: Russell Sage Foundation, 1960.

Senior, Clarence. *The Puerto Ricans: Strangers-Then Neighbors.* New York: Quadrangle, 1965.

Sexton, Patricia Cayo. *Spanish Harlem: An Anatomy of Poverty.* New York: Harper and Row, 1965.

Shapiro, Fred C., and James W. Sullivan. *Race Riot.* New York: Crowell, 1964.

Sherif, Muzafer, *et al. Intergroup Conflict and Cooperation: The Robbers Cave Experiment.* Norman Okla.: Institute of Group Relations, 1961.

Silverman, Arnold, and Stanley Leiberson. "Precipitants and Underlying Conditions of Race Riots," *American Sociological Review,* 30 (1965), 887–898.

Simon, Herbert. *Administrative Behavior.* New York: Macmillan, 1947.

Simpson, George E., and J. Milton Yinger. *Racial and Cultural Minorities: An Analysis of Prejudice and Discrimination.* New York: Harper's, 1953.

Sovern, Michael I. *Legal Restraints on Racial Discrimination in Employment.* New York: Twentieth Century Fund, 1966.

Stanley, David T., *et al. Professional Personnel for the City of New York.* Washington: The Brookings Institution, 1963.

Stern, Henry J. "Freedom When?: A Report on the City Commission on Human Rights Prepared for the Task Force on Economic Development to New York City." Typescript. New York: The Task Force, 1965.

Sutin, A. "The Experience of State Fair Employment Commissions: A Comparative Study," 18 *Vanderbilt Law Review* 965–1046 (1965).

Taeuber, Karl E., and Alma F. Taeuber. *Negroes in Cities.* Chicago: Aldine, 1965.

"Toward Equal Opportunity in Employment," 14 *Buffalo Law Review* (1964). (Entire issue, no. 1, is on this subject.)

United States Conference of Mayors. *Official Local Community Relations Commissions, National Survey Supplement.* Washington: Community Relations Service, 1965.

United States Equal Employment Opportunities Commission. *Hearings on Discrimination in White Collar Employment.* Washington: GPO, 1968.

United States Senate. Committee on the Judiciary. *Hearings on H.R. 42 (Anti-Riot Bill)*. 90th Cong., 1st Sess., pp. 784–785.

Wakefield, Dan. *Island in the City*. Boston: Houghton-Mifflin, 1959.

White, Walter. "Behind the Negro Riots," *New Republic,* August 16, 1943, pp. 220–222.

——. *A Man Called White*. New York: Viking, 1948.

Wicker, Tom, ed. *Report of the National Advisory Commission on Civil Disorders*. New York: Bantam, 1968.

Wilson, James Q. *Negro Politics*. Glencoe: The Free Press, 1960.

——. "The Strategy of Protest: Problems of Negro Civic Action," *Journal of Conflict Resolution* 5 (September 1961), 291–303.

Winter, R. K., Jr. "Improving the Economic Status of Negroes through Laws against Discrimination: A Reply to Professor Sovern," 34 *University of Chicago Law Review* 817–855 (1967).

Witherspoon, Joseph P. "Civil Rights Policy in the Federal System: Proposals for a Better Use of the Administrative Process," 74 *Yale Law Jouurnal* 1171–1244 (1965).

Zeitz, L. "Negro Attitudes toward Law," 19 *Rutgers Law Review* 294–316 (1965).

Index

*Race Relations and the New York
City Commission on Human Rights*

Designed by R. E. Rosenbaum.
Composed by Vail-Ballou Press, Inc.,
in 10 point linotype Times Roman, 3 points leaded,
with display lines in monotype Bulmer.
Printed letterpress from type by Vail-Ballou Press
on Warren's Number 66 text, 50 pound basis,
with the Cornell University Press watermark.
Bound by Vail-Ballou Press.